D1257676

DIRECTORS IN PERSPECTIVE

General editor: Christopher Innes

Roger Blin

DIRECTORS IN PERSPECTIVE

What characterizes modern theatre above all is continual stylistic innovation, in which theory and presentation have combined to create a wealth of new forms – naturalism, expressionism, epic theatre, etc. – in a way that has made directors the leading figures rather than dramatists. To a greater extent than is perhaps generally realized, it has been directors who have provided dramatic models for playwrights, though of course there are many different variations in this relationship. In some cases a dramatist's themes challenge a director to create new performance conditions (Stanislavski and Chekhov), or a dramatist turns director to formulate an appropriate style for his work (Brecht); alternatively a director writes plays to correspond with his theory (Artaud), or creates communal scripts out of exploratory work with actors (Chaikin, Grotowski). Some directors are identified with a single theory (Craig), others gave definitive shape to a range of styles (Reinhardt); the work of some has an ideological basis (Stein), while others work more pragmatically (Bergman).

Generally speaking, those directors who have contributed to what is distinctly "modern" in today's theatre stand in much the same relationship to the dramatic texts they work with, as composers do to librettists in opera. However, since theatrical performance is the most ephemeral of the arts and the only easily reproducible element is the text, critical attention has tended to focus on the playwright. This series is designed to redress the balance by providing an overview of selected directors' stage work: those who helped to formulate modern theories of drama. Their key productions have been reconstructed from promptbooks, reviews, scene-designs, photographs, diaries, correspondence and – where these productions are contemporary – documented by first-hand description, interviews with the director, etc. Apart from its intrinsic interest, this record allows a critical perspective, testing ideas against practical problems and achievements. In each case, too, the director's work is set in context by indicating the source of his ideas and their influence, the organization of his acting company and his relationship to the theatrical or political establishment, so as to bring out wider issues: the way theatre both reflects and influences assumptions about the nature of man and his social role.

Christopher Innes

TITLES IN SERIES

Adolphe Appia: Richard Beacham
Ingmar Bergman: Lise-Lone and Frederick J. Marker
Roger Blin: Odette Aslan
Joseph Chaikin: John Rudlin
E. Gordon Craig: Christopher Innes
Max Reinhardt: John Styan
Peter Stein: Michael Patterson
Bertholt Brecht: John Fuegi

FUTURE TITLES

André Antoine: Jean Chothia
Peter Brook: Albert Hunt and Geoffrey Reeves
Tyrone Guthrie: Ronald Bryden
Vsevelod Meyerhold: Robert Leach
Ariane Mnouchkine: Adrian Kiernauder
Harold Prince: Foster Hirsch
Constantin Stanislavski: Peter Holland and Vera Gottlieb
Giorgio Strehler: David Hirst
Andrzej Wajda: Maciej Karpinski

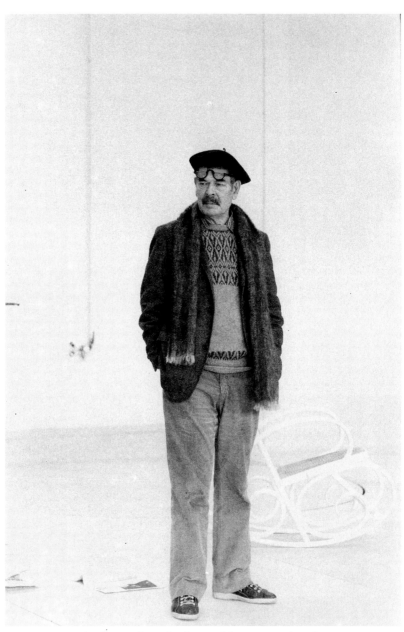

Roger Blin during rehearsals of *Triptych* by Max Frisch at the
Théâtre National de l'Odéon, 1983. Ph. Yves Chériaux

Roger Blin

and Twentieth-Century Playwrights

ODETTE ASLAN

Laboratoire de Recherches sur les Arts de Spectacle (CNRS)

TRANSLATED BY RUBY COHN

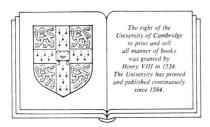

The right of the
University of Cambridge
to print and sell
all manner of books
was granted by
Henry VIII in 1534.
The University has printed
and published continuously
since 1584.

CAMBRIDGE UNIVERSITY PRESS

CAMBRIDGE

NEW YORK   NEW ROCHELLE   MELBOURNE   SYDNEY

Published by the Press Syndicate of the University of Cambridge
The Pitt Building, Trumpington Street, Cambridge CB2 1RP
32 East 57th Street, New York, NY 10022, USA
10 Stamford Road, Oakleigh, Melbourne 3166, Australia

First published 1988

Printed in Great Britain at
the University Press, Cambridge

British Library cataloguing in publication data
Aslan, Odette
Roger Blin : and twentieth-century
playwrights. – (Directors in perspective).
1. Blin, Roger 2. Theater – France –
Production and direction – History – 20th
century
I. Title II. Series
792'.0233'0924 PN2638.B/

Library of Congress cataloguing in publication data
Aslan, Odette.
Roger Blin : and twentieth century playwrights.
(Directors in perspective)
Bibliography
Includes index.
1. Blin, Roger, 1907– . 2. Theatrical producers
and directors – France – Biography. I Title.
II. Series.
PN2638.B56A8 1987 791.43'0233'0924 87-15162

ISBN 0 521 22440 3

SE

This book is dedicated
to Roger Blin
but also
according to his wish
to all those
who shared
with him
the joys
and pain
of that fertile period
in all the arts

What is a director? Nothing; he shouldn't be talked about; his personality shouldn't exist; he shouldn't seek a style; he should be rigorous about rendering the thought of the author, without adding anything. For that matter, authors should direct their own works; unfortunately, most of them can't do it. In the old days the director was an actor in the company who did the blocking; there was no talk about it. I put my name as director only because I was asked to, but I don't like it. I have no theory, and I try to have no characteristic style.

Blin, interview in *Arts*, 24 February 1950

Contents

Illustrations

xi

Acknowledgments

I warmly thank all who graciously helped me gather documents, memories, and materials:

Claude Accursi, André Acquart, Maurice Baquet, Jean-Louis Barrault, Alexis Barsacq, Mme A. Barsacq, Jean-Louis Bauer, Samuel Beckett, Simone Benmussa, François Billetdoux, Marcel Bozonnet, Catherine Cadou, Yves Chériaux, Claude Confortès, Jean-Marie Conty, Paul Crauchet, Alain Cuny, Jean Darcante, Gérard Darrieu, Jean Dasté, Marie-Hélène Dasté, Jean Duvignaud, Isabelle Famchon, Hervé Furic, Maurice Garrel, Georges Godebert, Bronislaw Horowicz, Maurice Jacquemont, André Julien, Hermine Karagheuz, Geneviève Latour, François Kuki, Robert Liensol, Sabine Lods, Gérard Lorin, Sarah Maldoror, Eduardo Manet, Jean Martin, Matias, Michèle Meunier, Lola Mouloudji, Rose-Marie Moudouès, Michèle Oppenot, Pierre Prévert, Jacques Seiler, Andrée Tainsy, Laurent Terzieff, Paule Thévenin, Pierrette Tison, Alexandre Trauner, Céline Zins.

Gabrielle Heller and the Austrian, French, Dutch, and Swiss centers of the International Theatre Institute; Cécile Giteau and the Departement of Arts du Spectacle at the Arsenal Library; Noelle Guibert and the Comédie-Française Library; the Rond-Point Theatre, the Odéon Theatre, the Schauspielhaus of Zurich, the Teatro Stabile of Turin.

I wish to thank all Roger Blin's friends and collaborators in theatre, film, radio, and television, who testified to the quality of his work and personality, thus helping me in my analysis of his director's choices and of his way of enhancing a play and its actors, while subjecting them to the utmost rigor. I hereby thank them and apologize to those whom I did not see, for everyone wanted to speak of him. It is rare to have such unanimity about a director, which is probably to be explained by the fact that Blin worked with those whom he respected and to whom he felt close.

Many thanks to Ruby Cohn without whom this book could not have been written. She is not only the translator but the initiator of the project through its completion.

O.A.

Introduction

To write a book about Roger Blin is a rash undertaking. There has been no extended examination of his work, since his modesty did not permit it. He kept no documents and made no director's notes. Even worse, he claimed that his direction aimed to be invisible, disappearing behind authors and actors. To include him in the context of Directors in Perspective is therefore a challenge, since Blin never had the opportunity to sustain his work continuously. With no hearth or home, with no theatre at his disposal where he could develop an audience, he worked here and there, waiting for a theatre that would agree to accept difficult works before they were understood.

Nevertheless he has contributed importantly to contemporary theatre. Discoverer of Beckett and explorer of Genet, Blin gave his support to young authors, fought for a new kind of dramatic writing, insisted on treating subversive subjects. He made his choices without bluster but without concessions, and he stuck to these choices tenaciously, ignoring tradition, fashion, and beaten paths. It is hoped that this book will break the relative silence surrounding this shy and solitary artist who refused worldly honors and disdained superficiality in order to dedicate himself to true communication and deep friendship based on mutual esteem. His sensitivity gave us today's theatre.

Even when he did not desire to be provocative, Roger Blin was a subversive agent: he did not fit into a mould; he is difficult to capture; he cannot be summarized by a formula. He thus questions the very basis of theatre. A natural doubter ("What's the use of your research?"), obstinate in his refusals ("What I do is not important"), he inspires a re-examination of conventional ideas.[1]

What is a director? Is his function a necessity or a usurpation? There have been many different conceptions of the director. From assistant to an actor in the difficult birth of a character, we have moved to a tyrant imposing personal ukases on a whole company. The exponent of poor theatre – four actors, a board, and spectators – has given way at times to a technocrat anxious to try many heavy-handed methods. From a simple mediator between the author's text and his interpreters, we have arrived at the idea of the director as "star" and even "superstar." How did this happen?

In 1878 a French work on theatre assigns the director the task of blocking movements of the actors and placing the properties on stage. This function "owes a great deal to Beaumarchais, to intelligent stage managers, to playwrights such as Dumas *fils* and Sardou."[2]

In 1885 another French scholar defines the director as " the stage manager specially assigned to directing," who controls the actors' movements and watches them rehearse.[3] This scholar distinguishes between human and material mise-en-scène. The director should respect the period of the play by choosing properties, planning the disposition of space, taking care of lighting and sound effects. In the theatre hierarchy, the managing director is on top – both an administrator and an artist – in charge of casting, repertory, and day-to-day notes. Under him is the director who gives orders on stage; and finally there is the stage manager who helps the managing director and looks after the stagehands. In many European companies the First Actor was the director; he was in charge of rehearsals, sensitive to the hidden life of a play, active in evoking that life for the other actors. This practice, based on enthusiasm for a work and closeness to the actors, might involve personal quirks on the part of those who played to the limelight, and this sometimes unbalanced a production.

For the Naturalists, the director insured the theatre's truth to life. At the Théâtre Libre, Antoine was influenced by the Meiningen productions (for a homogeneous ensemble and for crowd scenes) and by Zola's theories. The latter's *Naturalism in the Theatre* inspired Antoine to set naturalism on stage; in his *Conversation on Mise-en-Scène* (1903) Antoine insisted on the importance of the director in furnishing the proper background for the action, determining a "true" setting, and demanding true feeling from the actors. He therefore went to great pains to establish the exact milieu in which the characters would live – the material aspect of directing. For the non-material aspect, he focused on rhythm, on interpretation without hyperbole, and on the lighting which he called "the soul of the mise-en-scène."

Stanislavski remained close to the actor, and based his directing on that. External directing was useful to him only insofar as it aided the spiritual creation of the actor. For him, the director was the mediator, helping the actor. As the revolution against Naturalism progressed – Symbolism, Expressionism, Surrealism (and the Russian Revolution) swept away the old society with its theatre – the godlike director grew even more powerful. Analyses of the written work were developed within both a literary and ideological context. Some directors emphasized stage technology and others followed the path opened up by Appia, Craig, or Copeau. Adolphe Appia established a hierarchy of the elements of staging – the actor, space, light. Edward Gordon Craig insisted on the director as artist who coordinated all the elements of a production. With Appia and Craig, imbalances were supposed to disappear and be replaced by a governing concept that would orient the work toward perfection.

Jacques Copeau tended to be ascetic, preferring his bare boards to any kind of decoration. "We don't want to overstress the importance of sets and props."[4] For him the mise-en-scène was "the totality of movements, gestures, and attitudes; the harmony of faces, voices, and silences; it is the whole stage production stemming from a single mind who conceives, regulates, and harmonises it. The director invents and then maintains a secret bond between his characters, which is made visible – a mysterious series of relationships without which the play fails of its expression, despite excellent actors."

Five young theatremen of the next generation – Jean-Louis Barrault, Julien Bertheau, Sylvain Itkine, Raymond Rouleau, Jean Servais – formed a collective, the Company of Five, and issued a manifesto in 1936: "For us the director is the coordinating agent of the work (script and subject) and the elements of production (set, costumes, music, actors, and stylistic unity). He should be the main interpreter of the thought of the author, endowing it with theatre reality through his technical knowledge and authority."[5]

Theatre is a complex art requiring the collaboration of artists and technicians of different disciplines. It is often said that there are several plays and not a single work; there is the one written by the author, the one that the actors perform, and the one that the audience perceives. Today we are conscious of essential differences between a written text and its performance. But the author does not always see it this way. He may see a single reading of the work – his – and he imposes his phrasing and rhythm (which he dreams of being able to score musically), his esthetic conception, his understanding of the contents. In 1908 the Russian author Alexander Blok complained that he was dispossessed and betrayed: "The director is that invisible person who steals the author's play and then shows him to the nearest exit . . . Then the director takes it upon himself to explain the play to the actors, to the stupefaction of the author who later comes to see his play on stage."[6]

Futurists and Dadaists attacked language by denunciation and disarticulation. In the twentieth century the primacy of the word was threatened also by the importance given to visual elements. Erwin Piscator thought that the mise-en-scène was a science "that arises from the spatial division of the stage, from its plastic components; it is translated by the play of light as much as by intonations of the actors."[7] He viewed theatre as a way of offering historical and sociological perspective.

Whatever the political or esthetic allegiances of directors, whether they are influenced by Brecht, Artaud, or Grotowski, contemporary directors may be divided into two categories. There are those who create a new work out of the author's play; they bend it to their viewpoint, considering it a reservoir of possibilities, from which they choose one. (Thus we speak of Planchon's rather than Molière's *Tartuffe*.) They subdue all elements of the production to their viewpoint – actors' interpretation, deployment of space, conception of costumes, rhythms, etc. The whole is thus unified, and the result is often brilliant, even if an author is sometimes made to say what he never said. The viewpoint may be too personal, or a past author may become too contemporary, or a modern play may be bent away from its original meaning.

There are directors who object to this practice. They are more modest craftsmen, and are less concerned with carving a reputation for themselves. Often actors themselves, they continue the tradition of actor/head-of-a-company, helping colleagues perform a play, without any other intention than presenting it to the public in the best possible light. During rehearsals they offer the actors an outside eye to guide them. These directors know actors' problems from within, which is not always true of the other kind of director, who may be an expert in imagery.

These actor/directors also have visual imagination, and they too can exploit the resources of a sophisticated technology, but they do not make that the *sine qua non* of their production. They do not use such apparatus in a brilliant display that may smother the author's words; they do not shift the author's intentions; they do not indulge in a discourse parallel to the play; they do not make an exegesis based on the play. First and foremost, they bring the work to the stage. This necessary and sufficient process makes of them indispensable but discreet mediators, responsible for all elements of the performance, which they choose and coordinate. If they succeed in putting the work on stage, they do not yearn to be called "creators." They are men of the theatre who produce the plays of the authors. They leave it to the audience to draw their own ideological conclusions. Often playing in their own productions, these directors confront the work directly, without any other intermediary than their own sensitivity.

For Claude Régy, a well-known French director, the mise-en-scène means timing words in space: "One has to discover for each text how to extend words. Starting with the text, one has to listen for what whispers through our own unconscious [of actor or director] so as to prepare the ground for working on the unconscious of the audience."[8] An actress like Emmanuelle Riva increasingly appreciates "a mise-en-scène that does not call attention to itself, one in which the director does not display himself."[9] Moreover, there are discoverers and diviners who have a nose for new kinds of writing, who reveal what will be appreciated tomorrow, and who set on stage – the acid test – disturbing works that may become the classics of future generations.

It is clear that Roger Blin belonged to this race of discoverers and craftsmen. He was an actor helping other actors; he was a servant of authors, hostile to dramaturgical analysis and to overdependence on technology; he was a diviner, discovering authors who may (or may not) become famous; he directed very few works of the past. That is why speaking of him means simultaneously speaking of the authors he produced, the designers who placed his conceptions in stage space, the actors who shared his adventures, and the collaborators who took part in his productions. Continually helping others, concealing himself behind others, Roger Blin would not have permitted a study that focused on him alone. He belonged to a theatre in the process of being born, to a living and continuous stream that burst forth daily, and it is this stream that we will try to capture in its flow, with Blin at the center.

Stubbornly discreet, he makes analysis difficult. He rarely confided in anyone, or only peripherally; he communicated few specifics, or only jokingly; he did not plan his work methodically; he tried to produce an invisible mise-en-scène. Thus he seems a priori to destroy any impulse to study his work, since his hand cannot be seen in the production, or, if one does catch a glimpse of it, revelation would destroy Blin's intention.

Although memories and documents help constitute the basis of analysis, and can be integrated into an organized approach, they leave us perplexed before Roger Blin, who, by his temperament and behavior, denies the very possibility of a structured study. Coherent but visionary, logical but poetic, conscientious and yet not averse to a certain madness, he remains on the frontier of the intangible. He gave no instructions to those whom he was supposed to direct; he let things happen. Like a gardener, he brought to fruition. An alchemist, he titrated and weighed.

He raises doubts about our few criteria of theatre research. For that very reason it becomes essential to track what escapes us in theatre; what makes the theatre spring forth as theatre, independent of critical theories. Seeking to theorize about his practice would disguise its spontaneous, empirical, uncommented aspects. The alchemy of stage creation may derive from personal sensitivity, experience, meetings, external circumstances, intangibles, as much as from organized intention and profound reflection. That osmosis is difficult to capture; everything need not make sense.

It would be heresy to apply linguistic or semiological methods to a study of Blin's productions. He always bristled at "barbarous" words invading the theatrical discourse; he rebelled against theatre research itself; the important thing was to create theatre. However it should be possible to show "the primacy of listening" (to which semiologists are so attentive) in Blin's productions, where the technical apparatus never overpowered the actor. In a space that was deployed as cleanly as possible, without projections or complicated machinery, "without sand, water, or smoke" as he phrased it in 1983, gestures are discreet, and in the performance of the actors one senses "the tension between spontaneity and the control of signs," which Patrice Pavis calls "writing based on impulse."[10] An ideology was always in the background of Blin's choices, but one cannot imprison his creations in rigid codes, or claim to decode them by the projection of arbitrary ideas that would have displeased him. He feared that critical analyses would ossify the living performance. He detested the German dramaturg who was supposed to prepare his mise-en-scène scientifically; he caricatured him humorously as a man between fifty-five and sixty years old, with a head "shaped like a violin,"[11] who conceives the mise-en-scène at home and arrives at the first rehearsal with three hundred pages of notes to which everyone must conform. He positions himself in the middle of the orchestra and bellows orders from afar, through a microphone.

It is obvious that this is a prejudiced description which reflects the aversion of an impulsive craftsman to the director who claims to be in possession of the truth and does not work out his production in the warmth of the stage. A man like Brecht would not correspond to this description, since he was at once a theoretician and practitioner, and not a functionary of the intellect. For the director who displays his knowledge and power, Brecht substituted someone who entertains a dialectical relationship with the work, who arouses and organizes "the productive activity of the actors."[12] In 1963 Blin was hostile to the dramaturgomany that was beginning to be the rage in France. He appreciated Brecht; he detested Brechtians.

He preferred to act like an actor among actors. He worked like Dullin who was unable to finish an instruction: "You see, it's a little more . . . a little less . . ." and the actor understood. Or like Giorgio Strehler, more often on the stage than in the auditorium during rehearsals at the Piccolo Theatre of Milan. Rather than theorize, Blin jumped to the stage to demonstrate, without wanting to be imitated. He might take a metaphor from current life to clarify a situation, often he said nothing at all; he let the actor stray into an impasse and take note of it himself, then helped him to change his direction. Sometimes he found the actor's choice better than his own, and he adopted it. At the beginning he imposed nothing, although he maintained his basic convictions and his respect for the author. Blin was modest, considering himself a simple link in a chain, and he wanted his contribution to remain invisible. He proceeded by feel using the maieutic method of Socrates, and then disappeared.

Kind and timid, he was very firm in his refusals. He could say NO like no one else. NO to work by command. NO to stars who wanted to commercialize his undertaking. NO to a bourgeois repertory. NO to a painter who would simply design sets. NO to those who distorted the thought of Artaud, his friend. NO to all compromise. This stubbornness in refusal was used by director Sarah Maldoror when she cast Blin as the main character in her television production of Victor Serge's *Hospital of Leningrad*. Blin was a fearless man who sailed against the stream.

In this study he is quoted as often as possible. When he did consent to explain what he did, he revealed a keen, often corrosive mind. His thought was in advance of many of his contemporaries. Thirty years ago he seemed like a braggart with his *Godot*, and yet . . .

Even in his most recent productions there was no trace of the corporeal expression that is so widespread in contemporary theatre, causing actors to train on the floor. Aside from the paralytics or buried people of Beckett, Blin's actors' bodies are vertical, standing or seated; they are relaxed, but they are carriers of words before being expressive bodies. His revolution is elsewhere – in his ideological choices and his rejection of the classic tradition.

Like a tightrope-walker who ventures out on the stiff rope and triumphs over his discomfort, Blin revealed and brought to the stage works and authors who resist the usual *données* of theatre. Beckett is reserved; he slips away, almost hides his characters from the audience, and muffles their discourse. Genet proclaims his indifference to the public or his desire to mistreat it; he forbids the performance of his plays. Blin nevertheless succeeded in thrusting them upon the world. He knew exactly what to take from texts that seem more suitable for radio; he kept their musicality even while grappling with the individual problems of each production. In form he avoided realism. In content he was anchored in social reality. Impervious to fashion, to the snobbery of artistic movements, he may seem anachronistic when compared to certain directors, but he was actually abreast of recent experiments, ferreting out the unknown, ready to take new risks.

Although Blin never belonged to a school or a party, he enjoyed the company of the Surrealist poets. He was a friend of Antonin Artaud. He admired Soviet and German Expressionist films. He participated in the subversive theatre of the October Group; he supported causes like the Popular Front, the Resistance, and the Algerian Revolution. His commitment was personal. He didn't make a tribunal of the stage. The revolution that he sought in the theatre was the destruction of old forms and the inauguration of new writing. He denounced bourgeois art; he was eager to find new plays and new artistic forms. His taste spanned a wide gamut, from the mysterious abyss with its anguish, to the devastating laugh that denounces a rotten society. Blin fought for progress in the theatre, so that its form and content would correspond to the struggles of today's human beings. He therefore expected from playwrights a language that destroys bourgeois convention; he welcomed a questioning spirit and a sense of mockery. He had a taste for poetry; for him dramatic language was essentially literary but not esoteric. His choices are clear; neither Claudel, Giraudoux, nor Molière, but Strindberg, Adamov, Beckett, Genet. Draftsman and painter, visual and visionary, he had plastic gifts, a sense of color and lights; he sought beauty but not estheticism. He was enthusiastic about vocal research, about the musicality and resources of the human voice; he acted on radio, and he was interested in concrete music.

He was convinced of the centrality of the playwright, who brings to the production the yeast, the contents, the written form. Blin tried to be the servant/stage manager who transfers this written text to the mouths of the actors, in the simplest but most functional scenic space, under a light (in all senses of the word) that will show the play to best advantage. He refused to load the text with his own ego, his personal neuroses, or any kind of supertext. (In life as in his productions, his ascetic tendencies caused him to avoid useless luxury; he hated expensive machinery, gadgets, and mere techniques.) He relied on the actor rather than on sound effects. He was furious at the waste of money in subsidized theatre, when a successful production was taken off just because the program scheduled a specific number of performances. He told me in 1978: "In the old days they didn't close a production when it played to 75% capacity." In the world of show business, he remained a craftsman.

With his beard or moustache, depending on his role or the particular period of his life, puffing at his pipe to hide his shyness, he was sometimes rough, his eyelids heavy like a nightbird. During rehearsals he evaded questions. He was somewhat withdrawn, as though listening for an inner voice, and therefore unreachable; people were unwilling to interrupt this reverie, which was thought to contain some kind of foreknowledge. Since Blin made communication difficult, he often obtained deeper reflection, and he inspired artists to surpass themselves. He said more by silence than by discourse; he incited everyone to seek within himself.

The theatre is serious and works itself out seriously. For him as for his friend Artaud, theatre can be a surgical knife or a plague attacking outworn traditions and respectable ideas – to the jubilation of innovators.

Unlike certain colleagues, Blin's horizon was not limited to the theatre. He liked to be with friends and speak of other things, to share the time in which we live. In the literary cafés of Montparnasse or St-Germain-des-Prés he was at the center of artistic currents, meeting painters, poets, writers; he took part in discussion. When he entered a theatre, he carried those currents within him, that spirit of poetry and that group life, those social demands and that political awareness.

Indeed, he was also a graphic artist, and produced over 2,000 drawings. His schoolboy notebook testifies to a precocious gift of observation and surprising skill. Youthful studies show animals, self-portraits, nudes from his period at the Grande Chaumière. Gradually, a style emerges in which creatures with very long human legs and bird-heads are endowed with wings for flight. A few paintings show vivid colors – shaded reds, violets, washed out blue-greens. Boat hulls suggest departures. Then the graphics grow more complicated; they break down into many small tree-people and poisonous flowers among the animal forms. The people are composed of filaments and deformed bone-structures, of root-legs. Animals and plants combine in dreamlike ambiguity. The drawings turn into black gobs and splashes that then spread out into spidery lines; black on white, traces of dreams, frenzies. The pictures are experienced as exorcisms, screams. "If you know how to scream, you know how to draw," Blin joked while carefully inscribing date and signature at the bottom of a drawing he gave to a friend. The line quivers; it encloses bodies without legs, spreads curves, and produces fabulous hieroglyphics, black outpourings with a few color splashes.

Transferring his gift to theatre, Blin sketched several costumes. When intending to play Lucky in *Waiting for Godot*, he drew long widespread arms, sparse long hair. A grotesque character emerges from ample cuffs at the wrists, trousers too short, shredded at the bottom and held up by falling suspenders. For *King Christophe*, Blin drew women's headdresses and shawls falling in folds; uniforms with tight-chested white jackets and black hats with red stitching. For *The Screens* he produced for each actor a sketch for colored makeup.

One suspects that he gave his designers suggestions to orient them toward a pictorial universe that he himself never managed to put on stage. Only his subtle lighting, with its nuances of grey, red, or pale yellow, like a painter's palette, gives evidence of his ability to offer an appropriate atmosphere for each dramatic action. His attraction to the works of Genet, Valle-Inclàn, and Ghelderode (whom he wanted to direct at the Gaîté-Montparnasse) shows an affinity with writers whose words express images as much as ideas, and who draw these images from the depths of their own revolt.

To speak of Blin's productions is not necessarily to speak of ideas, but to go toward the source of a subtle path to the intangible, of a crystallization of dreams, of pictorial vision, of intimate vibrations. Yet Blin did not create performance art; he remained loyal to textual theatre. Artist of both the verbal and visual — that is the duality of Blin, irreducible, unclassifiable.

In this study what becomes evident is the inner coherence of a man of the theatre who refused to have a program, an explicit theory, a message, a distinctive style, but who nevertheless was completely committed to his convictions, both in life and the theatre. In spite of appearances, this craftsman left nothing to chance; he was also a polemicist whose choices are significant because he introduced what is sometimes called the anti-theatre of Beckett, the bomb of *The Screens* shortly after the Algerian War; with Genet's *Blacks* and Fugard's *Boesman and Lena* he opposed racism; with *Minamata* he stood up against industrial pollution and its criminal concealment, without abandoning theatrical form for agitprop. Roger Blin would have disliked this dissection. But I hope not to betray the very heart of his productions – their generous and sensitive life, his modesty of expression, the rigor and economy of his approach.

1   In search of Roger Blin

Son of a doctor, Roger Blin was born in the Paris suburb of Neuilly on 22 March 1907. While at university, he made the acquaintance of Surrealist poets, frequented dark movie-houses ("At midnight the Paramount was cheap"), played as an extra in films, wrote movie reviews, participated in the activities of the October Group (named for the October date of the Russian Revolution), began his career as theatre actor. This Surrealist period left a lasting mark upon Blin, as did his friendships with Jacques Prévert of the October Group and with Antonin Artaud whom he admired. "I met Prévert, Léger, and the others at the free Tribune of the Cinema. It was the first cine-club, with lively discussions and fights; there I saw the Surrealists for the first time; they came to boo some realistic film."[1]

Beginning in 1932, the October Group staged skits, parodies, and agitprop based on current events; it was a theatre of amateurs and semi-professionals who were hostile to official theatre and who wanted to participate in the class struggle. Jacques Prévert wrote a number of skits for them, usually directed by Lou Tchimoukow (Louis Bonin); the subjects were the economic crisis, unemployment, strikes, the Sino-Japanese War, Hitler's accession to power, the Popular Front. Among their productions were *The Battle of Fontenoy* (1932), *Phantoms, Current Events of 1933, The Scottsboro Boys, Nothing is Better Than Leather, The Palace of Mirages, Follow the Druid* (1935), *The Family Stovepipe, The Rise of Hitler, The Unemployed, The 14th of July,* and a revival of a Cervantes play previously performed in Jean-Louis Barrault's attic on rue des Grands-Augustins. All of these were presented outside of regular theatres, sometimes in department stores. Blin saw *Nothing is Better Than Leather* (plastic was beginning to replace leather) and *The Family Stovepipe*.

Blin broke with his background, lived marginally, and got on very well with the marginals of the October Group, which he himself described as "anti-colonial, anti-police, anti-military, anti-clerical, and to some degree anti-sociodemocratic."[2] The members of the October Group, led by Jacques Prévert, "discovered" Rimbaud and Lautréamont; above all, they discovered that corrosive laughter at outworn institutions led to mental and moral freedom. ("Prévert helped clean off my bourgeois upbringing," Blin told me in 1982.) He took part in the October Group "Breton Review" of 1935, whose purpose was political. Pseudo-Bretons in makeshift historic costumes paraded through the streets of the town of St-Cyr. Dressed in long pink underwear, surrounded by "mignons," Blin posed as King Henri III of France, with a (dyed) red-headed Queen Margot. October Group members dressed as unemployed Bretons, brandishing banners. French Communist Marcel Cachin gave a speech after the parade.

The skit *Follow the Druid* showed six scenes in the life of Breton workers and farmers of 1935, punctuated by a refrain from a song of sardine fisherwomen: "Turn, turn / little girls. / Turn around the factories. / Soon you'll be within them. / You'll be unhappy / and you'll have many children."[3] Blin spoke of the October Group as amateurs who didn't take themselves seriously: "We were *enfants terribles* who said funny things," Blin recalled.[4] He realized, however, that: "from a political viewpoint these skits were important, even in the puns, Spoonerisms, delirium, and dreamlike quality of Prévert." These skits infuriated the political Right who counter-attacked, wrote vituperative comments in the press, demanded that the Chamber of Deputies take action. But the Prévert band did not care. They participated in left-wing demonstrations, and secretly went to see the Eisenstein film *Potemkin* although it was officially forbidden in France until 1953.

"I had two ambitions then – to paint and write," Blin would tell theatreman Paul-Louis Mignon.[5] Like other members of the October Group, Blin wrote film criticism – in *La Revue du Cinéma* and in right-wing papers under a pseudonym; for example, defending Buñuel or the Soviets in the ultra-conservative *Action Française*. A long article might be devoted to Henry Langdon in some little out-of-the-way movie-house and then in two lines demolish something playing at the large Paramount.[6] Moreover, Blin was enthusiastic about *Hallelujah* (1929), made by King Vidor with black actors, and his friend Louis Chavance agreed, writing in *La Revue du Cinéma*: "One forgets that this film was made by a white person." As the critic Jean Cassou testified, in those early days of talking pictures black actors were more authentic than Hollywood's pale ones (in both senses of the word). In these reviews, Blin proved himself an ardent and severe polemicist.

Among movies Blin reviewed between 1928 and 1930, one might note *Money* by Marcel Lherbier, *The Man Who Sold his Appetite* by Okhlopov, *Land without Women* by Carmine Gallone, *Nights of Princes* by Marcel Lherbier, *The Works of Marey (1859–1904)* by R. Grimoin-Samson, *The Defender* by Alex Ryder, *Atlantis* by Jean Kemm. He admired the films of Murnau, particularly *Tabou* (1931), and he hated crude realism. He called bad films slush, and mercilessly criticized their faults. "A few theatrical scenes, a few sound-film discoveries, a few leftovers of silent film – all this clashes rather than harmonizes. After a striking opening, scenes are flattened by a dialogue that explains nothing and has no reason to stop" (*The Defender*).

He was indignant at a lack of proportion between set and characters: "A serious mistake in design deprives [the actor] Alcover of many good scenes; the glacial and overly rectilinear splendor of the hotel overpowers his plebeian silhouette; the man contradicts the wall, without suitable contrast" (*Money*).

Anti-conventional, open to many currents, Blin was not averse to a mixture of genres, and he preferred imperfection to a polished but cold style: ". . . one of the most interesting films of the season. Unexpected, fragmented, shifting back and forth between bad bits of American films and a German mystical drama, the film of Carmine Gallone [*Land without Women*] is a curious work that should be seen because of this mixture of styles."

He could summarize a scenario or reveal the visual logic of a sequence: "One, two, three, four. The tax-collector enters Café Bidard. A glance at the overturned chairs, a glance at the café-owner, his cowlick and pointed moustache, a glance at the owner's wife. Four gestures to adjust his monocle and cane. The girl arrives oddly made up, Hello." A simple indentation indicates a new shot, and Blin continues: "At the home of the banker Rapet four servants carry a single hardboiled egg. Monsieur has no appetite. Monsieur is rich; he can buy the appetite of someone else. Surely Professor Fouks will help him out, but Fouks is lost in the hallways . . . The beautiful jerky artifice of the beginning − a merry *Caligari*" (*The Man Who Sold his Appetite*).

One notes Blin's references, his attraction to Swedish movies and German Expressionist films, his rejection of Boulevard theatre and its leftovers in French film, his dislike of bad taste and self-indulgence. He analyzed acting in terms of psychological content: "Alcover acts authoritatively; he may be convulsed with anger or a plump Tartuffe in love; he moves his short arms and magnificent back. Sometimes he seems unhappy at failing to grasp this money that lacks concrete reality for his physical temperament" (*Money*).

"Conrad Veidt expands his part; some of his scenes are similar to those of his great mystic roles, but other scenes show him in a new way, embryonic, almost feminine. From the hysterical laugh that seizes him in a cabaret to the final madness, we feel him the prey of the sweetest and most terrible pains of love and destiny" (*Land without Women*).

Blin showed how mise-en-scène and montage in film are as important as the actors themselves: "At the beginning we see Emile and Jeanne Bidard at night, seated on a curb. Then in a very delicate succession of fadeouts, they change position with respect to one another. This ironic way of showing the poetry of a pure scene of love and distress is heartbreaking" (*The Man Who Sold his Appetite*).

As far as one can discover, Blin did not publish after this period, but he acted in about a hundred films − first as an extra, then in small parts. Pierre

Prévert, who knew him from the days of the October Group led by his brother Jacques, cast Blin in several films; he told me how impressed he was at the way Blin assumed a character with intense conviction and energy; the way Blin could mime a film that he had seen. Blin played in Aubert's *Guts in the Sun* (1958) with several actors whom he cast in Genet's *Blacks*. In 1974 Accursi cast him in the lead of *Dada at Heart*, a film that has still not been released, where Blin plays a disturbing creator of Dada spectacles. His spirit of opposition, nurtured on Surrealism, and his anti-establishment attitude are perfect for the part.

For Roger Blin to launch out on a career as actor is strange indeed, for he stuttered. A childhood fright made him aphasic for a time, and he subsequently stumbled over certain consonants. His father warned him to choose a profession that would not require him to speak, but Blin wanted to overcome his obstacle. "If my hands were cut off, I would probably have tried to be a sculptor."[7] This quip disguises a serious possible career for Blin – that of visual artist. If his meetings with Prévert and Artaud had not been decisive, Blin might have become a painter. It is also true that difficulties stimulated him. "I overcame my own stuttering by forcing myself to do exercises in front of a mirror. I owe a lot to the actors of the Comédie-Française; in listening to them at their matinées of poetry, with its purring sounds, I gradually found the way to master my own diction. Now I understand the mechanism perfectly, so that I have given and can give lessons in it."[8]

In 1927 or 1928 (his accounts vary) he met Antonin Artaud – a meeting that thrust him into a theatre career. Enthusiastic about the ideas of the founder of the Alfred Jarry Theatre, Blin offered Artaud a friendship that never weakened. He became Artaud's assistant during the production of his *Cenci* at the Folies Wagram in May 1935. For the first time Blin set foot on a professional stage; he played a banquet guest and one of the two assassins who at first did not dare to kill Cenci.[9] Artaud let Blin apply his own makeup, and he divided his face into four parts, colouring one red, another green, the third red, and the fourth green. Later he would conceive more elaborate makeup, but always unrealistic.

With Artaud, Blin discovered the theatre of cruelty, the violence of screams, physical theatre. He trained himself. "Artaud taught me to count on no one but myself," he later told me. Blin was fiercely protective of the hurt poet, the difficult person who was rejected by some and misunderstood by others. Although he was not Artaud's disciple, Blin showed the same moral intransigence, the same rejection of classical form and the repertory of the boulevards. He too appreciated a Jarryesque humor.

In 1930, during the filming of Jean Renoir's *Bitch*, Blin met Sylvain Itkine. With actors Deniaud and O'Brady, Itkine founded Group Mars that played at workers' meetings or in factories during strikes. Mars and October were the two main agitprop theatre movements in France.

We knew nothing of Brecht and the Lehrstücke, but we were already practicing Popular Theatre, that square circle, because we tried to perform significant material in the context of the future, and at the same time not to betray the poetic imagination, or even dream states. In form we wished to be clear, while allowing ourselves ellipses and daring stylization. [Itkine's purpose] was to harmonize his creative work and his revolutionary faith, both extended by humor.[10]

Itkine decided to produce Jarry's *Ubu Enchained* which was rediscovered by the Surrealists. Blin played one of the Freemen, then a Wrecker. Rehearsals lasted a year and a half, and they were important in Blin's apprenticeship. Itkine directed without ever being doctrinaire. "While urging us to discoveries, he made discoveries." The play was performed three times in a tiny experimental theatre at the Universal Exposition of 1937. Max Ernst did the collages of the set – *trompe-l'œil* backdrops with real objects like "a suspended tandem, symbol of marriage." This set was the surrealist basis of the production – 'the Ubic matter" in O'Brady's phrase. The production virulently attacked Ubu dictator, Ubu capitalist, Ubu bourgeois; the socio-political attack blended with an attack against outworn bourgeois theatre. "I was looking for an opportunity to revolt and declare war on the whole sick French theatre." The Freemen were bound by an enormous chain so that they disobeyed together; they spoke slowly in a lugubrious voice. Ubu struck Pissweet with a chain-and-ball; Pissweet fell into the arms of the first Freeman, who fell into the arms of the second Freeman, who fell ... etc. The Wreckers transformed the respectable salon into a prison cell. A Wrecker (Blin) poured water on Ubu who lay terrified under a mound of straw.[11]

Itkine's seriousness, professionalism, and exemplary ethics left a lasting impression on Blin. Itkine founded the acting company, the Scarlet Devil; he organized poetry readings with Eluard and the Surrealists; he saw a close link between poetry and theatre, which is evident in his essay on the dramaturgy of poetry; he had personal radiance and total commitment to all his undertakings, including the Resistance where he died horribly under torture. All this marked Blin indelibly, and he dreamed of offering homage to the prematurely dead Itkine by introducing a new generation to his work, such as *The Hussy*, where Ben Jonson is a character.

Blin met Jean-Louis Barrault in 1932, three years before Barrault's adaptation of Faulkner's *As I Lay Dying*, which aroused Artaud's admiration. At 7 rue des Grands-Augustins Barrault found three large attics where a whole group went to live, give readings, produce theatre pieces. "Tender anarchists in love with life" gathered at the Augustins attic; from the October Group came Prévert, Tchimoukow; also Marcel Duhamel, Robert Desnos,

1 Roger Blin in Barrault's adaptation of Knut Hamsun's *Hunger* at the Théâtre de l'Atelier, 1939. Ph. Lipnitzki/Viollet

Sylvain Itkine, writers like Gide; actors like Decroux, painters like Masson and Labisse. In that meeting-place ideas seethed. Jean-Louis Barrault recalled that period to me:

Artaud often requested: "Imitate me." It amused him, but then he grew irritated. He left crying: "They've stolen my personality." And he laughed up his sleeve. On 21 January, in collaboration with Breton, we very seriously celebrated the beheading of Louis XVI.

Margaritis and Caccia played cello and fake harmonica. I asked Prévert to adapt *The Wonder Show* of Cervantes. We needed a child, and Itkine suggested Mouloudji. [This child was found in the street and adopted by the group of Rue des Augustins.] He sang "O, how our childhood is sad," one of the first songs of Kosma. His first night in the attic he shifted from right to left in his bed, explaining that he was rocking himself.

In *The Wonder Show* Blin played a terribly seductive Don Juan smothered by old women. Barrault interpreted the wandering actor who aroused belief in non-existent marvels. Moulouijdi began his acting career.

In 1937 during the Spanish Civil War Blin played in Barrault's production of Cervantes' *Numantia*; he was a dead soldier who revived slowly, almost imperceptibly, in order to prophesy; one evening a woman spectator fainted – to Blin's pride. In the production Barrault blended the real and the fantastic; allegorical figures like Madness, War, Sickness brushed up against real people. Blin then played in Crommelynck's *Magnificent Cuckold* produced by Barrault in Lyon and in Brussels; in that production Stella was played by Madeleine Renaud, who was at that time a member of the Comédie-Française and therefore forbidden to play in Paris with any other company. A little later, in the prologue and epilogue of Laforgue's *Hamlet*, Blin lent his long silhouette – lengthened by top hat and umbrella – to the Narrator who was personified as Laforgue; Hamlet was played by Barrault. In a 1939 adaptation of Knut Hamsun's *Hunger* Blin played Barrault's double; while Barrault was preoccupied with the problem of the double, Blin recited a kind of nightmare poem where he used his mime skill and an invented language (drawing upon childhood games). In the meantime he appeared briefly in 1937 in an adaptation of an English novel about unemployment in 1848; Itkine and O'Brady were also in the cast. He played a leper in Lenormand's *Pacific*.

After taking part in the October Group, the Scarlet Devil Company, and Artaud's Theatre of Cruelty, he himself tried to found a company, but bad luck robbed him of the Gaîté-Montparnasse after two years. He was forced to act and direct in many different places, but this gave him a wide gamut of theatre experience.

Blin was irreverent, skeptical, but totally committed to his choices. He played only those parts in those plays with those directors in those theatres that corresponded to his social, political, and theatrical beliefs. Once, playing a matinée for which one was paid only half the evening wage, Blin took the stage with half his makeup on, and he spoke only one of every two words – to the fury of the manager. After World War II Blin reproached Barrault for taking over the Marigny, a bourgeois theatre. To another actor who returned to smaller theatres after a time on the boulevards, he remarked: "Ah, good. You're returning to the theatre."

His long flexible body, trained in mime by Barrault, and in dance as well, his youthful face with its strong personality and refusal of tradition – these rendered Blin at once unique and enigmatic. Though at first his features were not considered classical enough for leading roles, he soon became sought-after for films because of the mysterious aura he projected. He has confessed to loving Dostoyevskian mysticism, without ever speaking of his own anxieties.[12] He endowed his characters with a disturbing blend of anguish and detachment, a mocking skepticism and a serious purpose. In the theatre he portrayed strange characters, such as unshaven tramps, taciturn marginal people, or vociferous rebels – Synge's Playboy, Pinter's Caretaker, Valle-Inclàn's Sexton. With time, his face was etched with the mark of his struggles, his disdain for facile solutions, his hatred of compromise.

At Montparnasse or at St-Germain-des-Prés, he haunted the cafés, engaged in discussion with the writers Artaud, Pichette, or Queneau. He associated with painters and poets. He kept abreast of underground literature. As an actor, he took his own measure with unknown or difficult plays, such as *Epiphanies* by Henri Pichette. He sometimes played in his own productions – the Student in *Ghost Sonata*, Pozzo in *Waiting for Godot*. He also played the Envoy in Genet's *Balcony*, the Solitary One in Planchon's *Black Pig*. He joked that he could play only tramps and princes. And it is true that he could summon both distance and humanity toward the excluded, as well as earthy good nature. But his princes were demystified of their power, and his tramps were poetic vagabonds. Furthermore, he was not embarrassed by blasphemous authors nor by secretive writers.

Even a brief overview of Blin's theatre work shows how much it was tinged by death. From *Numantia* to *Bound East for Cardiff*, from the Assassin in *The Cenci* to the character of Destiny in the ballet *Rendez-vous*, from *Ghost Sonata* to *Triptych*, he played or directed those who are condemned, who are moribund, or who have passed to the other side of the screens. If he had the temperament to direct a terrible story such as that of *Minamata* (in which mercury pollutes the sea), if in Frisch's play he could reassure his actors with jokes, is it not because he brooded on death in his thoughts; by detachment from the trivialities here below, did he not acquire a certain serenity?

AFTER THE WAR

After the Liberation, the theatre seemed to explode. There was a burgeoning of authors, actors, little theatres outside of the main commercial thorough-fares. Although money was scarce, every kind of experiment seemed possible – existentialist, absurd, cabaret. Plays like Sartre's *No Exit* and Camus' *Caligula* were troubled about the human condition, while the power of language was evident in plays by Audiberti, Pichette, Vauthier.

In 1945 Roland Petit produced a ballet by Jacques Prévert, *Rendez-vous*. Kosma composed the music, and Picasso designed the curtain; Blin played one of two actors in the dance. In June 1947 the director Georges Vitaly won the prize for new companies with his production of Audiberti's *The Evil Run*, and decided to produce Pichette's *Epiphanies*. The manager of the Right Bank Théâtre Edward VII welcomed the idea because of the fame of the leading actors, Gérard Philipe and Maria Casarès. After two weeks he came to a rehearsal and asked the group to leave his theatre; Philipe thereupon rented the Left Bank Théâtre des Noctambules. In this dramatic poem in five parts the Poet is born, suffers, loves, is delirious, and dies. "It's a play; no, a poem; no, an orchestration; or rather a phonetic score."[13] The actors played in street clothes against backdrops of the Surrealist painter Matta. At the time it was scandalous to see a five-minute love scene on stage. Critic Jacques Lemarchand, ardent defender of new works, espoused the play's violent lyricism: "I've heard it said that this isn't theatre. We must listen to the cry of the poet."[14] Blin was cast as the Devil and Pichette rhapsodized about him as his ideal actor:

Whoever has felt his blood soar out of its usual circuit, and recalls Roger Blin in something beyond his usual theatre and film roles, can imagine how he contributed something new to the production . . . I attach great importance to faces, to eyes in faces, to the whole mass of human armaments . . . I ask the impossible of the leg and chest of the actor. I want him to be calm and torn apart by a bombshell, with different voices. I salute the way he burns the stageboards . . . the way he moves in the street and retains passion from it. I gravitate toward true actors . . . who are responsible, excited, brilliant, bearers of a time in which anything is possible; those who are natural, uprooted . . . erasers of skin-color, liberators of frontiers, those who are poetic and innovative . . . defenders of the tiniest right of the sun, welcomers of the fruit of the bird, of rain, snow, or flowers, those who bleed to guide a word to its destination.[15]

THE GAÎTÉ-MONTPARNASSE

A Greek alumna of Dullin, Christine Mavroides, and her painter husband, Thanos Tsingos, wanted to manage the small Gaîté-Montparnasse, but foreigners had no legal right to sign a lease. Roger Blin signed for them, partly hoping to direct his own productions. It was an old vaudeville theatre, near the well-known nightclub Bobino. Agnès Capri had already used it differently, mainly for the Grenier-Hussenot Company, which played *Orion the Killer* in 1946 and *Liliom* in 1947.

In 1949 Roger Blin directed Denis Johnston's *Moon on the Yellow River*. The scholar Maurice Bourgeois had introduced him to Irish literature, and Blin had played in or directed *In the Shadow of the Glen* and *The Playboy of the Western World*. He was attracted to Synge's characters, since they are marginal people, halfway between dream and reality. More generally, Blin responded to Irish humor. Johnston's *Moon on the Yellow River* took as its point of departure an actual event, but also dramatized its absurd side. In Johnston's play Irish villagers, preferring their kerosene lamps, dynamited an electric generator built by the English.

A few months later, Blin staged *Ghost Sonata* by Strindberg, on a double bill with Büchner's *Woyzeck*.[16] "I want to dire t theatre classics," Blin announced, but he would not do so. Most of his care?r would be devoted to works by new authors. And for that matter, what he means by "classics" are works of an international repertory – Strindberg, Büchner, and perhaps certain Elizabethans.

Ghost Sonata, already attractive to Artaud, could not fail to please Blin with its bizarre, almost monstrous, aspects. Strindberg was still relatively unknown to the French public. Critic Jacques Lemarchand underlined the importance of this production: "Those who haven't seen *Ghost Sonata* will claim in five years that they have seen it."[17] Lemarchand praised the sober, efficient set as well as a directorial conception that was naturalistic in some details but expressionist in its lighting, character grouping, and unusual interpretation. Among those who appreciated Blin's work was the writer Arthur Adamov, who wrote the program notes.

O'Brady, in the vampire part of the elderly cripple, moved disturbingly in his wheelchair; Christine Tsingos gave the old mummy a high-pitched parrot voice and an odd accent; Jean Martin as the servant Johansson moved as little as possible and limited gestures to his right hand, so that the character was disturbingly unnatural. Roger Blin played the uneasy Student who was something of a visionary. He encased his long body in a tight frockcoat and allowed himself few gestures; he was lost in a strange and increasingly suffocating world; he was himself strange, with a few bizarre, unbalanced gestures. Blin's production captured the uneasy atmosphere that bathes Strindberg's work; he suggested subterranean currents, halftones, scarcely perceptible vibrations.

In 1950, with the same basic cast, Blin directed *The Executioner is Impatient* by Jean Silvant, otherwise a well-known dance critic. In eight scenes like film-cuts, an Englishman, condemned to death, relives his life; the play was enlivened by Christine Tsingos as a drunken tramp, Jacques Dufilho as a prison guard, Pierre Latour as a judge, Jean Martin as a London cockney, and songs by Francis Lemarque – names that were later to be well known in Paris. On the double bill was *The Wife Unjustly Accused*, a play in the style of Japanese Noh, written by Jean Cocteau and directed by Sacha Pitoëff.

These productions were an early indication of Blin's refusal to be a "creative" director: "A director should render an author's thought without

2 O'Brady as Hummel, Roger Blin as the Student in Blin's production of Strindberg's *Ghost Sonata* at the Gaîté-Montparnasse, 1949. Ph. Lipnitzki/Viollet

adding anything." He was trying to have neither theories nor a distinctive style. He was drawn to works that upset him. How did he direct actors? As long as they have "studied grammar to be able to speak and classical dance to be able to move their bodies," let them express themselves. They have to have presence on the stage. In other words, that which cannot be explained or directed.

In these ventures the box-office take was small. *Ghost Sonata* played over a hundred times, but the house was never full. On Saturday evening, when the nearby Bobino was full, strays would wander in, thinking to find a merry production, and they would leave angrily. A fire destroyed sets. The theatre was soon bankrupt, and Roger Blin was sentenced to pay off its debts over a period of thirty years, thus precluding any possibility of forming his own company. But while at the Gaîté-Montparnasse, Blin was offered two manuscripts by Samuel Beckett – *Eleutheria* and *Waiting for Godot*. The second would shake the very foundations of modern theatre.

2 Beckett's plays

Today both author and play are famous. In 1949, however, while performing *Ghost Sonata*, Blin was told by Tristan Tzara of the existence of a play by Beckett which a number of theatre managers had refused. Tzara advised Beckett to offer it to Blin. "It was our last chance," Beckett told me. Suzanne Beckett brought the manuscript to the Gaîté-Montparnasse. Blin read *Godot* and was delighted. It was a play like no other, and with his sixth sense Blin felt how shocking it might prove. Different from anything on the boards, it questioned the very basis of theatre. Although well written, it sounded like everyday speech, avoiding literary circumlocutions; the dialogue consists of short, economical sentences, apart from a few tirades. Without metaphor or heavy-handed imagery, the style is sometimes lyrical. A blend of parody and gravity endows certain lines with heartrending immediacy, but by means of word-play, dry comedy, or even vulgarity, the author avoids sentimentality. Blin found the play "rich and unique in its nudity."[1] Though Blin later claimed that he did not then fully appreciate its resonance, he felt a need to direct it.[2]

Beckett then went several times to see *Ghost Sonata* and was sensitive to the director's respect for his author. Blin later joked that Beckett, without thought of commercial success, gave him the play because the theatre was empty. Blin knew how to read the work and stage it as a masterwork. Author and director were attuned to one another. Their friendship never lapsed.

Although Blin was nominally manager of the Gaîté, the Tsingos were actually in control and they did not want to produce *Godot*; for three years Blin sought a theatre and just enough money to pay a few actors. Several refused to have anything to do with it. A possibility fell through at the small Théâtre de Poche. Then a new subsidy was announced for aid toward production of a first play and writer Georges Neveux was on the committee of selection; he wrote Blin: "Dear Roger Blin, You are quite right to want to direct *Waiting for Godot*. It is an astonishing play; needless to say, I am fiercely for it. Cordially." The letter is dated 22 January 1952, but another year passed before *Godot* reached the stage. Jean-Marie Serreau welcomed it to his Théâtre de Babylone, but before then Blin had to make several cast changes. The subsidy was minimal, as was the set, in order to keep the money for the slender salaries of the actors. (Blin told me in 1968 that he might have produced *Eleutheria* rather than *Godot*, but it had too many characters.)

Reviewers were confused, and the most powerful of them, Jean-Jacques Gautier of *Figaro*, wrote no review at all. The writer Gabriel Marcel thought that it was not theatre, but he praised Blin's work, as did the sympathetic critic Jacques Lemarchand: "To arrive at such simplicity and force, one needs an intelligence of the heart and a kind of generosity without which talent and experience count for little. Enacting the part of rich Pozzo [Blin] arrives at a comic mixture that is not easily forgotten."[3]

One evening there was a near riot, with whistling and insults. Blin lowered the curtain before the end of the first act. There was a confrontation, but the discontented spectators left, and the show continued. Jean Anouilh coined an apposite phrase: "The *Pensées* of Pascal played by the Fratellini Clowns." The writer Audiberti was enthusiastic. Good reviews and word of mouth kept the show going for over a hundred performances; then there were tours, revivals, and the well-known success of the play in many languages; it has become one of the greatest, if not *the* greatest, classic of the twentieth century. It has been classified as anti-theatre and theatre of the absurd because it is said to have no plot, and the awaited character never appears. Blin quipped mischievously that the other characters have nothing to say to one another.

Some commentators overdramatize Beckett's purpose; others rob it of all drama. Pierre-Aimé Touchard (later head of the Comédie-Française) recalled that when he saw the second act of the play in 1954, he retrospectively understood the first, but he could not summarize it:

We were much closer then to the end of the war and the blow to our consciousness of atomic peril. It seemed to many of us that a new era had begun with Hiroshima and Nagasaki; that from then on one would say: before Hiroshima, after Hiroshima. This new era was one of cosmic fear; humanity might be on the brink of totally destroying itself. And we asked ourselves about the mystery of that destiny ... But the theatre continued as before Hiroshima. *Waiting for Godot* expressed our thought with unbelievable energy. What no contemporary human voice had yet been able to cry out, those miserable heroes sighed out in the dumb horror that humanity had been feeling for years.[4]

There has been a long series of exegeses of *Godot*, but all that needs to be noted here is that, among the many manuscripts submitted to Roger Blin when he managed the Gaîté-Montparnasse, he knew how to choose the one with a crucial treatment of man and the world. And at the same time he was sensitive to the novelty of its form – a blend of the comic and tragic. "After Beckett certain texts, especially theatre texts, have become unbearable. This is due mainly to his language which is at once sober and forceful in its tautness. I think that Beckett has revolutionized the form of dialogue. I think that after him there will inevitably be a greater stylistic rigor ... [He] has made a certain kind of theatre impossible, as Picasso has made a certain kind of painting impossible."[5] Today we can appreciate Blin's boldness. Not yet recognized as a director, he dared suggest that an unknown author would "junk three-quarters of the theatre of the past. That's a militant act on my part."[6]

In 1953 there was resistance, of course. Frustrated and disappointed, some people found the work hermetic, and they closed themselves off from a meaning that now seems clear to us. After thirty years the play has been digested and plagiarized. It is fundamentally theatrical, and nothing in its form surprises us any more. It is not revolutionary, but neither is it dated. Blin's revival at the Comédie-Française in 1978 showed how it can captivate today's audiences. It is of course received differently; we have evolved, and the context is different. It is characteristic of masterpieces to be anchored both in their own time and all time. To Blin's credit, he sensed this and fought to make it possible. In 1978 he agreed to work with the established Comédie-Française so as to reach another audience.

Beckett wrote the two plays – Eleuthéria and Waiting for Godot – while working on his fiction. He wrote Godot fairly quickly and revised small details until 1952. During Babylone rehearsals there were further revisions at Blin's suggestion, and these are evident in Beckett's English translation.[7] When Beckett directed the play in Germany, he made certain cuts, but Blin ignored them when he staged it in 1978.

After Godot Beckett attended rehearsals and even directed productions of his own plays. In manuscript and director's notebook he drew diagrams, sketches, musical notes; he did not stop at the words. For the original Godot, however, he did not write down descriptions of his characters and of their movements on stage. Watching Blin was his first participation in professional theatre, but Beckett did not subsequently imitate him. Beckett later composed a director's notebook before he began rehearsals, but Blin never did.

Blin was the ideal director to welcome Beckett to the stage. A connoisseur of texts, in love with words himself, familiar with research into sounds and rhythms, the servant of a work and obedient to its scenic directions, he tried to concretize to the best of his ability. He directed Godot with probity. He urged the actors to stick close to the text without permitting themselves any embellishment in stage business. More than a monolithic text or dialogue studded with scenic directions, Waiting for Godot is a wait, a silence through which false time flows; long stretches of silence are at times pierced by an exclamation, a question, a fragmentary phrase.

Every Beckett character "can be considered the beginning or continuation of any other."[8] The novel Mercier and Camier, which precedes Godot, prefigures the duality of Vladimir/Estragon, the complaining but inseparable couple. As Mercier, the big one, is vigorous, so Camier, the small one, is lethargic. Old friends in nightmare, traveling nowhere, they are overtaken by night; they dream of the horror of existence. In situations comparable to those of *Godot*, they exchange comparable remarks. In the novel's Mr Madden we can see the germ of Pozzo. There is also a tree and a reference to two thieves. The dialogue resembles that of vaudeville. (Blin will recall this novel when he directs *Godot* in 1978, for it is a kind of biography of the characters of that play.) *Mercier and Camier* is fiction with much dialogue. In *Godot* it is as though the narrative has fallen away, leaving phrases of a fragmentary dialogue; it is as though Beckett rejected the game of consecutive dramatic writing, and proceeded by flashes, by short intertwined sequences, each one developing an idea briefly: "Let's try and converse calmly." "Let's contradict each other." "Let's abuse each other." "Now let's make it up." "We could play at Pozzo and Lucky." There is no build-up in the action as there is in the so-called well-made play; rather all is re-examination, collage.

What do prisoners do in their cell? They recall their life, their arrest, their captivity. They no longer have anything but a crumbling vocabulary and an untrustworthy memory. All they can do is talk, filling their minds with something to make time pass while they continue to exist. Mercier and Camier, Vladimir and Estragon, are prisoners of human nature, condemned to live and die without knowing who or what condemns them. Wretched vagabonds, wanderers, poor, directionless, timeless, Vladimir and Estragon meet or see in a mirage an unusual couple, Pozzo/Lucky, joined by the materiality of a cord. One can pin labels on their reciprocal enslavement: master/slave of modern times, are Pozzo and Lucky an Auschwitz prisoner and his SS executioner? A Soviet dissident and the director of a psychiatric clinic? Or, beneath the appearance of a circus animal obeying his trainer, should we read the metaphor of every man suffering exploitation? "Not at all," protested Beckett, refusing to allow Blin to evoke social resonance from the Pozzo–Lucky couple. "Nevertheless the image of exploitation comes to mind when one reads the text," Blin has said.

Pozzo has power, property: a whip, a folding-chair, food, a pipe – illusory and transitory wealth; his valise contains nothing but sand that he nevertheless condemns his victim Lucky to carry. For them time passes more quickly than for Vladimir and Estragon, who are petrified and repeat themselves from one act to the next; in contrast, Pozzo goes blind, and Lucky dumb. Unless one exercises good will, "Nothing happens . . . it's terrible." Nothing happens; that was the most difficult thing to stage in 1953. The New Novel and the New Cinema had not yet appeared.

Nothing happens *on the surface* since Godot does not come, and the situation of Vladimir and Estragon remains unchanged – unless Pozzo, like a messiah, is not recognized as Godot. Beckett has a great deal happen, but without weaving a plot with its arbitrary climaxes and theatrical dénouement. He develops a series of gestures and humorous lines which pop up here and there in the stretches of stillness and silence: Estragon is hungry, Estragon is sleepy, Vladimir suggests that they do exercises, Vladimir finds Estragon's shoes, Pozzo and Lucky come to distract them in their wait; after their departure Vladimir and Estragon imitate them. All this is motivation for a variety of stage actions, a veritable series of stylistic exercises for actors and spectators.

Tramps or clowns?

Beckett does not mention tramps in the usual sense of the word. His generalized characters are wanderers without hearth or home. They have little to eat, and they keep their meagre provisions in their pockets. Estragon sleeps in a ditch and does not remove his shoes every day. They are near the end of their lives, near the end of a world. They find themselves in an unknown region, or in one that they do not recognize, but they are metaphysical vagabonds. Have critics since 1953 taken them for tramps because of their worn clothes, clodhoppers, and poverty? For critic Geneviève Serreau, Vladimir and Estragon are "clowns rather than tramps."[9] Another critic writes: "The clown is the pure actor and not the interpreter of a part; he performs his routine, which may be his personal parody of human behavior."[10] Beckett's characters often behave like clowns; they drop to the ground, perform their numbers, take part in a pantomime with three hats (a *commedia* number that inspired the Marx Brothers); they take leave with exaggerated politeness and judge their situation ironically. Their style and vocabulary are sometimes drawn from the circus: "Bags. (*He points at Lucky.*) Why? Always hold. (*He sags, panting.*) Never put down. (*He opens his hands, straightens up with relief.*) Why?"

Pozzo has a plosive, lively name, which cracks like a whip when it is pronounced, and he wields a trainer's whip. He improvises games: "If you asked me to sit down." He drops his tyrant role to play with the others, and he asks if he has played well. Phrases are repeated, as in circus entrances when clowns repeat several times to be sure that each section of the audience hears them. (Beckett does something similar in *Act Without Words 1* when a man is thrown from the right wing onto the stage, makes a few gestures, exits right; then he is thrown on the stage from the left wing, repeats the gestures, exits left, etc.)

Pozzo is an orator prating at his audience Vladimir and Estragon. Lucky performs two numbers, his dance and his monologue. Every night the characters will repeat their performance. Pozzo and Lucky are an entertainment for Vladimir and Estragon who take an inventory of Lucky; they do not view him as a suffering being but as an object for clown play. They juggle words and play with simple objects – shoes, hats, carrots, turnips, as well as with the tree that is at once a geographic signpost, a proof of life, a possibility of hanging. They have to play to escape the flow of time, to deceive their anguish, not to think. The actors themselves should not show this anguish, for the spectators will perceive it subtly through the course of the performance. Vladimir and Estragon play at playing rather than at living; they are frames for characters that shift from one attitude to another, from one game to another, like vaudevillians who move from one routine to the next, without any need for continuity.

Waiting for Godot is a parable of theatrical performance. In enacting Beckett's play, the actors are producing a diagram of performance, abstracted and therefore exemplary, concretized because lived as a conscious theatrical phenomenon. The anecdotal and emotional vanish, and yet if the spectator wants to be involved, he will find himself at the very heart of an existential quest.

Beckett is conscious of the clown resonances of Godot, and he has insisted upon them. He wanted Estragon/Latour's trousers to fall to his ankles and in the London production he insisted on keeping that gag in spite of the Lord Chamberlain's objection. For him, the grotesque and the tragic are inalienably linked. "Nothing is funnier than unhappiness," Nell will say in Endgame.

In contrast to minimal plot, there is a great deal of stage business. What to do while waiting? What to say to give one the impression of existing? Economy governs the dramatic construction: a single place, with a mound and a petrified tree; two symmetrical acts, five characters, sequences of brief phrases, succinct developments, few properties. Interest is continually revived between two pauses by various injections, just as it looks as though the characters have come to the end of their resources.

Lucky's monologue, sometimes considered senseless, proves to be a three-part construction – divine indifference, human reduction, and an inert cosmos – followed by a da capo in which the three themes reappear. Beckett insists on the right tone for each word and syllable: "My work is a question of fundamental sounds . . . realized as fully as possible."[11] Beckett also takes pains with gestures and their repetition. Estragon sleeps on his mound; he yearns for rest and immobility – his leitmotif. In contrast, Vladimir, drawn to the tree, moves, walks, and is never still. Their desires oppose their respective natures, for Vladimir wants to stay there to await Godot, whereas Estragon wants to leave. We are reminded of Beckett's fictional Molloy: "For me there have always been two fools, among others, one asking nothing better than to stay where he is and the other imagining that life might be slightly less horrible a little further on." It is always Estragon who falls asleep and Vladimir who walks around. At the very beginning Estragon is absorbed in a silent action; he tries in vain to take off his recalcitrant shoe. Vladimir enters, looks at the tree and then at Estragon. One character is troubled by his weariness, by his aching feet; the other is the prey of spiritual anxiety. The one is drawn to his mound, and the other to the tree.

The dialogue is often fragmentary, as though punctured by bad memory; it may be interrupted by a facetious detour, swerving from its initial direction; and then it may return to orbit through a logical remark. The human being, born to die, ignoring his immediate future, is turned in all directions but always brought back to an elemental level, with clarity and humor. In any case, it is without issue. The stage space is also without issue; it is a piece of ground where Estragon and Vladimir inevitably meet. The time of action is a cyclical time, repeated from one act to the next, repeated from one performance to the next. In detail and in overall structure the play is symmetrical.

If Beckett twists the neck of eloquence through his Estragon and Vladimir (at first performance, their conversational idiom shocked some spectators), he offers rhetorical possibilities to Pozzo, and this contrasts with Lucky who is like a motor starting up and turning in a void. Through their negations – "I don't remember," "I wasn't there," "They're not mine" – the characters refuse their own identity; they reject incarnation; they seem outside of themselves, but there is no sentimentality. Rather the play is an objective search into the furthest corners of the human condition. Beckett admits: "My little exploration has been that zone of being neglected by most authors."[12]

The venues

After a possible 1952 opening in the small Théâtre de Poche fell through, *Waiting for Godot* was at last produced in a theatre that was relatively unknown to Parisians. At 38 Boulevard Raspail, in an old dining-hall, a small theatre was built in 1952 by Jean-Marie Serreau, another pioneer of the French avant-garde. His Théâtre de Babylone was dedicated to experiment, but it was minimally equipped. Before *Godot* he had welcomed Strindberg's *Miss Julie* and revived his own production of Brecht's *Exception and the Rule*. (Brecht was practically unknown in France before the arrival of the Berliner Ensemble in 1954.)

After its success at the Babylone, *Godot* was revived at the Théâtre Hébertot in 1956, in Florence in 1961, at the Odéon in 1961, at the Grenier of

Toulouse in 1964, and at the Paris Récamier in 1970. Then Blin did another production at the Comédie-Française in 1978, which was revived at the Odéon in 1980. Created in a small avant-garde theatre of humble means, twenty-five years later *Godot* had at its disposal the luxury of the national subsidized theatre. The actors had changed, but the set and mise-en-scène of Blin preserved the same spirit. In other countries directors and designers moved far away from Beckett's asceticism. Beckett himself directed the play on a nearly bare stage at Berlin's Schiller Theatre in 1975.

Blin's mise-en-scène

The set
It is now famous: a tree, a mound. An almost empty stage on which four actors move. Nothing to rejoice the eye; a vision of the end of a world. Limited to poor theatre (the subsidy just covered the actors' meagre wages and the posters), Blin contrived a backdrop of odd pieces of light material stitched together. He designed a tree that his stage manager made by covering wire hangers with crepe paper, and stood the whole on a foam-rubber base. This dry, sickly tree was only a little taller than a man; it was ridiculous with its branch, or rather its section of broken branch, to which a few leaves were added in Act II. It would be truly difficult to hang oneself from it. At the back of the stage two people held oil cans with bulbs inside, but they did little with them. The lights gave a sense of ambience while lighting the actors' faces. Behind the backdrop someone else manipulated another oil can with a bulb, to show the rise of the moon at the end of each act.

After Blin moved to more richly endowed theatres, he had a cyclorama. He then asked the sculptor Giacometti to construct a pale, threadlike, slender tree which became a kind of symbol for the play. (The tree disappeared when Blin went to London to direct *The Blacks*.) When Blin directed at the Comédie-Française, he stressed Beckett's scenic indication of "A country road" and his designer Matias built an uneven ground, a kind of earthly dome marked by footsteps, with a rake of 10 percent. Blin raised the tree to show Vladimir and Estragon climbing toward it. Nor did he want the audience to lose any of the Act II scene in which the four actors are on the ground. Matias' rake delivered the visibility he needed.

A large cyclorama lit from behind was closed off by curtains on each side, as in the circus. When Pozzo and Lucky arrive, the curtain opens to admit them, but it closes behind them. They cross an unlit area, and begin to act only when they are brightly lit. This setting is the residue of an old discarded choice of Blin, who had been impressed in reading by the circus aspect of the play, so that he first thought of staging it as a circus ring. "I thought I'd bring the actors on like clowns, entering in dressing-gowns. At the back they would drop a curtain labeled HEAVEN or painted with something that would mean heaven. They would rub their feet with resin; they would bring on a tree in a pot. They would take off their dressing-gowns in the wings, and then the action would start; the only set would be that tree and a little red bench across the whole back."[13] Beckett was reluctant. It is true that the action sometimes resembles a clown show but also American vaudeville like that of Chaplin and Keaton. Beckett thought that too specific a reference to the circus might undermine the gravity of the play. Blin came to agree with Beckett, but he nevertheless sought to retain the play's circularity; it ends where it began, and it repeats infinitely; after turning round and round, Vladimir and Estragon return to their point of departure. Without actually playing in a theatre in the round, Blin had the actors move in circles. "The possession of space is tributary to the action described, but even more to the respiration of words and phrases. The musicality at many points is of primary importance in a text that rejects metaphor."[14]

The casts

Blin, being visual as well as visionary, had to see the cast in his mind's eye. He needed to imagine the character in some kind of model. When half awake or brooding about a work he was going to direct, he sometimes visualized by reference to theatre or films he had seen. Thus, thinking of actors, he envisioned an ideal cast of Vladimir played by Chaplin, Estragon by Keaton, Pozzo by Charles Laughton. He considered Vladimir for himself at one point, but at the Babylone he gave the part to Lucien Raimbourg, who fascinated him.[15] Raimbourg was not an actor but a vaudevillian, and he therefore had not formed the usual bad habits of actors; his playing was fresh, without inquiry into psychology. Naturally deep, very vivacious, he made the interpretation very human. Perhaps Blin unconsciously recalled Steinbeck's *Of Mice and Men* in which "the little one directs the big one."[16] (In 1945 a dramatization had played at the Hébertot theatre.) Since Raimbourg was small, Blin sought a larger Estragon and found him in Pierre Latour, an actor who had played with him in other avant-garde productions, an actor who could be at once humorous and disturbing.

In 1972 the Comédie-Française asked Blin to direct *Godot* at the Odéon, but Blin refused because he could not have Raimbourg as Vladimir; at the time it was impossible for an actor to play a single role at the Comédie. After Raimbourg's death in 1975 Blin agreed to direct there, and he did so in 1978. He then balanced the production in the other direction, choosing a tall actor for Vladimir and a small one for Estragon who could thus come to Vladimir for protection. The image was more direct.

When he started writing, Beckett had no names for the master/slave couple. In his manuscript he had first noted that the two men were, respectively, big and small, and there too the casts evolved gradually. In September 1952, actor Jean Martin met Roger Blin who told him: "I'm directing a play. There was a part for you, but unfortunately I'm playing it because I like it. It has only one line." Said Martin: "Then I have no regrets." "Oh but yes, have a look." And he showed Martin the six-page monologue.

Between the time when a production was scheduled at the Poche and the actual opening at the Babylone, Blin was refused by a number of actors. The play was difficult to understand, and they didn't know how to approach it. They feared a failure, and they predicted to Blin: "You won't make a cent." Actually, Blin himself was surprised the first time that he saw a full house in

3 The original cast in Blin's production of *Waiting for Godot* at the Théâtre de Babylone, 1953; Lucky (Jean Martin), Vladimir (Lucien Raimbourg), Estragon (Pierre Latour), Pozzo (Roger Blin), tree by Gerstein. Ph. Bernand

the 240 seats of the Babylone. Was it an illusion or a misunderstanding? He did not dare to believe his eyes.

In casting, Blin had to deal with Beckett's preferences. Blin himself wanted a corpulent actor to fulfil the one indication the author gave him for Pozzo – "a mass of flesh." And yet Beckett wanted Blin to play Pozzo. Did that finally happen because of Beckett's desire or because the actor who rehearsed Pozzo was inadequate? Jean Martin recalled: "One day Roger called me to the Babylone. The actor playing Pozzo just couldn't manage it. Since Blin knew what had to be done and knew the part by heart, Raimbourg and Latour urged him to play it and to look for someone else for Lucky. I read the play, and I found it wonderful." Blin therefore played Pozzo in spite of himself. He thought that he had neither the appearance nor the bluster that were necessary (nor perhaps the temperament of a despot). Afterwards Pozzo was played by a number of heavier actors, and in 1965 Blin declared: "From now on I'll play Estragon."[17] But he never did.

Lucky was first played by Jean Martin, who was memorably haunting. Since his stage trembling began to afflict him offstage, he did not wish to continue too long in the part, and Blin cast a number of other actors in his different productions.

Costumes

Beckett gave only one scenic description in this area; all four characters wear bowler hats. Is this the influence of silent film comics, or is it the residue of bourgeois dignity? Pozzo is rich, or has been, since he claims to be the lord of the place, the proprietor of the land, and perhaps even Godot. Blin saw him as a gentleman-farmer, like John Bull in English etchings. The character also reminded him of Chaplin in *Limelight*. Blin played him in gleaming costume, riding-breeches, checked greatcoat, boots, and gray bowler.

Lucky has to have long white hair hidden under his hat. Jean Martin's physique suggested a Surrealistic costume to Blin; striped body-stocking, black trousers that were cut off at the calf, eighteenth-century livery with gold trimming. Martin found that costume. Lucky's bare feet were shod with old boots, resembling those in a Van Gogh painting that Blin recalled. Intellectual Vladimir wore formal attire with tails (Blin's father's wedding-jacket), an old pink undershirt, a shirt-front attached by strings, a wing collar, a loose necktie. Estragon had a patched jacket, a loose scarf, an old dented bowler, worn shoes that were obviously too big. None of the characters was particularly ragged, and their clothes contrasted with their situation. They stubbornly conveyed an image of civilization in a landscape of the end of the world. Shabby but dignified tramps, they might be gloomy and anxious but not desperate. These metaphysical clowns and their costumes set the tone for other casts.

Except for Pozzo's, the costumes were made of leftovers, suggesting something of the tramp and something of the clown; but since they were dark, they were dignified. Like the tree, these costumes are part of the *Godot* legend. Twenty years later Beckett came to think that Pozzo and Lucky should also be tramps, and Blin incorporated this into his production of 1978, where Pozzo was unshaven in a worn costume.

How to play *Waiting for Godot*

The first actors had so much difficulty because they had a long way to go. Accustomed to a wordy text whose momentum would carry them along; accustomed also to calculate emotional effects in order to display them at a given moment, they found themselves now before a fragmented form, whittled down to a minimum. They could find no springboard; they had to proceed slowly, constantly stopping. It was impossible to identify with or even incarnate a character. There was no continuity to the dialogue; each line was short and short-stopped. What to invent to avoid monotony? What to substitute for psychological consistency? What was the deep meaning of the play? "I didn't want to bother the actors with metaphysical notions. I made them play the basic level, concretely," Blin recalled in 1978.

Blin was very respectful of all Beckett's scenic directions. Occasionally, he suggested a slight cut or a bit of business. Beckett did not always agree, but he did allow Vladimir and Estragon to step on Pozzo and Lucky on the ground: ". . . all mankind is us . . ."

Although these characters are almost bodiless because their lines are so skeletal, although they are at grips with the human condition, Blin started with their specific physical pain. Estragon's feet hurt, and when your feet hurt, your whole body is tired. You stop, you sit down, you do not want to get up again. Thus Estragon is lethargic and fixed on himself: "I see him as large – a block of rejection, of silence, which is occasionally broken by ingenuous flashes; in his permanent sleep there are occasional extraordinary insights."[18] The first Estragon, Pierre Latour, achieved some distance from his character by cool comedy, and a sulky response to Vladimir's exhortations. At the Odéon revival in 1961 Etienne Bierry varied between banter and exhaustion.

Vladimir has prostate trouble, so he is bent double, or he has to run into the wings to relieve himself. He moves back and forth, voluble and mobile. Never discouraged, Vladimir tries to placate Estragon; he reactivates their slim hope. Raimbourg plays without seeming to play, humming the words between his teeth. He jumps around, full of guile and tricks. He is close to the knotty tree of the set. Blin explained to me in 1978:

There is a certain cruelty in the Vladimir/Estragon relationship, but also a certain tenderness. Their friendship is not based on much. Like a couple, they are bound together by habit; they can't bear each other, but they cannot separate. Beckett told me that in this filth that surrounds us [in spite of his pessimism about the human condition] there are nevertheless moments when one can take someone's hand, when something authentic happens. Vladimir and Estragon are immature; they are floating corks; they don't take their fate into their hands. Estragon's aching feet may be real or fictional; he wants to make himself interesting. Vladimir has one obsession – to watch for Godot's arrival. I make him watch left, right, front, and back.

In Lucky's monologue Jean Martin began by delivering his text slowly, syllable by syllable, in a monotonous tone that gradually became choppy. Then his pace picked up like a machine run amuck; his voice emitted sharp uncontrolled notes, repeated syllables making the discourse skid, an acceleration leading to incomprehensibility. His frenzy increased when Pozzo wanted to interrupt him.

Retrospectively, it is surprising to note that Lucky has nothing to say, outside of his monologue. During performance, one has the feeling that the four roles are approximately equal. This proves that one acts just as much without a text. Lucky is on stage for the same length of time as Pozzo, and the impact of his presence or his stage business is just as visible and important. Actor Jean Martin explained:

I couldn't stand there doing nothing, except for a monologue. To justify the logorrhea and the trembling, I consulted a doctor friend about Parkinson's disease. When I started the trembling at rehearsal, Roger was not very enthusiastic. I adopted an uncomfortable position, on one toe, with the other foot raised, and was unbalanced with my basket and valise. Beckett didn't object. When the costume-fitter fainted after the monologue, Roger told me: "You were right; that's what has to be done."

Martin frothed, capered, trembled.

Since then our sensibility has evolved. We can manage today with more schematic acting for Lucky. Less studied, and less Artaudesque, he still moves us as much. We are no longer in the context of after-Auschwitz or after-Hiroshima, and we recognize the master/slave couple without naturalism. In 1970 actor Michel Robin had the skew look of a shackled intellectual whom one could not silence; and he recited like a thinking top. In 1978 Riquier was an awkward puppet near collapse, rather than a suffering victim; he was ready to laugh at himself. Beckett does not like to exhibit physical suffering any more than social conflict. He seeks allusive acting, theatrical acting. In 1953, however, Jean Martin was haunting.

Pozzo is the oldest. He is worn out; all his strength is in his voice. He is full of bluster and false heartiness. He treats his folding chair like a throne; he eats daintily; he cracks his whip. Without these signs of power and wealth, invested in his props, he would be no one of any significance. Blin played him against type, with moustache, husky voice, and a pillow at his stomach; an

Italian described him to Blin as "a skinny one inside a fat one." His shouts contrasted with his distracting seriousness. He lost his temper, but his eyelids showed his depression. Like Vladimir with Estragon, he is part of a pair. Without Lucky's reactions to his words and gestures, his personality would collapse. More than a character, he is a function.

Having entered their characters through corporeal conditioning, the actors had to play the situation with great caution. They had to make the dialogue play and not try to display themselves. They had to learn how to pause precisely, to respect the silences, to work with real time since the duration of *Godot* is the duration of the performance. "It's all a matter of respecting the pauses and repetitions. That's what carries the truth of the play," said Blin in 1978.

In 1957 critic Madeleine Chapsal noted the effect this produces: "For long stretches of time, uneasiness spreads through the theatre. The public is accustomed to listen to words in artificial groupings, which are not recognizable like this, dragged in their materiality through the silence."[19] For that audience there was no trace of the experimental theatre of the 1920s and 1930s. It was not until the late 1960s with the abandonment of classical delivery that new ruptures, slowing down, disconnection gained acceptance.

Roger Blin knew how to fill time with an object or to fill the time between two actions with the actor alone, without making him look like a fool. An actor showing Vladimir or Estragon alone on stage is both concretely and allegorically alone in the world. Sometimes deprived of words, the actors are forced to project lines point-blank into the immediacy of the situation. The reflexes of a mime or clown are needed, rather than the actor accustomed to build a scene; there is no crescendo, no *savoir-faire* to show. The actor has to be there, without a part to play, as Alain Robbe-Grillet has masterfully shown.[20] To be at grips with the inevitable, helped by a few slim words; to express the unnameable, to quote Beckett's title of a novel. The actors would have profited from training in Futurist or Surrealist texts — broken and disjunctive — but that repertory had not been approached by professional French actors, as was evident when Ionesco's first plays were staged.

Unlike trained actors, Raimbourg entered fully into these short, spontaneous lines, even if the larger meaning escaped him. Sometimes the work seemed closed to him, but he let himself be directed by Blin. The indications were always concrete, couched in terms of daily life; there was no whisper of metaphysics.

Rehearsals lasted over a year, through changes of venue and cast. Beckett came only to the last rehearsals, and Raimbourg testified: "I've never in my life met someone so profoundly human, so modest and yet so clear in explaining what he could see or not see in the characters through the acting."[21]

Beckett did not yet have the stage experience that he subsequently acquired. Although Blin respected his scenic directions, he occasionally commented when a movement or pause would be more evident to a reader than an audience, and he suggested that one might have to proceed differently, in harmony with the actor or the concrete needs of the performance. But Beckett was already maniacally exigent about breathing and pronunciation. He wanted the quintessence of stylization, but actors tend towards mimesis. While expressing the humanity of these characters, they had to preserve a certain irony towards themselves. They had to be detached from themselves and not evade the situation.

In occasionally playing down the comic, Blin avoided both the farcical and the tearful. "If there are gags, it's in line with Beckett's intention. I wanted to keep Beckett's sober tone, so that the tragic would appear only in the slow pace of the action, up to the dreamlike atmosphere of the last moments."

Later Beckett himself directed *Godot* in Berlin, and he did not hesitate to emphasize the comic. Blin commented to me in 1978: "Beckett's Berlin mise-en-scène was very funny, but I personally could never eradicate my first impression of the play – that of cruelty."

Toulouse

Blin directed a revival of *Waiting for Godot* at the Grenier de Toulouse in 1964. The director knew the play well and gradually guided the actors. "You need to be very fit to play Beckett's decrepits," Blin said at that time.[22] Slowly, he revealed new facets of each role, and he showed by example. Incapable of theorizing, he jumped to the stage to give the actors the general direction. He showed the trembling and panting of Lucky, without asking the Toulouse actor to imitate the high-pitched voice of Jean Martin. He showed how Pozzo might treat his folding-chair like a throne, how Vladimir might waddle painfully. He was attentive to the specific qualities of the actors in Toulouse. He let them play with a slight southern accent, and he let Vladimir sing a dialect lullaby of Languedoc.

At the Comédie-Française

What did it mean when someone as unconventional as Blin agreed to work for so official an institution? Essentially, it was a matter of seeking a new generation and a new kind of audience. Again Blin contrasted his Vladimir and Estragon – a low voice for the latter and a high one for the former. As in Beckett's 1975 Berlin production, their costumes linked them, the one wearing striped trousers and the other a striped jacket. Estragon looked like a Callot etching, hands almost soldered to his pockets and jacket unbuttoned,

face unshaven, hat over his eyes, plunged in sulks. He accented certain
syllables strangely. He made fun of Pozzo in imitating him, taking positions
from *commedia dell'arte*. When he was seated, chest forward, heavy, hands
hanging, he seemed to fall asleep without being at rest. All his energy was
cerebral. Vladimir bent his knees when he wanted to affirm an idea; he was
compared to a penguin crossed with a crow, whereas Estragon resembled a
barking badger. (In 1953, however, only Lucky summoned animal compari-
sons – to a dog barking at the moon or a horse in harness.) Face to face,
Vladimir and Estragon moved their necks and chins; they bent their bodies.
On their knees they were nose to nose. They twisted and played to forget the
tragic aspect of their situation, as clowns can enjoy each moment. Estragon
was contorted in mockery while Vladimir offstage suffered from prostate
pain. To show that he was out of breath, Estragon placed his hand on his
heart, as though to contain its beating. He was obstinate in his refusals, sulky
in his friendship, intransigent. He moved his head a great deal, and took
advantage of his mobile face. The two friends resorted to vocal nuances –
crescendos and de-crescendos; they chanted five variants on: "Do you
want to get rid of him?" They alternated questions and answers. They
imitated circus pronunciation of certain words, with false naiveté. They used
the wide resources of their vocal skills. They showed off facets of Beckettian

4 Rehearsal of Blin's 1978 production of *Godot* at the Comédie-
Française, with Beckett present. Ph. Hermine Karagheuz

syntax – short assonant phrases, those that dovetail, those that break off.

Lucky had stiff arms and a jerky walk; he seemed on the point of expiring. He was a trembling robot, a skeletal figure. When he was humiliated, he seemed to withdraw into himself and disappear; he lowered his head, hid his neck, and scowled. With clenched jaws, he mixed several tones in his monologue, and this alternation of deep voice and falsetto added to the schizophrenic incoherence. With vitreous eyes – Blin explained it as the dissolution of matter – and mouth wide open in the mute scenes, he thought before each banal movement which he had difficulty completing. When he was opposed, his hands would wring, his lips tremble. He watched grimly when Estragon imitated him. At one moment he moved only his eyes, and in the next moment he broke into somersaults. He moved his long limbs like a camel discovering water. Pozzo didn't know what to do with himself before this pitiful display. He hid his face in the cape of his coat. Or he raised his voice and imposed his authority on the others.

5 Scene from Blin's 1978 production of *Godot* at the Comédie-Française. Set by Matias. Vladimir (Michel Aumont), Estragon (Jean-Paul Roussillon), Lucky collapsed in the centre (Georges Riquier), and Pozzo (François Chaumette). Ph. Hermine Karagheuz

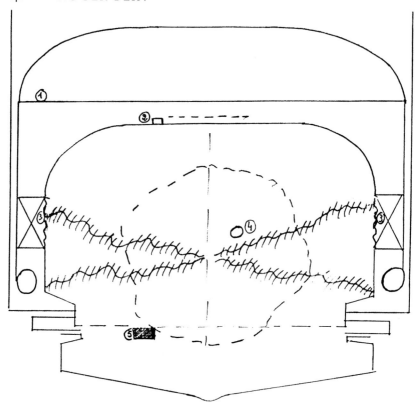

6 Details of Blin's production of *Godot* at the Comédie-Française,
1978, suggested by Ludmila Hols' notebook in the Archives of
the Comédie-Française
(1) dark gray, transparent backcloth (2) moon projected from left
to right (3) side drops for entrances and exits of Pozzo/Lucky
(4) the tree (5) the stone (which replaces the mound of the text)
Shading shows the paths taken by Pozzo and Lucky. The stage
has a 10 percent rake.   (From Ludmila Hols' drawing)
N.B. Although some positions are strictly fixed – primarily those
that are spotlit – the actors' paths are more rounded and flexible
than indicated in the sketch. [O.A.]

A few sequences of the 1978 *Godot*

Beckett meticulously noted all stage movements. What then is Roger Blin's
contribution to what may seem like directing *avant la lettre*? He respects and
completes the author's directions.

Beckett	*Blin*
Estragon, sitting on a stone, is trying to take off his boot. He pulls at it with both hands, panting. He gives up, exhausted, rests, tries again. As before.	Estragon sits down on the stone, lifts his left foot, sighs twice while he puts it on his right knee. Third sigh. He uncrosses his left leg.
Enter Vladimir . . . advancing with short, stiff strides, legs wide apart.	Vladimir enters and stops near the tree. He acts like a philosopher, looking around without seeing. He moves forward and then notices Estragon.
V: I'm glad to see you back . . . We'll have to celebrate this. But how? (*He reflects.*)	Neutral tone. V ponders, his right elbow bent, his hand on his face.
V: (*hurt, coldly*) May one inquire where His Highness spent the night?	V is hurt but not devastated. He withdraws.
V: (*admiringly*) A ditch!	V pretends surprise.

Ludmila Hols noted these comments of Blin:

Time seems suspended. There is neither beginning or end in this play that might have 21 acts. There is real friendship between E and V, but they also play at friendship. Their games fail. They fear to keep still; they dread silence. Circus play always underlies their actions. They are children with no sense of responsibility, children who would bicker like a married couple. V tries to catch the eye of E, who does not look at him, except when they meet in a game. When truth bursts forth, it is a cry.

V: Sometimes I feel it coming all the same. Then I go all queer. (*He takes off his hat, peers inside it, feels about inside it, shakes it, puts it on again.*)	Principle of a code for V and E. One takes off his hat, the other his shoe. V postpones a solution to his problem.
. . .	
E: That would be too bad, really too bad. (*Pause.*) Wouldn't it, Didi, be really too bad? (*Pause.*) When you think of the beauty of the way. (*Pause.*) And the goodness of the wayfarers. (*Pause. Wheedling.*) Wouldn't it, Didi?	Whining, childish, E pulls at the tail of V's jacket.
First entrance of Pozzo/Lucky.	E rubs his head against V's right hip.

V and E are upstage center. The right curtain is opened for their entrance, the left curtain for Lucky's exit after crossing the stage. Lucky looks like the cartoon dog Pluto. In his right hand he carries a suitcase, in his left hand a basket and a folding-stool. A coat is draped over his left arm. Whenever he is not burdened with baggage, he trembles. P stops near center stage. He is an enormous, old, panting, worldly, pretentious squire. Extremely vulnerable, he shifts from humiliation to fury.

L exits on the left, and his fall can be heard after Pozzo jerks the rope brutally. The baggage falls. V wants to rush to L's assistance, but E stops him for the aside:

E: Is that him?

V: Who?

E: (*trying to remember the name*) Er. . .

V: Godot?

E goes downstage, pulling V.

P: You took me for Godot.

P moves towards E who, after each word, retreats a little to the right.

The place called The Board is at the center of a circle; an imaginary line from upstage to downstage marks the poles. Pozzo asserts his status by dominating the primary axis, but he retreats to the circumference to eat undisturbed.

L cries "like a melancholy dog" – Blin's simile – and during his dance, when P pulls him forward, he will use the central axis. L is front and center, V and E as spectators sit on the stone. P is positioned almost symmetrically on the other side of the stage. A triangular tension is established between the exhibitor P, the exhibited L, and the spectators V and E. L dances like a classical ballerina and fights against an invisible net that covers and binds him. He falls with syncopated movements.

Ordered to think, L looks at P to please him, then casts a circular look at V and E, and at the audience. Blin noted: "He will take wicked pleasure in making Pozzo suffer." For Lucky's monologue, Blin asked his actor not to make the syntax clear and to move at odd times. While V and E, impatient at the worthlessness of L's performance, move about and around the circumference and then exit, Pozzo tries to escape from this logorrhea though remaining in the same spot; he covers his ears and then hides his head in the cape of his coat.

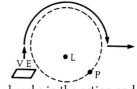

The humor and wit of the director reside in tiny breaks in the action and compensate for the anguish produced by the text at certain points. E pontificates like a Buddha with a solemn gesture of his right hand: "We are all born mad. Some of us remain so." V uses the exaggerated gestures and intonations of a tragic actor when E leaves him: "Gogo! Come back!" The latter takes a clown-like posture – legs bent, hand shading his eyes: "Do you see anything coming?"

The exchange of insults is set like a match. They glare at each other from a distance: "Moron! Vermin! Abortion! Sewer-rat." Insulted by the word "cuckold" (not in the English text), E looks indignantly at the audience, then flings forth: "Architect." V doubles over as if hit in the stomach, and E turns in a victorious circle. Reconciling, each moves one step toward the other at each line. P's line: "Is there anything I can do to cheer them up? I have given them bones . . ." provokes "a storm under the skull."

Trying on the Shoes
This is a pretext for a clown game, with E hopping on one foot.

V: Pull up your trousers.	E does not move.
E: (*staggers*) I can't.	
V pulls up the trousers, looks at the leg, lets it go.	V insists. E lifts his right leg.
V: The other. (*E gives the same leg.*) The other, pig! (*E gives the other leg. Triumphantly.*)	V goes to the right above E, who again gives his right leg. E lifts his right leg, which V slaps.
	E changes quickly and lifts his left leg.
There's the wound! Beginning to fester!	V, happy, hurting E, hits the wound and runs toward the central axis.
E: And what about it?	
V: (*letting go the leg*): Where are your boots?	
. . .	Sure of himself, V looks at the shoes and turns on his heel, humming. He completes his triumph by going downstage toward the shoes, then upstage to the left.
V: There they are!	

Willy-nilly, E finally tries the shoes on and admits that they nearly fit him, but he rebels violently against laces. Letting his blood circulate in his feet represents his last claim to liberty.

Minimal light cues

In Act I three changes bring full lights on the playing area. The fourth change accompanies the ascent of the moon; the fifth one projects a bluish atmosphere for the scene with the Boy; then a spot lights E's shoes, downstage center. At the end of the act three light changes restore darkness. In Act II a new light on the shoes, before bringing the lights up on the rest of the stage; slight fade on P's exit, on the moonrise; bluish atmosphere for the Boy, lowering the lights except for the moon and the shoes; final darkness.

At the end of each act a white ironic moon rose like a balloon. The work seemed much easier to understand; it involved less suffering than at its creation. Gone was the heavy atmosphere, existential anguish, interminable waiting, nightmare vision grounded in Lucky. *Waiting for Godot* had become a theatre piece. While remaining faithful to Beckett and his first mise-en-scène, Blin took account of the personality of these actors and their pleasure in acting.

During a revival in 1980 their interpretation matured and acquired more gravity, especially at the end of Act II, when Vladimir asks himself; "Was I sleeping while the others suffered? Am I sleeping now?" Blin commented: "Spectators who saw the play twenty-five years ago were afraid that they wouldn't feel the same effect in seeing it again. But they told me that they recaptured the spirit. As for the younger generation who were afraid it would be old hat, they were struck by the work's modernity, by its form." I had asked Roger about the audience reaction to his mise-en-scène. He answered about the reception of Beckett's work.

ENDGAME

If the play is not exactly a continuation of *Waiting for Godot*, picking up the same characters at a later stage, it is nevertheless a logical extension of their situation. Hamm has almost finished playing; he hasn't long to wait for everything to finish. In *Waiting for Godot* there is no end to waiting. In *Endgame* there is no end to finishing. In 1957 the public did not yet know that Beckett would tend increasingly to the minimal, paradoxically driving theatre performance towards annihilation, reducing it to no more than a breath. In *Endgame* the characters still appear corporeally on stage, in a kind of place and a kind of situation. But it is as though, from one work to the next, Beckett envisages a reduced human being, caught between birth and death, with scarcely a life between the two, except for memories and distorting commentaries that contradict one another. Whereas bourgeois convention hides physical accidents, Beckett emphasizes them. Crippling infirmities attack the body as though old age were perceptible from adolescence on; as though the future were visibly inscribed in the present, and all of existence were a process of putrefaction. But these infirmities are symbolic.

It is up to the actor confined to his wheelchair (Hamm) or incapable of bending his knees (Clov) to transform these primary physical handicaps into symbols. Comparably, there is nothing realistic about this room in which

Hamm revolves in thought, nor about the empty planet that Clov scrutinizes with his glass. Hamm projects his own mortality upon the world. He will die without descendants; the sin of being born will be expiated forever; after Hamm there will be no living being on earth; no insect or blade of grass. Or so he thinks.

This austere work did not please any Paris theatre manager. Blin rehearsed for a month at the Théâtre de l'Œuvre in the hope of playing weekly on its dark night, but he was soon invited to leave. Then the enterprising British director George Devine invited him to open the play in French in London: six performances at the Royal Court played to full houses in April 1957. By the end of April Blin was able to open at the small Studio des Champs Elysées in Paris. In 1968 he revived *Endgame* at the Alpha Theatre.

Between script and performance there is always the gap of the actor's corporeality, that corporeality that Beckett tries tenaciously to reduce. Hamm's parents are already legless cripples whose heads alone emerge from their respective ashbins. In *Happy Days* Winnie is buried in the earth to her waist. In *Not I* we see only a mouth. In *Play* we see heads only when the light shines upon them. All that remains before final extinction are broken words and frantic breaths. And yet Beckett is not moving toward radio writing (in spite of *All That Fall, Embers,* and *Cascando*); he continues to write for the stage. He creates tension between what is possible in the theatre and his own increasingly ascetic writing. A theatrical mise-en-scène is the concretization of thought, but Beckett is ingenious in destroying action and dramatic progression. He tends toward the static, and he reduces all to a bare minimum, to the very limit of the possible. The actor feels himself forced, pressed, and, at the extreme, excluded.

In *Endgame* the end is in the beginning. The actor is reduced to a kind of filter for thought; he has to transmit it orally without any stage business. It is almost pure thought – these words that are at once human and bodiless. The writing may be influenced by the analogy of the play to a game of chess (with its resonances of the chess-games of Marcel Duchamp), and by the humorous way the playwright depicts an extreme situation. Analogy and repetition cooperate to build a circular structure that satisfies the mind, but is a nightmare for actors who fear to bore the audience, and who usually seize upon a nuance, variation, or rhythmic change to gain attention. Beckett is opposed to such subterfuges; let the audience listen only if they want to. Today we are more accustomed to his work, but for the audience of 1957, even after *Waiting for Godot, Endgame* was a severe trial.

While adhering to Beckett's thought, Roger Blin did all he could to endow Hamm with singular intensity. There was therefore a slight gap between the first performances and the wish of the author. Blin saw Hamm like a King Lear (which was also the reading of Jan Kott, author of *Shakespeare our Contemporary*), but Beckett says it never occurred to him. For Blin Hamm was nevertheless a tragic character and a violent tyrant. He and Martin realized that they were too loud at the Royal Court: "The English like acting in undertones," commented Blin in 1968.

To what extent should he resist or accede to Beckett in order for the French to accept *Endgame*? Blin sought harmonics and paid attention to transitions; Beckett wanted aridity and even monotony. Actor Jean Martin told me: "At rehearsals Beckett paid close attention to the music of the words. He viewed

7 Hamm (Roger Blin) and Clov (Jean Martin), in a scene from Beckett's *Endgame* at the Studio des Champs-Elysées, 1957. Ph. Bernand

the performance like a Mondrian painting. Each time a phrase was repeated it should be spoken in the same way, without variation and without crescendo. There must be no effort to be dramatic." The horror of living was not to be shown as suffering but as mere testimony. Blin and Martin wasted no self-pity on their fate. They brought out the humor and dignity of Hamm and Clov, but it was hard to pass without transition from anger to laughter. They respected the syntax, pauses, alliteration, but to the spoken words they added business. "We tried to say and play it carnally."[23] Blin thought in 1968 that Beckett might be satisfied with actors who would merely utter naked words, without psychology.

This anti-psychological acting that we understand better today was not the only problem. One wonders what audience Beckett had in mind. He would have liked Hamm to speak with his back to the audience, in a voice at the very threshold of audibility.[24] Martin thinks that: "Beckett's dream would be the departure of the audience after five minutes of performance." In the last thirty years we have seen enough Beckett imitators to know that Beckett is unique in his strange blend of extreme economy with a revelation of the most intimate wounds, of sarcastic ridicule with an underlying tenderness, of a humorous viewpoint with implacable nihilism.

One of the main props of *Endgame*, the ashbin, exemplifies all these aspects in its polyvalence. It is not merely the container to which Hamm condemns his parents. The ashbin is the dwelling of old age; it shelters and hides inevitable infirmities. (Hamm is halfway there; he is still mobile if someone pushes his wheelchair, but his legs are inert under his blanket.) When the cover of the ashbin is lifted, the sovereign intellect emerges, but unfortunately Nagg is essentially limited to asking for his pap. In this regression to infancy, the ashbin is like a cradle; what is left of the body is still vertical before succumbing to the horizontal coffin. The ashbin already resembles a coffin, for it is a closed container when the cover is on. And yet the cover can be removed if there is a knock to request it, and then there is communication with the living. When this immense eyelid of the cover closes again, it is time to sleep. Far from insisting on the decay of age, and blasphemy toward parents, Beckett makes of it a poem of images. The ashbin is a marvelously theatrical object; it permits Nagg and Nell to enter and exit without moving or being moved. Their presence or absence is decided by the raising or lowering of the cover which thus acts like a door of the set. This inhabited prop is a place-within-a-place. By convention it is forgotten, but then it is rediscovered when animated by language. The exiguity of this place does not allow the actor to curl up and remain there for a long period. A theatre property, the ashbin is also a magician's container; the back is false, and it leads in Blin's production to a hole in the stage wall. The actors come unperceived from the wings and kneel in the ashbins until they are called upon to speak.

In Blin's production Nagg/Georges Adet wore a funny nightcap and imitated a toothless old man; Christine Tsingos as Nell (the Mummy of Blin's *Ghost Sonata*) had a sharp high voice. The faltering voices, the dazed smiles, the imprisonment in ashbins showed these characters to be vulnerable and abandoned by life; nevertheless they can summon vigor and animosity toward the cruelty of Hamm. Finally the ashbin becomes a grave when Nell no longer answers the knock on the cover.

Hamm is like a monarch in his carriage when Clov pushes him in his wheelchair. In London Blin wore a luxurious velvet robe trimmed with fur; it covered him down to the ankles; he wore a wig and side-whiskers, resembling Francis Bacon's portraits of popes, which he discovered soon afterwards. He sat majestically in a Gothic chair. In Carouge, Switzerland, he staged the play in a deconsecrated chapel over which arched a kind of cupola with flying buttresses.[25] The formal nobility of the text was his reason for this pomp, and he spoke Hamm's lines slowly, majestically.

For Beckett, however, Hamm was a bourgeois in bathrobe, seated in an ordinary chair in an empty room in a gray light. At the 1968 revival Blin revised his conception and wore a robe which was once sumptuous but was now reduced to rags. Beckett eliminated some details that seemed to wink to the audience ("I see a multitude in transports of joy"); he eliminated the blood-stained handkerchief which too obviously alluded to the veil of Veronica, replacing it with a dirty handkerchief. Blin attenuated the Lear aspect of his part, feeling that Hamm could also be a former convict.

Clov wore frayed trousers that were too short for his long legs, a dirty sweater with long sleeves, and old shoes that grated on the floor. Nagg and Nell were in faded nightshirts. The white makeup of Clov, Nagg, and Nell contributed to the overall impression of grayness and decay. Dusty, they would soon be ashes.

"Since Beckett wrote *Endgame* for us, we had to enter his design," said actor Jean Martin. After the Pozzo–Lucky couple, that of Hamm–Clov shows the master–slave relationship. Hamm was blind, like Pozzo in Act II of *Godot*, but he was also paralyzed in his chair. He could move only his arms and chest. He was entirely dependent upon Clov, and yet he maintained his authority and dictatorial power. His dark glasses hid his expression; his straggly beard and his toque gave him a disturbing appearance. His breathing was based on the fact that he was blind and immobile. All his energy was concentrated in his facial muscles, in his hands, and in his imperious voice; he broke out unexpectedly at times.

Hamm's power is limited to his family and domesticity. He rules over Clov (even though he is dependent on him); over his dog; and over his parents in their ashbins. Blin gave Hamm terse and sarcastic intonations; he was both inside and outside the character of Hamm. Although Blin was not drawn to alienation, he did practice it to some degree in this black humor directed against himself. His terse and pitiless intonations were followed by musical passages composed in the pleasure of the discourse, and they cast doubt on the seriousness of what preceded. Like Clov, the audience shifted from fright to stupefaction before bad faith, tricks, and the ingenuity of a tyrant who manifests the stubborn rage or insouciance of an immature person. To some extent, the intransigence and the cruelty towards Clov remind one of an Artaudesque character, based on nerves; at other times one could detect the mocking affection of Blin towards a human being and his destiny. A few gestures helped his verbal rendition – a lowered eyelid, a sullen droop of the lip, a hand that punctuated an exclamation by striking the armrest, or that gripped the toy dog tightly. Even though Hamm cannot move through space himself, he does so with Clov's help. A sonic space is created on the basis of his proximity to Clov; of his attention to Nagg; or of his plunge into his own thoughts. He would be less disturbing if we could see his eyes. Blin's own fiery temperament blended with his physical fixity to yield an atmosphere of menace. When actor André Julien assumed the part of Clov, he was so fascinated by Blin's Hamm that he had to be careful lest he neglect his own role. Beckett wanted Blin to give Hamm three voices in his narrative – the narrator, the beggar, and the character who answers the beggar; for the rest of the part, neither realism nor subtle nuance.

Clov was bloodless; tall, he was elongated by his glass to a huge spider. He submits to the undertow of commands and counter-commands; he skips in and retreats, performs useless and endless manoeuvres. More rebellious than Lucky, he knows how to wound Hamm, and he does not obey him immediately. His lapses are quickly reprimanded, and he then drags himself around again. He scarcely lifts his feet from the ground, even when he hurries, and his rapidity is inversely proportional to his efficacy. Hamm thinks and speaks; Clov moves, but neither in the direction nor at the time desired by Hamm. They work in dissociation, companions in spite of themselves; ill coupled, they erupt in tensions and rhythmic breaks of the performance: a performance in which Blin wanted to "weave a spiderweb between the characters and the audience."[26] The spectator should not be able to escape from what he is shown, from the uneasiness aroused. In this endgame, at the conclusion of a vaguely defined contest (life? dominance? an invention?) in which Hamm and Clov take turns in scoring points, it is unclear who has the last word. Will Clov remain? Will he leave? It is left in doubt. At the end of this ritual the actors do not bow. Behind the safety curtain, they should not seek applause.

For *Endgame* Blin did not speak of an invisible mise-en-scène but active humility. It was not a question of directing a play, and incidentally consenting to take a part as well. He was fascinated by the character of Hamm. Each day he felt himself influenced by the role that he would interpret in the evening.

During the Paris performances the *Arts* critic commented on the "convulsive maturity" of the actors,[27] the deterioration of their bodies, and the jangle of their nerves. Critic Jean Duvignaud rendered a vivid homage to the main actors: "Never before the role of Hamm has Blin been so powerful, so sure of himself, so full of a mocking force that provokes demons to be devoured by one another. One might say that in this role he gathers his previous parts from *Ghost Sonata* to *Hamlet* of Laforgue. At his side the tortured servant Jean Martin steps out of a strange universe where gestures become strange rites and suspicious signals of another world."[28]

HAPPY DAYS

"It is an even more difficult play than *Waiting for Godot*. It does away with thirty years of stupidity. Beckett is subversive, like all shy people."[29] *Happy Days* had its première in 1961 in New York, directed by Alan Schneider, and

8 Madeleine Renaud as Winnie in Blin's production of Beckett's *Happy Days* at the Théâtre Récamier, 1970. Set by Matias. Ph. Nicolas Treatt

Peter Brook reviewed it in *Encore*.[30] This woman alone in the middle of the stage, buried to her waist, seemed to him as powerful an image as Vladimir and Estragon under their tree, or Nagg and Nell in their ashbins. It was the concretization of an idea.

In Paris Blin directed the play in 1963 at the Odéon Theatre, with Madeleine Renaud who is tender and tiny. For twenty years she has made the play live, taking it on tour, and moving with it from the Petit-Orsay Theatre to the Rond-Point in Paris. After Nell, buried in an ashbin in *Endgame*, here is Winnie, eventually buried to her neck and doomed. But she is not desperate; she is grateful for the life that was given her. She is not unduly troubled. "Her nature is stubbornly turned toward optimism; she is damned to hope," said Jean-Louis Barrault. She is a prisoner of her little hillock, at the centre of a vast expanse of scorched grass, into which she sinks a little more deeply each day.

This is one of the few Beckett plays with a woman as protagonist. Her husband, who can only crawl, lives in a hole, and can scarcely extend his arm to her. She tries to communicate with him, but he can utter only brief interjections. Awakened each morning by a bell, she does not wish to see the horror that surrounds her; nor does she admit her decrepitude. She smiles. A French critic has said: "Never has the reference to the Book of Job been more evident, for Winnie in the depths of her suffering is possessed by an inexplicable joy."[31]

At first Beckett thought of the play for a man, but only a woman could take from her bag the many small objects that fill her life, and keep her occupied from morning till nightfall. So the character of Winnie took form, with her pathetic feminine vanity that does not permit her to neglect her appearance; she dedicates stubborn care to her toilette, with humor and smiling resignation. Blin commented: "Beckett has never gone so far in emotional intensity that is dramatic beauty. It's always that way. Every time that one says he can't surpass himself, he does so. His secret? He expresses his preoccupations with ever greater rigor, economy, and asceticism."[32]

Beckett described Winnie as a woman in her fifties, "Blonde for preference, plump, ample bosom." American actress Ruth White corresponded to this description, whereas Madeleine Renaud was quite different, svelte and not fleshy, full of charm and not mocking. But Blin had to choose between an actress who answered the physical description and one who could manage an extraordinary monologue that was full of traps. Blin suggested the role to Madeleine Renaud because of her experience with classical plays at the Comédie-Française and the many roles she played in the Renaud–Barrault Company. Beckett agreed and was present at all rehearsals. As usual, he did not want direct expression of suffering, anxiety, or despair.

It was a frightening text to memorize and speak; there was a gamut of feeling in it. Winnie shifts from the tiniest triviality to the tragic. In Act I she is a bird-brain, a "bourgeois who chatters in her hole as if she were still in a tea-room."[33] In Act II she is buried to her neck, and the situation is painful. "The unique quality should not come from the appearance of the actress or from her ability to caricature, but from the play alone ... Tenderness and sensitivity must be glimpsed through this dizzying monologue, this mad sequence of anecdotes. This is all the more necessary because the playwright has burdened his character with all kinds of small weaknesses."[34]

The situation is given at the start, with its arid set and buried woman awaiting death. What has to be played is her relationship with the different objects of her bag, her last riches whose use punctuates the hours of her life like the performance of a ritual. She engages in a dialogue of the deaf with her husband who can scarcely answer her or approach her. Pauses, manipulation of objects, are the essence of the performance.

The set is more important than in *Waiting for Godot* or *Endgame*. From the very beginning it has to be clear that this is the end of the world, whereas in *Waiting for Godot* and *Endgame* one could still hope that something might happen. Here, nothing. Everything is played out. This is the beginning of the last hours of life. Maybe the atomic bomb has been dropped in the vicinity.[35] All possible suspense is eliminated. Therefore the set is suffocating. It prefigures final annihilation, but it permits the audience to be present at a theatre performance without suffering.

For this kind of play the large Théâtre de l'Odéon was gigantic, and the Petit-Odéon was too small. The solution was to reduce the size of the large theatre to the orchestra and the first balcony by curtaining off the second and third balconies. The set of designer Matias was built far downstage so that Madeleine Renaud was as close as possible to the audience. In a blinding light the expanse of scorched grass swelled up into a kind of hillock from whose steep sides emerged the torso of the actress. The artificial backdrop described by Beckett was supposed to represent a horizon where earth met sky. Matias built a soft uneven ground without grass but with a rough surface so that the objects from the sack would not roll down the incline. At the back was a hole for Willie, with a wooden frame to hold on to. "Matias painted the sky in violent orange; the ground was also orange, and very brightly lit, forcing one to look toward the centre of the action, that is to say to the character who is surrounded by a paler orange mixed with gray and pink. One is compelled to look at that little head in that immensity."[36] In Act II the spectator had no choice but to look at the head of the actress; the audience is fixed upon her words and facial expressions. Beckett pushes theatre performance to an extreme limit when "that tiny head could suddenly become a film closeup because of the attention it commands, the fascination it exercises."[37]

Before the play opens Madeleine Renaud entered the foam-rubber hillock in the dark, to look as though she was buried in it. She sat on a hidden quilt and could move her torso forward, sideward, or backward. In Act II only her head was visible, fixed; she could no longer depend on anything but facial expressions.

Winnie is supposed to wear a low-cut blouse and a pearl necklace, leaving her arms and shoulders bare. There is something carnal about her. Flesh is reluctant to die and therefore displays itself, but Madeleine Renaud is more modest. Graceful, with her feathered hat or bare-headed, she is dressed up. She clasps her hands, sighs with happiness, remains open-mouthed in the silence; she puts on and takes off her spectacles; she performs small gestures without ever succumbing to metaphysical anxiety. She does not think of death; for her the play is a love story. In an everyday voice – or poetic when she quotes verse – she becomes the young girl evoking her first ball, or she becomes the good housewife attentive to keeping order in her possessions and appearance. She mentions with some humor that her husband is not much use to her, but after all he is there. Toward the end the rhythm slows down; memory weakens.

To despair Beckett opposes everyday courage, tenderness, and small reciprocal help: "The fact that *ego* looks at *id* diminishes animal despair . . . With Beckett everything is dignified and controlled; the fiasco has to be concealed. You have to look at the débâcle from a distance. You have to retreat with the honors of war."[38]

Of the husband we see only the end of an arm or a straw boater on a skull. From the charming white parasol to the black revolver, Winnie has a miscellaneous collection of objects – toothbrush, bottle, comb, hand-mirror, spectacles, magnifying glass. Above all she has words to fill time. Pensive, melancholy, ironic, the actress wanders in the byways of a discourse without logical sequence, through nuances and repetitions.

Roger Blin did not want to be known as the director of the production. "What would people say? It's a play without entrances and exits. My work consisted of seeking, with Madeleine Renaud, a stylized diction for a text built on the head of a needle."[39] Nevertheless, a director was needed to orchestrate that duet and the sound of the bell – also stylized since it might be a vague echo of an external power – so as to build a performance out of near immobility and a discourse blending pauses with tiny cadences, without boring the audience. To help the actress build her character while taking into account the strict directions of Beckett: do this gesture here, count two seconds there, emphasize that syllable; all of it should harmonize naturally.

To deal practically – and humorously – with the words of Willie in his hole, and to make him occasionally visible to the audience. In short, it is thanks to the director that the play becomes a performance.

"I work differently with different actors: some are lazy, others too intellectual . . . Madeleine Renaud was perfectly open and available, like a student. She felt the play intimately but the expression was rather new to her . . . When she discovered the ant, her first reaction was joyful. I said to her: 'Careful. For Beckett that's not it; but rather, down with life.' It's a reaction of disgust and horror."[40]

The playwright must have liked the interpretation of the actress, with its lack of exaggeration. She did not dramatize unduly. She spoke her lines with scarcely a movement of the body. She wore an ingenuous smile that made middle age loveable. She emphasized the pleasure of still being alive, even though deprived of motion. She left it to the words alone to speak of decrepitude and death, while she welled up with tenderness in the life of a couple.

Happy Days was performed at the Venice Festival in April 1963 before it came to Paris. In 1965 the Teatro Stabile of Turin asked Roger Blin to direct an Italian version with the actress Laura Adani. There were great linguistic difficulties. Blin explained: "Beckett often constructs phrases without verbs; sometimes there is a single word followed by a period, and then the following word contradicts it, or confirms it, or modifies it slightly . . . In Italian, a language that I love, it isn't possible to drop articles, verbs, and to cut the phrases to the bone."[41]

The character of Winnie can be played differently, depending on whether the smile, tenderness, and faith battle with a desperate situation; or whether despair is tinged with a smile, tenderness, and faith. Madeleine Renaud played it the first way (for her *Happy Days* is a love story); Laura Adani chose the second. It is not only a question of a brighter or darker version of the play. In this work that blends the comic and the tragic, where the words themselves are both comic and tragic, Laura Adani was bitter where Madeleine Renaud was ironic.

By 1965 Blin had been directing Beckett for thirteen years. He had directed Genet's *Blacks* and would move on to *The Screens* the next year. He was never to direct Brecht, but in 1965 he declared that his favorite playwrights were Beckett, Genet, "and also Brecht."[42]

3   Genet's Plays

Genet subtitled *The Blacks* "a clown show," and this term embraces the grotesque, the tragic, and the heavy makeup or masks. Genet's characters are variously masked; black actors playing Blacks masked as Whites to stand for Whites condemned to watch the performance on the stage, they disappear and reappear, playing in and interrupting the action, playing themselves and playing on us. Each time that they take off and put on their masks, we are fooled.

White spectators invited to the theatre as a captive audience in a ceremony, we are present at only part of the ceremony, a mere show that conceals or masks the event that takes place offstage – a matter of justice which concerns the Blacks alone. We learn this from Newport News, a different kind of character who was first played by black actor Robert Liensol. This enigmatic role surprised Blin, but when Genet came to a rehearsal, he explained to Liensol that he didn't want to expand this role or offstage events, since he felt that "an African writer should deal with that."

Genet was not primarily a political author, but his theatre serves him as a personal outlet and as a platform for attacking us. His own unjust treatment (infant abandoned by his mother, placed by welfare agencies on a farm, unjustly accused of stealing, becoming a thief to justify his condemnation, homosexual exposed to reproval) provoked his pitiless condemnation of our society: "I know it and testify to it; social order is maintained only at the price of an infernal curse leveled against people to whom I feel close; whether it pleases you or not, the vilest and most insignificant of these is dearer to me than any bourgeois."[1] Genet declared himself "the interpreter of human refuse." As a poet, he spat imprecations and oaths – furiously but generously, although he would deny the latter. He spoke in the name of others: Blacks, Arabs, the disinherited. In his imagination he transformed himself and became as others saw him. In *The Blacks* the Blacks play themselves as white racists imagine them, and the Whites are shown as the Blacks imagine them. Genet offers us not characters but reflections. Perhaps that is the basis of his "clown show" – defiance of the audience. This theatre of reproval, which places the true concerns of the Blacks offstage in the wings, also prevents the performance from becoming what we are accustomed to. The playwright assaults us, once we enter the theatre. He offers us a mirror instead of a theatre plot, a fiction. He drags us through artifice and destroys that artifice; this is what French critic Bernard Dort calls "Genet's battle with the theatre."[2] He destroys our conception of performance, of theatre convention, and substitutes his ritual of justice. He wrote not for but against his audience as well as himself. He disdained commercialization. A single performance would suffice to accomplish this exorcism, which is like the explosion of a bomb. The usual theatre performance bored him; he dreamed of a unique event.

As Whites with collective responsibility for the condition of the Blacks, we have to listen to our own trial by representatives of those whom we once reduced to slavery. In 1958 Genet treated the situation as though the Blacks had already won their fight for independence, but were still struggling against residual colonization; he prefaced *The Blacks* with these words: "This play... written by a white man is intended for a white audience, but if – which is unlikely – it is ever performed before a black audience, then a white person, male or female, should be invited every evening. The organizer of the show should welcome him formally, dress him in ceremonial costume and lead him to his seat."[3] This symbolic White will be the audience. A projector will be focused on him. And if no White accepts this role "Let white masks be distributed to the black spectators as they enter the theatre. And if the Blacks refuse, then let a dummy be used." The play is not intended for a black audience. It does not incite them to rebel, but is itself a rebellion against the white civilization that for centuries has been guilty of racism and oppression. The play accuses and condemns that decadent society that escapes execution only by dying of its own deep and irreversible putrefaction.

Certain critics indulged in temporal or geographic displacements to escape the play's immediacy. In France one critic evoked "the most joyous [period] of Surrealism, about 1925 when all hopes centered on a gigantic bloodbath in the West by hordes of the Great Mogol or the Grand Lama." Another critic recalled *The Diaboliques* of Barbey d'Aurevilly or *The Garden of Tortures* of Mirbeau, or Jean Lorrain. Still others compared the play to the contemporary situation in Algeria (American Herbert Blau in *Encore*) or the crisis in the Belgian Congo (Jean Selz).[4] No one mentioned French colonialism in black Africa.

Political play? Committed play? *The Blacks* is no more a diatribe for the Blacks than *The Maids* is a plea for servants. Let no one expect entertainment, however; the work sparks thought. What color are Blacks? A Black can be white, like Genet; he feels himself their brother; he has the same problems: "I have searched the continents," he says in *Thieves' Journal*, "and Blacks surround me... Blacks recognize me, and I am of their tribe." The problem is existential. Since they are outcasts, let them persist to the point of madness in what they are condemned to be. Let them claim blackness, darkness, stench. Up to now, Blacks existed only through the eyes of the Whites; they were the mere reflection of the imagination of Whites "since they merge us with an image and drown us in it." You see me as black, and I am therefore black. Let us be black to the very end, cries Genet, and above all let us not take the Whites as models, for there is nothing exemplary about them. The entire effort of the Blacks should be bent toward getting rid of the white view of them; they should go to the point of inventing a new language to express their negritude; they should even invent love.

Yesterday's slaves parody their masters. With lucidity and mockery, they play Whites seen by Blacks, but if the ceremony is serious, is the murder imaginary? There is no (white) corpse in the catafalque, but there is a (black) death offstage. They plead guilty to a murder without a corpse. All around them a battle is in preparation. Intermediate, between the abortive revolution of *The Balcony* and the Arab war in *The Screens*, this battle gives way on stage to a verbal contest: "We have tried to filch your fine language," warns Archibald. "By stretching language, we'll distort it sufficiently to wrap ourselves in it and hide." By language they construct between the audience and the offstage militants what Richard Coe calls a "smoke-screen."[5]

Genet's words about the writing of black George Jackson could be turned upon himself; in this subtle battle the Black's "hatred of Whites can be expressed only by that language which belongs equally to Black and White, but over which the White extends his jurisdiction of grammarian." And that becomes "a new source of anguish for the Black, to think that if he writes a masterpiece, his enemy's language is enriched; another jewel is chiseled by a Black in hate and love. He thus has only one resort – to accept this language but to corrupt it so cunningly that the Whites will be trapped in it." Into it he puts "all his obsessions and all his hatred of the Whites. It is a difficult task that seems to be contradicted by that of the revolutionary."[6]

Under Genet's trowel, as a master of this exercise, the Blacks of *The Blacks* become lyrical; "Nostrils, enormous conches, glory of my race, sunless shafts, tunnels, yawning grottoes where sniffing battalions lie at rest." It is in a verbal duel that Felicity (Africa) conquers the White Queen. The sides are drawn. The Whites attend their own funeral. Rather than take up arms, the Blacks perform theatre to reflect themselves: "We'll see ourselves – big black narcissists – slowly disappearing into its waters."

For Genet theatre and fiction were rites. He proceeded gravely; he worked at a purified and chiseled language. "Some day I want to bring the French language to a pinacle of heat and intensity. I'll get there."[7]

The language of *The Blacks* is undeniably successful. Balanced and chaotic, melodious and harsh, it attains a plenitude of varied rhythms. However, it demands effort to read or listen to Genet; not to be bothered by the complications of his syntactical detours or the vigor of his terms. What has sometimes been called obscene is exaggeration. In dwelling on scatological words, Genet sublimates them. He polishes rough words, or invents them for the pleasure of their sounds, as Lope de Vega or Ronsard polished hyperbole in a precious style. He is comparable to the great style of Villon, to the plainsong of Cocteau. When a reporter for *Playboy* reminded him: "You once wrote that poetry is the art of using excrement and making the reader eat it," Genet retorted that as a writer he demanded freedom of expression, and that he was only transcending a vocabulary forged long before him.[8] However, he admitted that he had passed the period when obscene words served him as a weapon against society.

The Blacks called forth a dazzling variety of epithets – ceremony, verbal magic, incantation, plainsong, incarnation, rupture. Most commentators considered the play an event, a miracle, a pinacle of contemporary theatre, an extraordinary play that upset all the rules, disturbed reflexes, and defied judgment.[9] It was a theatre ritual that " spoke a language . . . not heard for many hundreds of years on the European stage."[10]

In 1971 Richard Coe wrote that this work wanted to be an explosion of hate and violence, that the incantatory ritual, music, dance, masks, should arouse the hatred of the audience and transform the actors into symbols.[11] But in performance it is the theatricality that is uppermost, a theatricality inscribed in the very structure of the play. There is constant tension in the violence with which Blacks and Whites confront each other on the stage. The White is the enemy who strengthens the Blacks' hatred; they spit on his effigy; they exist through him and he through them. For Genet shadow reveals the nature of light, and Blacks reveal the nature of the Whites; decadent, effeminate, Whites are already conquered. It is the Blacks who are strong and virile. This conflict is concretized in the bodies of the actors who enact "something stormy, heated, and amazingly real under the sparkle of their verbal lyricism."[12]

The will to destroy performance conventions reinforces theatricality. The actor who finishes his scene remains on stage; each of the actors announces his name, his role; he transforms himself before us. The actors imitate wind and leaves; roaring evokes a forest; ceremonies are multiplied. In 1959 all this was decidedly new.

Blin's production

With characteristic humor, Blin recalled in 1966 that as early as 1931, the year of the French Colonial Exposition, he had welcomed "savages" brought from Africa and Melanasia to be exhibited in cages. He wrote an article that was discussed in the Chamber of Deputies – already.[13] Twenty-five years later he was working with the Griots, a black company.

Four black students at the Drama School of Rue Blanche had produced Sartre's *No Exit* in 1956–7; they wanted to form a company, and they asked for help from Roger Blin, who had played with some of them in the film *Guts in the Sun*. (This was 1957, when Blin was working on Beckett's *Endgame*.) Blin helped the Griots articulate better and develop their own nature; they practiced on poems of black francophone writers – Aimé Césaire, Léopold Sédar Senghor, René Depestre. At the Vieux-Colombier Theatre they gave a public reading of Césaire's *And the Dogs Are Quiet*; Blin directed them in performances of Pushkin's *Stone Guest* and of *Daughter of the Gods* by the African Abdou Anda Ka (comparable, according to Blin, to Synge's *Deirdre of the Sorrows*); they played at the International Festival of Student Theatre at Parme, then at Royaumont, and then in a barn in the Haute-Savoie. This was followed by a dramatic montage of Jean-Jacques Morvan, "a kind of cycle of tradition, colonization, and liberation."[14] Blin either directed or supervised these performances. Eight years after the company was founded, the Griots had twenty-five people, with their own director Robert Liensol, their aims and bylaws: "Not to copy French actors in any way. To affirm and develop our personality of black actors; to popularize the best black and universal dramatic works. To found a black acting school for a black theatre."[15]

Through his humor and sensitivity Blin understood, and made himself understood by, these enthusiastic and sometimes touchy young blacks. Without offending them, he guided them toward seizing the essence of the phenomenon of theatre, toward being more aware of their choice of texts, toward a deep examination of their culture. Undidactic, his teaching was much more important than diction exercises and reading aloud, to which he resorted to help their elocution.

If we recall the context of the times, that is to say when colonialism was still strong, it was a daring enterprise to produce *The Blacks*. Negritude was not recognized, and Blin helped show the way. Since then, various African countries have achieved independence; we have learned to be interested in black culture; black power was manifested in the United States; a militant black theatre has appeared. But more than twenty years ago, before francophone black countries achieved their independence, actress Sarah Maldoror recalled that "to yell on a Paris stage 'Death to the Whites!' – we were crazy." Genet nearly opposed the production: "He thought that everything he had written until then was meaningless. He probably reacted like certain painters who have several periods, and think that the last one is better than the preceding ones."[16] Blin persisted.

For *The Blacks* Blin joined black Parisians to the nucleus of the Griot

Company. He did not choose an easy path in producing an explosive playwright who was still relatively unknown, with a company unknown to most audiences, in a small theatre that was also unknown (in the area today occupied by the University of Paris VII). In 1956 the Théâtre de Lutèce was an empty building near the Arènes de Lutèce. This was converted to a rudimentary theatre with two hundred seats. Directors such as Bourseiller, Steiger, and Serreau produced plays by Arrabal and Brecht for tiny audiences. When Lucie Germain took over the management of the theatre, her friend from Algeria André Acquart remodelled it, and the success of *The Blacks* gave it notoriety. Acquart re-covered the façade of the building, painting the theatre walls red, but he left the stage black. He mounted lights on a metal cross-beam and installed a television circuit so that the technician could communicate with the stage from the basement, which was the only place for the technical apparatus. Since no one expected the play to be a success, the actors were paid a percentage of the box office. The management had cause to regret this.

Black actors of different origins – African, American, Parisian – had different accents that had to be unified to some extent. Genet did not accept the popular myth that blacks spoke *petit nègre*, and he used a fine classical language with occasional archaic syntax. There was a combination of preciousness and extreme vulgarity that offended some actors: "One actress withdrew rather than utter the phrase: 'My mother shat me standing up.'"[17]

It was a stroke of luck for the black actors to be part of the Blin/Genet undertaking, but they had to confront several kinds of difficulties: a playwright who was disapproved of and an aggressive theme against the white race. A few of them, married to whites, experienced personal conflict; or they feared that they would not be able to perform on their return to Africa because they had acted in a play written by a white.[18] In the play they had to go beyond their negritude and even mock it when they had taken such pains to achieve its recognition. They feared that the play-within-the-play would be misunderstood and they would be taken as savages in Paris. In short, an offstage psychodrama might have taken place, and rather than direct, Blin first had to win over his actors. After introducing them to the theatre in general, he had to win them over to the theatre of Genet.

Blin's stylized mise-en-scène for *The Blacks* created a special tone. The delivery was never prosaic: the gestures were never vulgar. The silhouettes, the way of showing blackness, of arching their backs, of smiling – all this was neither realistic nor parodic. It derived from the actors' authentic selves even while they added a daring self-examination. Nothing was merely said or acted literally. The blacks played at being blacker, playing upon themselves. The whites kept their characters at a distance, or exaggerated them ironically.

Nothing was diluted. Raw words were spoken either violently or suavely, and tender words mockingly. Speech accelerated in frenzy, but at times it slowed down arbitrarily. At the moment of his execution, the Valet danced "The Death of the Swan." (In his 1982 production, Peter Stein borrowed Blin's idea.) After having played upon reflections of reflections, Blin transformed the general laughter at the end of the play into a frenzied dance lasting several minutes before the final minuet. He encouraged exaggeration. He brought the grotesque just short of madness, in harmony with the verbal delirium created by Genet: "What I appreciate in Roger is his way of dreaming, of opening horizons that I wouldn't have seen without someone like him, without that kind of madness," his designer said.

Blin gave up his "invisible" mise-en-scène. Although he did not like the usual form of the play-within-the-play, suspecting it of self-indulgence, he accepted it in this play, and even emphasized its boundaries. "If the audience approves of the play physically, they have to see the cracks in that approval, and the credibility should be interrupted so that the audience is constantly reminded that thirteen actors are amusing themselves. All of that dictates a visible mise-en-scène."[19]

Blin saw to it that the ceremonial aspect was in screaming contrast with the real, that the humor clashed with the ceremonial. Through the acting, he underlined the (somewhat sadistic) jubilation of the punished pupil taking his revenge through his punishment, of the poet who surpasses his reality through writing. He arranged counterpoints; the Mozart minuet followed fury; "The Death of the Swan," mimed by the Valet, accompanied the condemnation to death of the Whites.

Set and costumes

Through the director Jean-Marie Serreau Blin made the acquaintance of André Acquart. *The Blacks* was the beginning of a lasting collaboration between them. Acquart has said: "For me scenography is a projection of my painting and sculpture. I make abstract designs; when the actor arrives, he makes them work. Roger Blin arranges the blocking so simply that it seems to flow from a source; it makes my scenography obvious."

For *The Blacks* Blin thought to keep to Genet's scenic directions – a few tiers on risers at different levels – but Acquart proposed a more elaborate design: "I wanted the actors to move on airborne constructions; one wouldn't know how they moved there in their colored costumes. I used metal tubing, as in everyday life. I don't like decorative elements."

The tubing was arranged at heights so that it could serve as a staircase. Asbestos cloth was twisted and pasted around the tubing, looking like raw material which sparkled in the light. The top platform was occupied by the Queen and her court; another platform was only a step high. The platforms were made of triangular pieces. This set offered a balcony to the Whites, allowing them to look down on the Blacks playing on the ground below the platforms. The White Queen had a gold armchair; the dignitaries of her court had stools, but the Valet remained standing. The Black Queen, slightly raised on her lower platform, had an armchair resembling that of the White Queen. At stage front a white sheet on two chairs represented the catafalque covered with irises, roses, gladiolas, and arum lilies. On the ground was a large shoeshine box. There was nothing else on stage. This arrangement suited the play-within-the-play; the actors below could play for those above; seen by the audience, both groups played directly for one another and indirectly for the audience.

Genet was not able to see *The Blacks* in Paris, or perhaps he slipped in one evening without letting anyone know. He did attend performances in London with the same mise-en-scène, with English-speaking Blacks. André Acquart was somewhat anxious about the changes he had introduced, but Genet reassured him: "As long as you found a better solution than mine, that's perfect." In the second edition of *The Blacks* Genet noted: "I am keeping the description of the set as I imagined it, but if it is compared with what André Acquart has designed, it will be seen that his should be followed. Also his costumes." When one is aware of how exigent Genet was, one can appreciate the 1959 production. Genet found that Blin's mise-en-scène "is the realm of perfection. To imitate him would degrade him. His mise-en-scène can only serve as an example of daring and rigor."

The lighting enhanced the atmosphere; it left areas in shadow, thereby creating nests of anxiety, and that anxiety extended to what was seen under bright lights; occasionally one sensed a quick silhouette in the shadow; on the curtain above the White court, painted heads suggested a surrounding crowd.

The costumes of the black women were magnificent; displaced by a century, the gowns were made of old curtains or tablecloths, re-dyed. Instead of ribbons, there was visible exuberance in large tassels, or tapestry fringes. Through these rough materials the evening gowns took part in a grotesque ceremony; the Black Queen, as majestic as a singer of negro spirituals, wore heavy trimming and delicate jewels. The young women in lace blouses had slim waists and sensual hips. Their silhouettes were delicately balanced on high heels.

Black actors playing Blacks were in full dress, with white lace jabots, flowered vests, and yellow shoes. Only Newport News wore informal dress: everyday trousers and wool sweater, barefoot. During the performance,

Diouf put on a skirt, a hilarious white mask of a woman with eyelashes of a vamp and long braids; he took up knitting in his white gloves.

Blacks playing Whites wore caricatural half-masks made by Claude Acquart (from clay and paper) to his father's design; they resembled European masks that Acquart had seen made by black Africans. Claude Acquart also made the rag dolls that mocked the White court. From under the skirt of Diouf, masked as a white woman, were taken the Governor, the Valet, the Judge, the Missionary, and the Queen as dolls about two feet high. These dolls were hung on the court platform, ridiculing members of the court and reducing them to puppets. One thinks of exorcism. The White Queen had a half-mask with large pointed nose; the corners of her mouth were drawn down, giving her a sad expression that was contradicted by her exaggeratedly long eyelashes. This mask forced her to lower her head when watching something, and it influenced her to act with a certain gaucheness. Neither her crown nor sceptre, which were rather soft and formless, lent her

9 Scene from Blin's production of Genet's *Blacks* at Théâtre de Lutèce, 1959. Set by Acquart. Lower left, the Blacks; at right the "White" court; at center the Governor, and above them Diouf. Ph. Acquart

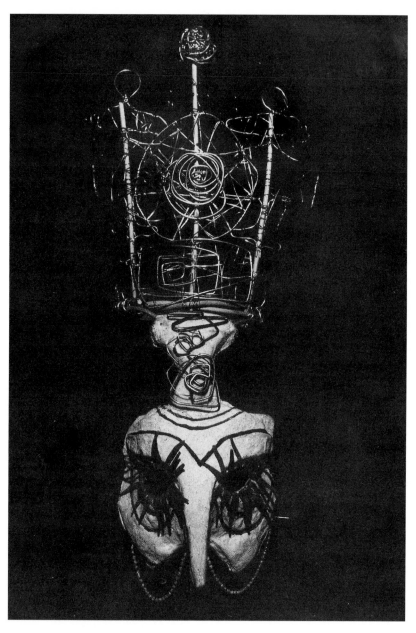

10 Mask of the White Queen, constructed by Acquart for Blin's production of Genet's *Blacks* at Théâtre de Lutèce, 1959. Ph. Acquart

dignity. Rosettes speckled her feathered blouse, and long gloves covered her bare arms. Worldly elegance was undermined by mockery. When she was almost drowned in shadow, the Queen appeared like a giant insect robbed of all power. The Governor, in colonial helmet, wore a dented mask with thick eyebrows and moustache; his stiff beard was made of fur. The Missionary, with two lines crossed on his chasuble, had sleeves widened at the wrist, so that his movements gave the impression he was going to fly. His fingers were covered with rings. The Judge had an ermine collar in the form of petals, and an odd-shaped toque. The Valet was in livery with striped waistcoat, powdered and curled wig, white stockings; he always stood near the Queen. His half-mask had a comically turned-up nose. On his arm he had a white napkin which he played with like a scarf or a handkerchief to wipe the tears of the Queen; or he would place it carelessly on the support of the platform as on a rail.

Each member of the court was plainly, according to Genet's specifications, "a masked negro whose mask represents the face of a white person. The mask is worn in such a way that the audience sees a wide black band all around it, and even the actor's kinky hair." The other Blacks painted black backgrounds on their faces. One of them shines his face by rubbing it with a chamois-cloth, as one would a shoe.

Rehearsals lasted a year and a half. Actor Robert Liensol told me that Blin worked slowly: "He corrects gradually. He has an extraordinary patience and power of listening. He accepted our individual suggestions; he encouraged our spontaneity, while imposing rigor. Sometimes he did not say anything throughout a whole rehearsal. All the group movements were his suggestions." The group movements involved all the looks, reactions, shifts of position which were common to the black and white groups; the reactions of the two groups toward one another, for example, the bows from one level to the other, the dances around the catafalque, the exit of the members of the court. All these movements had to be coordinated.

I asked Robert Liensol whether the black actors easily accepted wearing masks in the theatre. He retorted that there might have been a problem if they were ritual masks, but there was no problem at all in wearing masks that ridiculed the Whites; that didn't break any taboo. Technically, the half-masks did not hamper pronunciation. Masked acting tends toward exaggeration, forcing the actors to go to their very limits. This exaggeration is in harmony with that of the clown show. Defiance, insolence, and mockery are exacerbated in the articulation of a phrase, in the provocative corporeal undulations that can be grotesque, in changes of the voice.

Reception of the production

The small Lutèce theatre was full every evening, but the audience, disturbed, did not know whether to laugh or whistle. A few years earlier Genet had bragged: "I'm going to write other plays – one on Blacks, and you'll see how they talk; people will be thunderstruck."[20] Thunderstruck they were. The uniqueness of the theme, the impact of the mise-en-scène, the deliberate provocation of the author, and the rigor of Blin aroused enthusiasm, enchantment, or irritation. "We are scorched," *Le Havre libre*; the *Témoignage chrétien* reporter was struck by images, ideas, and symbols; Jean-Jacques Gautier, the powerful reviewer of *Figaro*, felt highly insulted: "I don't know whether the work of thousands of French in Africa deserves this sarcasm, these gibes, this joyous charge." The critic of the Communist *Lettres françaises* wrote that Genet had bypassed the major subject of colonialism and that his characters were too allegorical, whereas for the reviewer of *Arts*: "These Blacks are mere allegories, phantoms born of the contempt, rage, and repulsion of Jean Genet for a social order that he entirely rejects." One has to seek beyond the satire of colonialism to understand "this hothouse poetry, this plainsong."

To read a work by Genet is one thing; to accept it in the theatre is another. *The Blacks* served as trail-blazer for the scandal of *The Screens*. Because Genet offered an unacceptable mirror to the society of his time, his virulence was much worse than a committed work would be. He has said: "I think that direct action, the fight against colonialism, will do more for the Negroes than any play. I tried in these plays [*The Blacks, The Maids*] to give voice to something deeply buried, something that Negroes and other alienated people were unable to express . . . It may be that I've written these plays against *myself*. It may be that *I'm* the White, the Employer, the Clergy."[21] But the audience was nevertheless the target. Blin suspected that the critics and public would react more or less violently. Ionesco felt himself attacked and left before the end of the performance.

There was unanimity about the mise-en-scène. It is probably the production for which Blin received most praise: "A mise-en-scène as cruel as the text, brutal and shocking, as taught by Artaud," in *Le Monde*. "There cannot be a mise-en-scène different from Blin's" in *Libération*. "A masterwork of intelligence and adroitness" in *France-Observateur*. A production that surpasses all others of the season, full of fury, faith, and fervor. From *Figaro* to *France ouvrière* the critics were unanimous in their verdict on the acting. As usual, it was Jacques Lemarchand who was most sensitive to the hallucinatory production which "tears us away from our usual audience habits." It is "one of the truest successes of Roger Blin who managed to master – not to order it, for this would have deprived Genet's play of a great deal of its power of

11 Scene from Blin's production of Genet's *Blacks* at Théâtre de Lutèce, 1959. Set by Acquart. The black clown-show actors mockingly bow to the "White" court on high. Ph. Ernst Scheidegger

enchantment – the poet's inspiration." Lemarchand was sensitive to a ceremony that is not stiff, to the way Blin respected the Griots, to the way he served Genet's text as he must have dreamed.[22] Blin was faithful to the scenic directions even when he transposed them, faithful at the same time and going further than the mere words of the text, while harmonizing deeply with the most secret aspects of the work.

The following year Blin directed *The Blacks* at the Royal Court Theatre in London, with open casting rather than a given company. Since then he has not again directed *The Blacks*. Genet joked to Blin that perhaps it would be revived in ten thousand years.[23]

THE SCREENS

The Screens takes place in Algeria, and since it was written in 1958 when insurrection was rife in the French colony, one might think that the play is militantly revolutionary, were the author not deliberately outside of any party. *The Screens* was published in 1961 but couldn't be performed in Paris because the Algerian War militated against such criticism of colonialism and Western attitudes. A production could not be scheduled until 1966, four years after the Treaty of Evian, but the right-wing press and certain veterans' organizations felt themselves attacked by the play. Coming after the furor over *The Deputy*[24], the criticism of *The Screens* shows how theatre can still inflame public opinion when it conflicts with attitudes, historical circumstances, government policies. When Patrice Chéreau produced *The Screens* in 1983 in a completely different context, the play was ancient history, and its impact came entirely from its theatrical qualities and stage power. In 1966 these aspects were virtually ignored in the climate of political passion.

After *The Maids* and *The Blacks* Jean Genet achieved a certain reputation in the theatre, even if he was not unanimously accepted. Production of *The Screens* was at first deferred and then announced as THE event of the year. Presented as the work of a poet and not a militant, it contains rebellion against any establishment, and, whether or not Genet desired it, it evokes a stormy time of rebellion, a war for independence, and a right-wing reaction.

Indirectly, it denounces the evils of racism. At the time it was written, *The Screens* predicted the Algerian victory which many French still refused to believe. For all these reasons, no theatre manager wanted to have anything to do with it. In 1959 the Minister of the Interior refused to allow its production at the Vieux-Colombier Theatre. Moreover, its language was sometimes obscure (tirades, long hyperbolic sentences) and sometimes obscene (a crude vocabulary even though lyrically phrased). The play demanded a large budget, a cast of about a hundred, a variety of costumes, and many screens. It could be produced only in a subsidized theatre, but the subject was much too explosive for that.

The Screens therefore opened abroad in a German translation (directed by Hans Lietzau in Berlin in 1961), then was played in English (Peter Brook in London), in Swedish (P. V. Carlsson in Stockholm), and in German in Vienna (Leon Epp).[25] After the Treaty of Evian and its implications, Jean-Louis Barrault agreed to have Blin direct it at his Odéon-Théâtre de France in 1966. The complex set would remain on stage for a given number of performances, preventing the usual repertory playing of the Renaud–Barrault Company.

Since Genet did not expect the play to be performed, he did not hesitate to jettison all kinds of norms; it would last over five hours, if played in its entirety. The plot is not clearly developed, everything criss-crosses. The Algerian revolution is seen only distantly, through allusion to a mythical rebel, to fires, and to sabotage, but Genet's universe spreads out before us, with his personal obsessions. As in the case of The Blacks, the excluded are given a voice. The Screens is a political play to the extent that it denounces the alienation of colonized peoples, but it does not militate in favor of any particular party. Genet has explained: "Perhaps it was homosexuality that made me realize Algerians are no different from other men."[26] One scene of the play seemed particularly abrasive: Genet was accused of insulting the French army, but he judged all Western civilization as criminal and decadent.

After he stopped writing for the theatre, Genet spoke out for the Black Panthers, the Palestinians, the German Red Band, and he can be considered a committed writer. In 1961, although on the side of the Algerians, he forbade Roger Blin to politicize the performance of The Screens. His focus was poetic; the story of a thief and traitor who glories in his crimes.

Because Blin had joined other intellectuals in signing the Manifesto of 121, which supported the right to insubordination in the Algerian War, he was barred from state radio, television and theatres. He therefore viewed it as poetic justice that he should have the opportunity to direct The Screens in a national theatre. He thought that the production of the play might aid acceptance of the Evian agreements, since mockery might weaken the convictions of those who were still reluctant. But he also predicted that, even more than The Blacks, The Screens would offend people. Along with the pleasure of displaying the beauties of Genet's text, this prospect delighted him[27] – and indeed performances were interrupted, the right-wing press exploded, veterans considered themselves insulted, and André Malraux had to defend the play in the Chamber of Deputies. Two years before the events of 1968 at the Odéon, the same theatre was invaded by paratroopers and cordoned off by police. Today we are indifferent to the politics. During the last two decades homosexuality has been treated in novels and films, without shocking anyone. We are no longer frightened of slang and obscenities. It is therefore difficult to recapture that climate of hostility that surrounded *The Screens*.

The play had several changes of title. Written in 1958, first it was *It Still Moves*; then it was *The Mothers*. The second suggests a matriarchal regime governed by four women – the Mother of Saïd, Kadidja the Passionnaria of the Revolution, old Ommou Mother of her people, and the Mother of the One Condemned to Death. When the play was discussed with Blin, it acquired the title of *The Screens*, under which it was published in 1961, and which testifies to stage preoccupations, confirming the method of visually inscribing the action on the set. Places were suggested by drawings on the screens – a palm tree for the desert, a fountain for a village square. Light screens were folded and unfolded to change the scene from the living to the dead.

Genet used an actual event as the springboard; an Algerian worker in France was robbed of the pittance he had saved; back home he could therefore buy only the ugliest (and therefore cheapest) woman as wife. Genet inscribed this incident in a fresco of seventeen scenes. Saïd is at once the young agricultural laborer and the anti-heroic thief who will not reform. He lives with his mother and wife in an area where the colonists are in power, but where the slowly developing revolt makes the army uneasy. This permits the playwright to show civilian and military French society, as well as the native population and its rebels. Criticizing fiercely, Genet spared no one – the colonists, for their imperialism, racism, and stupidity; the Arabs, because they are imitating the organization of the very people whom they want to banish.

This work was flung full face at an audience still relatively unfamiliar with the inverted universe of Genet, and his usual targets. They reacted strongly against attacks on characters reduced to puppets. Genet's denunciation of Western society actually cut far more deeply than mere insult to the French army.

Saïd forces his wife, Leïla, to hide her face under a hood. Genet thus exaggerates the veil of Arab women through which one can see. He disfigures the ugly woman a second time with a hood pierced by eye-holes. Since Saïd is at the bottom of the social ladder, he places Leïla even lower. Having named her as his wife, Saïd repudiates her immediately, unable to stand her ugliness. She is the mirror in which he sees the image of his poverty, the shame of his situation. She submits to all kinds of humiliation at the hands of her husband, her mother-in-law, the villagers; she turns that humiliation to her glory. In Genet's mythology every couple is a failure. Saïd can show no tenderness for Leïla.

The Mother rules over the household. Rejected by the women of the village, she takes refuge in the exorcism of laughter at intolerable situations.

The trio of Saïd, Leïla and the Mother constitute the Family of Nettles, exposed to the hostility of the village, rejected, excluded. These nettles that grow in sewage prick anyone who approaches; they symbolize the proud waste in this Arab community to which Genet felt close, since he was excluded from the French community. These people glorify their unhappiness and choice of Evil. The Mother will rise to crime, strangling a French soldier almost without noticing it in her dance of exaltation and of sexual excitement at the contact of this foreign skin. She will be irritated at thus earning the esteem of the Arabs for a murder that she didn't intend to commit. Crime chose her, without any patriotic intention on her part.

Saïd is alienated from his colleagues at work on the property of Sir Harold. The colonists are not only French but also English and Dutch. Employer and workers mock Saïd, provoke him, harass him. He steals a jacket and is put in effective quarantine. He thinks only of obtaining money to go to the brothel, while waiting to buy another wife. He continues his career of thief, tries to go to prison, is proud of it. Leïla also wants to be someone and to gain the esteem of her husband; she walks in his footsteps, commits petty larceny, but leaves enough clues so that she too is arrested and joins Saïd in prison.

The rebellion spreads: fires are lit; orchards are burned without a clue as to the guilty ones. Uneasiness grows in the colony. Civilians and military officers are shown as virtual puppets vainly trying to maintain their prestige. They resemble the clients of *The Balcony* who rise on cothurni and broaden their shoulders. In flight, these characters shed false stomachs and buttocks. The army is not flattered; its officers are without illusions. Everything is falling apart; Western civilization is rotting from the inside. The brothel where Warda worked at being an image of the prostitute is also disintegrating. And even though Genet is on the side of the Arab rebels, they are not presented favorably; Genet reproaches them with having models and trying to build a new institution. In *The Blacks* he wanted the Blacks to declare their negritude without imitating Whites, and in *The Screens* he wants the Arabs to assume their own personality. He agrees with Frantz Fanon who advises the Algerians not to imitate Europe: "Humanity expects something else from us than this caricatural imitation . . . We mustn't reflect even an idealized image of their society and their thought, for which they sometimes feel a great nausea."[28] Genet explained: "Everything happens as though the rebels were saying: 'We are going to prove to the regime we just overthrew that we can do as well as they.' And then they imitate academically."[29]

Saïd is preoccupied only with his descent (for Genet an ascension) to Hell. He takes no part in the Arab revolution, and this contradicts those who persist in seeing *The Screens* as a political play. Even if Saïd is poor, dirty, and illiterate, he is not the prototype of the Third World. He cannot be used by any party. As in *The Balcony*, revolutionary conflict is only a backdrop. Genet does not plead the cause of the victims of colonization; he sings in hatred as in *Miracle of the Rose*: "I don't love the oppressed. I love those whom I love, who are always beautiful and sometimes oppressed but dignified in the revolution." In short, it is not because the Arabs are rebels that they have Genet's sympathy. He supported all those who stand up against society – the solitary and the minorities. His whole life and his work were made up of refusal; that is the source of his strength. He rejected compromise, conventions, clichés. He was a rebel at many levels. He argued, he accused, he enclosed himself in disapproval, and he affirmed it proudly. He raised his head and burst out laughing.

It is on his sense of the absolute and of laughter that an interpretation of *The Screens* has to be based. Laughter spreads and gives the characters the right to say anything. This energetic laughter balances a gamut of oaths, deeply felt phrases, joyously fierce relationships between the characters. Hatred and power struggles link Arabs and colonists, the colonists themselves, the Mother and the women of the village, Saïd and Leïla; these bonds will weaken only with the destruction of that society, with death. The Arabs express their rebellion against the Europeans by enraged designs on the screens; the Mother defies her enemies and covers them with insults; Saïd insults his wife and expresses his abortive tenderness by wounding phrases. Saïd refuses to serve the Algerian revolt and disappears. Leïla, increasingly joyous at her humiliations, plunges into the shades of night and death.

In *The Screens* we find Genet's symbols and obsessions – the holiness of Evil and the glory of abjection, poetically phrased. Song has to magnify evil in a theatrical act that is "an active explosion," a homage to death through beauty. This beauty may be present in fecal matter, or in suffering, which are transformed and transcended. Genet cautioned against reading the play ideologically. He refused to situate the play in a precise historical period, celebrating any given cause; the play embraces a century and a half of colonization. "It is a spectacle . . . a celebration for the Dead . . . Everything should work together to break down whatever separates us from the dead. We must do everything possible towards creating the feeling that we have worked for them, and that we have succeeded."[30]

All great poets have written of death, but it plays a special role for Genet. Invisible, insidious, it is always present. In the play a rebel is killed, and his spirit is consulted in the cemetery. Under her golden skirts the prostitute Warda is a living skeleton. The Dead watch the living and follow their struggles. The living of the early scenes gradually enter the platform of the Dead. And Leïla asks: "Is death a lady who'll come and get me or is it a place you have to go?"

This play is set during a century that saw the growth of colonization and its disappearance; it is a reminder of the Middle Ages with its *danse macabre*, of the mysteries of Eleusis that fascinated Artaud. Genet incites us to think of the intangible death immanent in us, which will claim us some day. Yet this death is light-hearted; it leads to Nirvana and a wisdom that the living lack. In the realm of the dead all opponents are reconciled, and quarrels end. Saïd does not arrive there; he has entered a realm where none can reach him.

Even those who were horrified by the play, or were impervious to its meaning, were sensitive to the luxurious and magical language, bristling with obscenities as well as the most refined phrases. All the characters use obscenities, even the General who wants to behave like an aristocrat; even the "distinguished" Vamp, and Sir Harold's son. At times of danger vulgarity triumphs over decorum: "If [obscene words] exist, they have to be used. Otherwise they shouldn't have been invented. If I didn't use them, these words would exist in a state of apathy. The role of the artist is to impart value to words."[31] The language has been polished by a jeweler in love with it, who has moreover read Proust, Nerval, and Mallarmé. Words sing–laugh–cry; they make jokes. "Night is beginning to drizzle," says the Gendarme. "Oh! Palms!" says the Vamp, quoting from a Saint-John Perse poem. "Here I am seated in the Arab night," says the Legionnaire. "Here I hang my dignity, here my sadness, here my gravity," murmurs Leïla, the poor Arab. As a footnote to the Rabelaisian vocabulary that acts like an exorcism, or through it, Genet uses words to magnify the beauty of ugliness and misery.

A series of games move the play forward and underlie its rhythms. In the first scene the game of the valise, that of the shoes, of the dance, of the storm – all these confirm theatricality and ludic pleasure. Genet offers subplots that nourish the main action and its dynamic. A game is often focused on an object. The Mother and Saïd play with a valise; they speak of it and handle it as though it were full of precious gifts; at the end of the scene they show the interior to the audience, with a great burst of laughter; the valise is empty. Leïla imitates a cockerel, then an entire barnyard; on the screens she draws a clock, a vase, a palm tree; she creates the environment – not without humor and mockery.

In his scenic directions or comments during rehearsals (later published as *Letters to Roger Blin*) Genet suggested that the actors execute hieratic gestures. Maybe he thought of the serious dances of Indonesia or of Chinese opera. It would not be the first time he was influenced by oriental theatre. In his Preface to *The Maids* he wrote: "I find Western theatre too crude after what I've been told of Japanese, Chinese, or Balinese ceremonies and after the idea in my head. One can only dream of an art that would be a deep blend of active symbols, able to offer an audience a language in which nothing would be said but everything felt."[32]

In *The Screens* he asked for extremely precise acting, with each gesture visible and realism banished. He was thinking of the artifice of Chinese actors, building their inflexions and gestures into a kind of score. Genet demanded a vocal score ranging from murmurs to cries. Today we can conceive of such demands because we are more familiar with oriental techniques, Grotowskian scoring, and other research. But in 1966 the actors of *The Screens* were astonished.

Outside of the hieratic and controlled expression, Genet made other demands. Nothing should be ordinary, affected, or pretty. The set should arise from delirium, madness; costumes should be accoutrements and trappings; the actors should be made up, masked; they should give the best of themselves in a raw light in which abjection should astonish and performance should be dazzling. "I don't believe you should anticipate more than four or five performances . . . If the actors and actresses delve deeply within themselves, they will not be able to hold out for very long . . . A single performance properly staged ought to suffice (but that one should be prepared for six more months)."[33]

Genet told Jean-Marie Serreau that the spectator had to earn the performance. He envisioned a production to which the spectator had walked more than twenty miles, climbed a hill, and could see the show only on tiptoe. This is the insoluble contradiction: Genet multiplied directions for a play that he did not want played. He dreamed of transforming theatrical raw materials into a ceremony offered to a "beyond." In *The Studio of Giacometti* he wrote that the work of art was an offering to the dead; art possesses "a strange power of penetrating this domain of death, of perhaps seeping through the porous walls of the realm of shadows."

The living have the right only to a reflection of performance, of the ceremonial event. Genet wanted more than the usual performance; he desired a creative theatre, stronger than life, joining death. The work is revolutionary in its form; it explodes norms and taboos. The conditions of production are also revolutionary, for Genet wanted to ignore commercialism, break down habits, force participants to reflect, to ask questions, to question the very basis of theatre. Without seeming to, these requirements predicted the revolt of May 1968 in the life of the university, society, politics, and the arts. It required a seriousness and ethic that were unprecedented in Western theatre.

Intractable, Genet did not yield. He never considered himself as the simple provider of a text. Present at all stages of the enterprise, cooperative, anxious to learn about theatre, he came to several rehearsals, did not hesitate to interrupt them, and fulminated against whatever displeased him. He consented to cuts, encouraged Blin against actors who resisted their parts. Finally, in homage to his director, he published the letters he sent during the work so as to guide Blin (or impose new difficulties). During the course of rehearsals, Genet sometimes sensed flaws, but he couldn't make himself understood in professional terms ("I don't know your jargon!"); nor could he help the actors surmount their difficulties. Blin served as mediator.

In this unique meeting of playwright and director, there was mutual esteem. They addressed each other as *vous* and listened attentively to one another's suggestions. Was Blin having difficulty because he was too kind and wouldn't fluster an actor or bang his fist on the table when there was outside irritation? Then Genet would shoulder his way in, yell, or send telegrams. Would someone accuse Genet's text of scatology? Blin would roar and argue sharply. In life both men cared little for outside opinion. Genet was always ready to depart, living as he did from hotel room to hotel room, with a single valise containing a change of clothes and some books. For years Blin lived in a modest apartment where bookcases were collapsing under the load of books. They had the same scorn for everyday life.

Genet's letters to Blin were written to solve problems, to insist on his exigencies, to refer to specific actors and characters; they were published to reinforce publicly his admiration for Blin in a theatre where he knew the director to be somewhat controversial; these letters have today become a kind of exercise book to which theatre people refer as a source of inspiration, comparable to Artaud's *Theatre and Its Double*.

When the second series of twenty performances began, Genet decided that he had said all he had to say; that his presence was no longer of help; he disappeared.

The production

For five years Blin wanted to direct *The Screens*, imagining it even though production was not possible, until Jean-Louis Barrault welcomed him to the Odéon. This was luck because it meant financing, but it was also a handicap because there might not have been so much disturbance at a non-subsidized theatre. From summer 1965 on, Blin, Genet, and designer André Acquart met to talk about the mise-en-scène and especially the set. Genet's directions were followed: platforms at different heights, and mobile screens. The final set differed little from the first sketches.

In casting 65 actors in 110 parts, Blin dipped into the permanent company of Renaud and Barrault, who themselves wanted to play. From outside the company he called on Maria Casarès for the Mother, Paule Annen for Leïla, as well as other actors for parts refused by company members.

Amidou, who played Saïd, was hired by the company for a year. He alone was an Arab "so that there will be stylization, distance with respect to the real; the other Arab parts will be played by French actors. Genet didn't want

Arab actors. There was Amidou alone who sounded the basic note. I made the actors up like Japanese."[34]

In December 1965, Maria Casarès and Amidou met several times with Genet who spoke to them about their parts. Rehearsals began in January with "the Family of Nettles." Three months of work before including the rest of the company permitted the establishment of the style of acting by research into the creative possibilities of the actor. When actual rehearsals began, the Family of Nettles was a kind of inspiration to the other actors, so that Blin didn't have to explain things to them. To his dismay, a few actors were committed to touring, and could rehearse for only two weeks. Tania Balachova as Ommou had to be replaced because Genet found her too realistic, and she memorized her lines too slowly. The handsome Sergeant was cast very late. Barrault's actors were used to quick assimilation, but Blin would have preferred more time and depth.

The length of the text was another difficulty. Blin would have liked to play it without cuts, perhaps in two evenings as was done in Stockholm. He was told that this was not possible in Paris. With Genet's consent, he therefore made a certain number of cuts that brought the performance down to about four hours, including intermission. The only purpose of the cuts was to decrease the length of the performance, and not to dilute the frankness of the language, or to simplify difficulties. He cut a few long passages, eliminated a

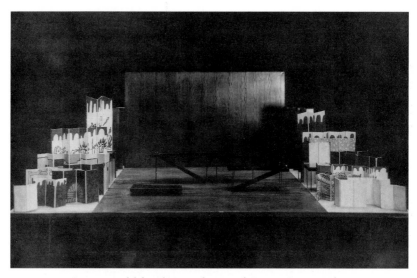

12 Acquart model for Blin's production of Genet's *Screens* at the Odéon-Théâtre de France, 1966. At the center are platforms on different levels, and at the sides the painted screens that will be slid onto the stage as needed. Ph. Acquart

few minor roles, and did away with the seventh scene (the Cadi dispensing justice). During rehearsals Blin several times shifted the cuts of the twelfth and seventeenth scenes, for the equilibrium was delicate. Genet changed the dénouement several times. Finally Blin tuned the triumphant cry of the Mother when Saïd dies, and he restored the two final lines of the play:

THE MOTHER: Saïd, I'll simply have to wait for him.
KADIDJA: Don't bother. He'll no more be back than will Leïla.

It was essential to end before midnight so as to avoid costly overtime wages for the stagehands, but it was a pity to cut the caricature Figures who were to reappear in the final scene and watch it from below. (The Figures were the Soldier, the Vamp, the General, the Academician, the Banker, the Girl Taking Communion, the Photographer, who acted like marionettes dressed in 1840's costumes, and whose voices were recorded, so as to make them seem even more mechanical.) These Figures would stand between the audience and the actors in the last scene: they represented society, and the audience is forced to recognize itself in these Figures, who replaced spectators costumed as extras, which Genet would have liked to add to the crowd on stage. He wrote: ". . . a certain space would have to be reserved directly on-stage for a certain number of walk-ons – motionless and silent – who would be part of the audience, having donned costumes designed by the costume designer – the notables on one side of the stage, and the common-law convicts on the other, masked and chained, guarded by armed soldiers."[35]

Genet didn't believe that his play would be performed, but once having embarked on its performance, he conceived of circumstances far from Western theatre custom; he suggested that spectators be allowed to enter and leave the play during the performance without bothering anybody. He wanted them to stand, or even approach the stage, as one approaches or moves back from a painting. He also imagined that the performance could take place in the open, with platforms at different heights and painted screens carried by stagehands. To play at the Theatre of France in the Odéon, however, Blin and Acquart departed from this idea; they installed several levels of platforms and movable screens.

Genet has given no explanation of the meaning of the screens. He wanted them to function visually; the actor would carry and design his own set on stage. This was a principle of theatricality. Starting there, we can give them other meanings. For Barrault the screens hide the selfishness, hypocrisy, and other vices of a society of which Genet disapproves. They are also screens that separate us from death, thus recalling Cocteau's *Orpheus*.

The action unfolds in many places: the square of an Algerian village, a trough, a hovel, a brothel, a cemetery, a prison, an orange grove, a court, a highway, a mountainous country, a desert, the domain of the Dead. The screens not only evoke these places, but they also suggest time; with a painted sun or a quarter-moon, Blin shows the passing of day into night, or night into day. The screens show designs in action – the flames in the orange grove, the Arab revolution. The screens preserve the memory of earlier scenes; the revolutionary designs remain on stage. They bound the playing space. Flexible as the screens desired by Craig, they appear, disappear, hide, reveal. By being folded and disappearing into the darkness, they erase a playing area. All the usual realistic props have disappeared in favor of designing objects on stage.

The whole set is composed of mobile screens and platforms connected by bridges. Acquart wanted the three platforms to be raised or lowered, but only two small ones could be moved in this way. Using an existing elevator, the largest platform was installed upstage. These platforms provided very little room for the actors to move, and Blin could not raise the brothel as high as he wanted. Genet designated a step-ladder for hoisting Warda, but there would have been no room for it, nor for a table and chairs. The solution was to have the brothel clients on the ground; then they crawled to the feet of Warda, the empress-prostitute.

The number of screens was slightly reduced. In the text Warda bursts through three screens in order to die; Blin had her burst through a single one. Nevertheless, there remained twenty-seven screens:

the sun-screen
the brothel-screen
the screen of Saïd's first house
the palm-orchard screen
the village-screen
the wall-screen (Saïd's second house)
the three screens of the orange orchard
the two prison-screens for Saïd and Leïla
the large transparent screen
the Blankensee-screen
five town-walls with their designs
the highway-screen with the dragon of sleep
the black screen with the crescent moon
the trough-screen
six screens that the Dead burst through

At first, the head of the Odéon shop considered these screens as conventional frames to be flown on pulleys. However, Genet and Blin, inspired by oriental theatre, wanted the screens to appear and disappear laterally, rolling silently on wheels, guided by actors during performances. The personnel of this subsidized theatre were disturbed by the number of movements required during the four hours of performance, by the way the stagehands had to function visibly within the whole. Blin wanted small screens to be manipulated by children, but the Labor Department would not authorize children to be in an "immoral" play; for the same reason the part of the Boy was cut.

In his scenic directions, Genet specifies: "One or more real objects must always be on the stage, in contrast with the objects drawn in *trompe-l'œil* on each screen." Blin and Acquart dropped some of the objects in order to avoid burdening the platforms and to purify the performance, but they did keep the red wheelbarrow, the bicycle, and the sprinkler. The milestone in the first scene was eliminated, and the pile of stones was painted on a screen. The red wheelbarrow was to appear in the palm orchard of the fourth scene, but Blin introduced it in the third scene at Saïd's house. Thus, the wheelbarrow linked the two scenes, emphasizing the continuity of Saïd's humiliations. For the same reason Blin introduced old Ommou in the twelfth scene, to show her position among the Arabs, although the text introduces her in the fourteenth scene. Genet had conflicting instructions: "Each scene, and each section within a scene, must be perfected and played as rigorously and with as much discipline as if it were a short play. Without any smudges. And without there being the slightest suggestion that another scene, or section within a scene, is to follow those that have gone before."[36]

Deployment of screens and platforms

Genet (Frechtman translation)	Blin/Acquart
I. Four-panelled screen. Painted on the screen: a palm tree, an Arab grave. At the foot of the screen, a rock-pile. Left, a milestone.	The platforms lie flat, as do the raked walkways to reach them. A screen representing a road appears. No palm tree, nor painted grave. No rock-pile, no milestone. A round stain for the sun.
II. The brothel. Two screens. Seated at a table covered with multicolored cloth are three clients . . . Nearby on a wicker dummy, a gold petticoat and cloak.	Two white screens. A straw dummy. No table. The brothel clients are lying on the ground.
III. A four-panelled screen. [Saïd's first house] Drawn: an oven, four pots, a frying-pan, a table. Objects: a bucket, a very low stool.	No recognizable object drawn. The Mother has a bucket in her hand. The wheelbarrow of the fourth scene is already on stage.
IV. The screen – five panels – depicts a field of palmettos. A round, yellow, tissue-paper sun painted on a very blue sky. In front of the parapet a red wheelbarrow.	On an eight-panelled screen are painted dwarf palms; a paper sun is glued on. An actor will peel it off to represent evening.

V. A four-panelled screen represents the front of the prison: with a big door and, on each side, a low barred window. Object: a palm tree.

Platform 2 rises. Leïla and the Mother climb the ramp (the hills). No screen. No palm tree. The two women come down with Saïd. The platform drops.

VI. A five-panelled screen spread open against the back wall represents the square of an Arab village; a painted palm tree, the grave of a marabout . . . A blazing sun is painted on a very blue sky. Object: an open umbrella, upside down, leaning against the screen.

A nine-panelled screen is brought on, without figurative drawing. Ochre surfaces, walls, ramparts. No sun painted, but in order to protect themselves from the supposed sun, each woman opens a big black umbrella.

VII.

Scene cut by Blin.

VIII. A five-panelled screen representing the cemetery. R, a cypress tree. Painted on the screen, C, a tombstone. In the dark sky, a crescent moon and a constellation.

No screen. Madani sets the boundaries of the tomb by placing a little rug in the middle of the acting area.

IX. The screen (four panels) represents a rampart. Objects: a three-legged table, a tin dishpan.

The first platform rises. On it a screen with a painted rampart. Leïla will draw a clock on it.
No table. At the foot of the screen the lamp brought by Leïla under her skirt.

X. Three screens, five panels each, painted with orange-trees and a darkened sky.

Three screens are an orange plantation, with two chairs for the colonists. The first platform is again lowered. Crackling accompanies the sight of fire.

XI. On the floor of the stage, two three-panelled screens, one screen to the left, one screen to the right, which represent the prison. Both Leïla and Saïd are at the foot of their screen. On a high platform appears the screen of the Blankensees, with a painted window and a balcony. On an even higher platform, a sky blue screen, transparent or opaque, before which the Legionnaires will accoutre themselves.

Two screens are the prison, downstage right and left. Isolated on each side of the stage, Saïd and Leïla whisper, even while extending their voices toward one another.
The first platform rises, and on it is placed the screen of the Blankensees. With the rest of the stage dark, the lights go up on the upstage platform, raised ten feet high. The screen that hid the arrival of the Lieutenant and the Legionnaires is removed.

XII. The screen (six panels) represents a kind of long, high, white crenelated rampart. Above, on a platform, appears a second screen, all gilded. On this platform stands a very tall dummy . . . on which are pinned all kinds of decorations. Near it, a field-glass, mounted on a tripod . . . From the L wing, rear, emerges a screen similar to the first . . . but the second one is larger and will top the one already on stage.

From the start there are three rampart screens. All the platforms rise. A tall dummy and a tripod are on the upper platform.

Two other very tall screens are brought in. Altogether 23 panels of screens can be drawn upon.

XIII. A five-panelled screen represents a field, with a cactus, both painted green. Object: a milestone. Beginning of the exodus.
A black screen on which the Mother draws a crescent moon. A third screen represents a mountainous region.
The fleeing colonists, Saïd and Leïla, the Mother, the Legionnaires cross without seeing each other, and ignore each other.

All the platforms remain raised till the end. On the back of the highway-screen is Leïla's dragon of sleep. No cactus, no milestone.
Above, on the black screen, the Mother draws the moon, and the Lieutenant a mountainous landscape.
Each light change illuminates only the acting area. Pierre and the Mother, speaking in the dark of night, are on different platforms.

XIV. Two screens: First screen . . . the brothel. Second screen . . . the village watering-trough.
(Object: a bicycle.) Behind this screen, one can see the screens of scene XII, covered with drawings . . .
Sudden appearance of Saïd who eludes his pursuers.

Cf. Genet. Ommou will enter from above, like a star.

On the upper level a screen moves to reveal Saïd briefly.

XV. A series of transparent white paper screens arranged one behind the other at intervals of about three feet.

Three single-panelled screens to be punctured by the new Dead. The Legionnaires crawl from one level to the other without seeing each other. After the Lieutenant's death, they disappear above.
After the dialogue about the flies, the Mother and Kadidja exit below. Leïla descends from the middle platform, without meeting anyone. She dies in her hooped dress that seems to swallow her, and, tumbling over herself, she exits.

On the upper level, a paper screen for the mother.

XVI. The screens are set up on two levels. Above, again the many white screens that the Dead will burst through. Below, on the floor of the stage . . . an unlighted screen. This will be the brothel. . . . Six women knit. . . . Through the transparent screen representing the brothel, one can see the dead Warda being washed, while a second actress plays the part of Warda joining the Dead on the upper level.

On the first platform are the knitters and the five-panelled screen representing a trough. On the upper level the Dead. Each new arrival is an event for the Dead already there. The following arrive by puncturing a screen: some Legionnaires, Warda, the Sergeant. Warda's toilette takes place in public, in front of the brothel-screen, but above, Warda is simultaneously among the Dead.

XVII. Three platforms. On the upper level, white paper screens. On the middle level, one screen for the prison and one for the grocery store. On the lower level one screen for the brothel, one for the village square, and one for Lalla's house. One by one, the actors draw what the screen is supposed to represent.

No prison-screen nor grocery-store. On a supplementary level, at the bottom of the stage, the Figures were to be placed. Except for Lalla, who draws a vase and then the huge stem of a rose with very visible thorns, no actor draws on the screens.

In summary, for Scenes I, II, III, IV, VI, VIII, and the beginning of X, the platforms are at stage level, almost invisible. During Scene V the second platform rises and descends. During Scene IX the first platform also rises and descends. From Scenes X to XII the four levels move, changing during the course of the performance. From Scenes XIII to XVII, the four levels are used, but not always systematically. Some platforms are bare; on others, screens slide laterally. Characters change places in the dark, new screens bring new colors, distract the eye, return to the wings, to be replaced by others. Like Genet, Blin and Acquart preserve the confusion of levels. They do not set a fixed structure where the Arabs are always on the same side, and the Europeans always on the other; or where the living are on the lower level only, and the Dead on the upper level. The places intertwine, change in a phantasmagoria. Each scene offers a new, autonomous vision. Horizontal and vertical planes take turns. Vehement when they are on the ground, the living grow dull when they are perched on the upper level among the Dead, or when they are seen below in their final throes. They are separated by some distance from the area of action. The uppermost platform carries an operetta-like army, cut off from reality, led by a hallucinated Lieutenant.

Blin always takes great care with the spectators' sightlines, rendering each detail clearly. Sir Harold and Blankensee are seated at stage left when an arsonist sets fire to an orange tree on the right in Scene X. From above and from the front, he lights the actors and the screens concerned area by area. On each side of the stage lie the waiting screens, used to reveal what is new or to recall a previous scene. Groups isolated on a particular platform remain relatively static. Circulation on the floor is rendered difficult by the platform supports, and on the upper levels by the narrowness of the platforms. There is diversity in the actors' strange attire, the ballet of the screens, the succession of characters in the action, the play of lights and colors, the verbal ruptures.

The designs on the screens were conceived by Acquart's son, and Genet had him modify several for the second set of performances, mainly in color, to make them look like the inventions of mad people. Screens and designs constituted a set in action, contributing to the phantasmagoria without undue dependence on sophisticated technology. When the Mother climbs the road leading to the prison, a platform rises, forming an abstraction of a hill. In the thirteenth scene, to conceal the exit of Saïd and Leïla, the highway-screen folds up, showing its back on which the dragon is painted; the dragon of sleep envelops the couple. Otherwise light changes hid scene-changes. Changing screens in the dark yielded a pleasing effect. The sequence of volumes and colors was a show in itself. The fire in the orange-grove was created by a stagehand moving red and yellow ribbons behind the painted trees. For the screens of the Dead a projector was aimed on the silhouette preparing to burst through the screen from behind; the shadow increased in size up to the point of breakthrough. Acquart's set permitted Blin to direct poetically: "Poetry is the only path to reality. In this way realism becomes surrealism. It should give the impression of 'jamais vu.' A Louis XV salon is truly realistic only in a desert . . . We have to return to ideograms. If a black screen crosses the stage, that means that night is falling. But audiences have grown so lazy."[37] Blin included several elements of stylization: a circle of red or yellow paper pasted on a screen represented the sun; an actor tore it off when night came. Barrault manoeuvred a small carpet to show the tomb of Si Slimane. Although this seemed naive at the time to sophisticated Paris, it anticipated the modern stylization of acting.

Costumes and makeup

Acquart wanted bright colors. He agreed with the orange specified for Kadidja, and he replaced the Gendarme's cap by a colonial hat; he invented a death-robe for Leïla by lining her dress with flexible foam rubber that made it look as though Leïla was sinking into the sewer. The cloak of the brothel empress Warda was stuffed with polyester, and coins were glued to her dress. Most of the cloth was treated, glued, sculpted, painted by every imaginable procedure. The uniforms of the French soldiers were not khaki, but greenish; they were made of a fragile cloth that frequently had to be mended. Genet had thought of American uniforms for the Algerian soldiers, but Acquart chose ochre, since the screens of the Algerian village were white and ochre. Most difficult to costume was the French Lieutenant; it took twelve different sketches. Genet wanted an 1830 uniform, and Acquart gradually simplified it, adding a long red scarf that symbolized death.

To avoid the actor's having to make up their arms and legs, they wore fine leotards. Nevertheless, Barrault conscientiously made his hands up. All the actors painted their faces according to a Japanese model designed by Blin, and this makeup replaced the masks at first envisaged by Genet. Blin explained to me in 1966: "Masks immobilize part of the face. I don't mind a masked character, but I'm somewhat bothered by the mask-character who has a kind of phantom face. I'm even bothered by a half-mask with an obscene moving mouth below, under an immobile forehead and the rest of the face immobile. I preferred a makeup that was almost a painting, with bright colors and well-marked features. The prostitutes have a greenish makeup and emerald-colored paint around their eyes. Acquart gave Si Slimane a vein on his cheek."

Genet described some of the makeup:

Kadidja: Her face purple, almost black. The colour of Negroes' lips, more or less. Her wrinkles, which are numerous, will be white.

Ommou: a yellow face ravaged by many wrinkles "that will make her face resemble a full moon, if possible covered with craters and lunar seas like the Sea of Serenity."

Warda: sky blue hair, with a very high, Marie-Antoinette-type chignon propped by hatpins.[38]

Blin had the Dead slash their faces on stage with an oblique white line; this was a humorous and symbolic gesture, calling attention to theatre and de-dramatizing the beyond.

Actors at grips with Genet

For The Screens Genet specified precise, taut acting, without useless gestures. He insisted on "the playing within the play." By putting on her highheeled shoes, the Mother becomes another person; she dances for Saïd who claps his hands; they imitate a storm, lightning; they create a spectacle. Leïla plays with trousers that represent Saïd; the needle comes alive and pricks her. The Mother and Leïla imitate the clucking of hens and roosters; they become a barnyard; they bark and become dogs. The pigskin glove of Sir Harold is a surrogate authority. Saïd and Habib imitate the noise of the wind and create a sound setting. Everything happens on stage, before the spectator; neither the audience nor the actors should forget that they are in a theatre.

All these details bear on the very idea of theatre and the profession of acting. May 1968 had not yet sowed the seeds of rebellion, and Genet's demands were surprising for actors in a company accustomed to playing great playwrights in a so-called classical style. In *The Screens*, the actors had to have physically trained bodies, while also speaking a difficult text. They had to be officiating priests at a ceremony, rather than actors, and at the same time utter obscenities. They had to be their own stagehands, carry and design the

13 Saïd (Amidou) and Habib (Jean-Pierre Granval) in Scene IV of Blin's production of Genet's *Screens* at the Odéon-Théâtre de France, 1966. Behind Saïd's head is a paper sun pasted on the palm-screen. Above the screen is the pigskin glove of Sir Harold. Ph. Acquart

14 Makeup and coiffure for Warda (Ingeborg Kloiber) for Blin's
production of Genet's *Screens* at the State Theatre of Essen,
Germany, 1967. Ph. Acquart

set, make themselves ugly. It was not only their acting style that had to change, but their whole behavior. Genet was not satisfied with a mere brilliant acting performance; he wanted actors "in danger of death." Rather than forgetting the play between scenes, actors were to concentrate and not leave the stage ceremony even if they were not actually on stage at the moment. Genet ordered Blin: "Make all the actors work. I have the impression that they think they can do everything." If they had that illusion, it was quickly dissipated.

Genet liked to make people uncomfortable, especially actors. Far from helping or encouraging them, he robbed them of assurance and proved to them that they could not perform even the simplest action. He provoked them with increasing difficulties; he dared them and continually increased his demands. In *The Balcony* he imagined the actors perched on soles twenty inches high: "How can they walk without breaking their necks, without scratching their legs in the laces and trains of their skirts? Let them learn how."[39] In *The Screens* he refused to relieve the soldiers of tin cups that annoyed them. They were supposed to enter noiselessly in spite of hobnailed boots. He would not hear of felt soles to create silence artificially. It was up to the actors to find the solution in themselves; they should come on stage silently, like thieves breaking into a house. Soldiers watched by an enemy depended on silence to save their lives.

Genet cared little for a well-modulated voice; he wanted a voice that the actor had never used before; the actor should invent, search deep within himself. Everyday, banal, mechanical intonations were forbidden. On stage the actor should speak artificially, since everything on stage is artifice, but well-planned and creative artifice rendered with all his force and all the power of his presence. He should be there, without any possible evasion; he should assume each situation, word, and silence.

Actress Maria Casarès recalled: "When I said: 'under the moon,' I had to think of it." When she wasn't thinking of it wholly, Genet sensed it: "Moon! It's not a table, or a chair, or whatever! It's a moon!" That day he struck Casarès with his cane.[40]

At the beginning of rehearsals, Genet forbade any gesture by the actors. Later they could work at a few and then keep to them. Thus Genet wanted to avoid clichés; he preferred gestures that contrasted with the words but did not draw upon everyday reality or anarchic spontaneity. He did not want gestures felt by the actor, but an individual corporeal score – "show and utter what is usually unnoticed." This desired effect of strangeness is not at all like Brechtian estrangement, but arises from a taste for stage exploration; it is a joyous invention of new expression. "Nothing is known in advance, and nothing is learned. Everything has to be discovered and named. And there is no question of forgetting or being absent. The actor has to be present for each word because each word and gesture must be reinvented, and thus from invention to invention one approaches this secret world which we discover by living it."[41]

Genet was not interested in mere spectacle. He sought the quintessence of theatre, the essential gesture that could be accomplished only on the stage. In 1975 he would write to director of *The Balcony*, Antoine Bourseiller: "Every theatre performance, every spectacle is fantasy. The fantasy of which I speak does not need mirrors, sumptuous cloths, or baroque furniture; it is in a voice that breaks on one word rather than another, but you have to find the word and the voice. [Fantasy] is in a gesture that is out of place at that moment . . ."

15 The Mother (Maria Casarès) at left and Kadidja (Germaine Kerjean) at right, with the Arabs who have drawn their revolt on the screens in Blin's production of Genet's *Screens* at the Odéon-Théâtre de France, 1966. Set by Acquart. Ph. Acquart

Genet would ask an actor point blank why his body was resting when it should be participating in the stage action. During silences the actors should "dream of the death of their son or their beloved mother, or of a criminal robbing them or of being seen naked in public." It is necessary to discover gestures "at the boundaries of death," to commit oneself to a universe in which "morality is replaced by stage esthetics," in the hope of approaching the sacred.

After playing in *The Screens* actors should be transformed. Genet wrote to Blin that the actors "should not get over it, in whatever sense you want to give that phrase." Blin must thus be ready for strong-arm tactics, arsenic or blows, Genet joked. The least of his remarks at rehearsals was vitriolic; he knew nothing of nuance or caution. He wanted tough actors, without useless modesty, without pity for themselves or their characters. He wanted intelligent animals who would transform an animal cry into an artistic spark. Exterior life must no longer exist, for the theatre absorbs everything, and the actor had to be at the service of the world of Genet. He wrote: "I go to the theatre to see myself on stage [reconstituted as a character or through many characters in a story] as I wouldn't dare see myself or dream myself to be, and yet as I know myself to be."[42]

The function of actors is therefore to take on gestures and properties which allow them "to show me to myself naked, in solitude and joy." The creative, inventive, ceremonious actor celebrates a black mass dedicated to an author for whom normal values are inverted. The actor's work, beyond the play and the part, investigates the biography of the playwright. Roger Blin helped in this initiation.

In *The Screens* human space and time are abolished. "On stage you are going nowhere." "The stage represents nothing." "When you hear a character come in from the left, look toward the right; theatrical space is boundless." Time? The paratroops in Algeria wear the uniforms of the troops of Marsh. Bugeaud who left to conquer Algeria in 1836; they continue the tradition. Living and dead are the same; they simply change floors. The eye of the Dead on the living fixes them at the point of death. All the characters are beyond their lives and can laugh at themselves. They have gone beyond problems, past wars, and they can appreciate the inanity of existence. Genet wrote: "Whatever separates us from the dead must be transcended" and "I see the stage as a place which is closely related to death."[43]

In such a play the actors have enormous responsibilities. They are charged with anchoring the characters in their own bodies, but the unwarned spectator, while looking at these bodies, must also know that he is to be cut off from the real, dragged into a fantastic world where rags are royal, where the lead of makeshift habitations is turned into gold, spittle into diamonds.

No gesture or inflexion must be borrowed from realism, or the whole edifice crumbles. The slender structure hangs together because of energy and refusal of the ordinary. The performance has to dazzle and scintillate with a rare gleam. It is a celebration, an offering to the dead; it will demand great effort to radiate. It is not a simple stage play, but a metaphysical enterprise. That is why Genet wanted at first to authorize a single performance, one unique act, a union of life and death. Show me what I know myself to be, he demanded in his other plays. Show me arriving among the Dead, he demanded here.

The difficulty of performance arises not only from the huge cast, the large number of costumes (and the budget that implies), but also from the dovetailing of scenes, the difficulties of syntax, and the problems of the set. But then the play was designed to be unperformable; the incandescence of a poetic action goes beyond the theatre as we know it. Roger Blin allowed us to enter this poetic dream, this theatrical experience.

Blin's work

Genet's special world and his complicated syntax required clarification. Blin tried to carve a path between Genet's requirements and the actors' anxiety. Paule Annen, Leïla, read the play several times, perceiving many levels, sensing that "we couldn't play it like other plays."[44] When she first read the manuscript, Maria Casarès, the Mother, was both fascinated and confused: "It was necessary to go around it; to find a door or a window to get inside, and not always by reason . . . Genet's text withdraws if you try to pin a label on it; since there are several possibilities, that encourages invention. I never before had to work with such a living text. Every word has to live, and every object carries its own weight. You need breath, vitality, and joy even in tragic passages." The manuscript seemed so difficult to Casarès that she nearly gave up the part. Then Genet explained to her: "You see, the Mother can resemble . . . a Marseille fishwife." That image gave the actress her voice, bearing, and walk. And Genet's presence enabled her to find the profound cry with which she begins her speech: "Saïd! Saïd! You're not going to give in?"[45]

Blin tried to orchestrate the laughter: "There was the broken laughter of Paule Annen, the famous laugh of Casarès, that kind of quavering chuckle in the barnyard scene where they imitate the cries of birds, turkeys, ducks. And then the laugh of the Dead."[46]

From the start Blin would not allow anyone to call the play vulgar or obscene. He considered *The Screens* a long, beautiful, highly imaged poem that was also full of humor, "like a tragedy with burlesque language." It was "a declaration of anti-realism for truth of another kind, proving that anything can be dared and meaningful, outside of realism."[47] He therefore conceived of a poetic mise-en-scène, in its largest meaning. Separated in space, each in a prison cell, Saïd and Leïla coordinate their movements, as though they were next to one another. Split between two actors, the soldier Pierre arrives below in the realm of the Dead, and his corpse is dragged on high by the Mother, in parallel movements. One character does not look at another to whom he is speaking; instead he looks in the opposite direction, or toward the audience, into the distance. The death of Kadidja is stylized; she falls to her knees, then remains inclined slightly backwards, supported by two Arab women. The dead General is propped up and made to walk, turned round and round. This detail pleased Genet so that he elaborated it, making the General turn more and more quickly "until he reaches the speed of light." In the fourteenth scene the jealous knitting women move with small jerky steps under narrow sheaths, resembling six rings of a serpent; at each rotation around Warda's corpse they whisper agressively: "Let us knit, let us knit." The Legionnaires would have to cover hundreds of yards if they advanced as often and as long as the Lieutenant ordered. Blin did not want them to use the mime of walking in one spot; he preferred a stylized crawl. He did not practice either abstract mime or corporeal expression, but subtle suggestion. He would have liked the actors to make more use of the set, as if it were the rigging on a ship, supports in space upon which to impose the images of the edge of a ravine, a pile of stones, the lip of a well, a mast, etc. But their imaginations were not up to it. Together Blin and Genet fought against the realistic spirit of the actors. The latter remarked during a rehearsal: "Nothing should be heard when the crowd crosses the stage, especially not the boards. Your hands and feet remain prosaic. When you walk on stage, you look as though you are going somewhere, as in life. But on stage, you are going nowhere." The instructions were easy to understand but difficult to perform. Blin explained to me in 1966: "There was no school in France to teach this; it was not a matter of teaching one form of dance rather than another, but of finding attitudes corresponding to the beauty of the text."

Genet wanted the actors to be transformed into animals, for example sublimated dogs that would correspond to their barking. He requested:

. . . for the mother: very small steps but great authority in her gestures; then suddenly, large steps; for Ommou: that she tear each of her steps from the mud; for Warda: her cothurni should be so heavy that she cannot walk; fasten her to the stage; for the Arabs drawing the revolution in the twelfth scene, a different walk for each of them; one with hands in his pockets, touching the screens as he sways; another very firm and decided; a third finishing on one leg; a fourth one amused and dancing a street dance; for the natives trembling before the son of Sir Harold, each one should practice making all his limbs tremble so that they could give a sorrowful impression of fright. They should tremble from head to foot, from shoulders to hands; the trembling should evoke a field of rye in a strong wind, or the flight of a flock of partridges.[48]

Blin helped the actors to concretize these directions, or at least to be inspired by them. He also prevented any recourse to sentimentality. He saw to it that Saïd was set off from the other characters. Toward Leïla, Saïd played the strong man. When he told her: "Kindness drowned me," he rejected her with a kick. Toward the Mother, Saïd played the man of authority. When he commanded: "Put on your shoes. . . . Dance!" she played submission. Toward his employer Saïd was humble, the humblest of farmworkers: "Oh yes, Sir!" but he did not pity himself or his fate. He felt himself cut off from the other workers. Blin introduced a fight provoked by Saïd. Toward Habib, the most intelligent farmworker, Saïd showed fright; Habib turned him around with his arms spread out, like one who is crucified.

Development of Scenes I, X, XI, XII, XV
Scene I

Saïd and his mother, on the road leading to the village home of Leïla, the fiancée. Unenthusiastically, Saïd is going to get married. The stage looks quite empty to the spectator who does not see the platforms lying flat; there seem to be no props. Saïd enters; behind him an invisible stagehand slides in a five-panelled screen decorated with a sun and abstract floral patterns. This screen, placed on the floor behind the first two platforms, and brightly lit, seems to radiate heat. It is smaller than the width of the stage. It is a metonymic element suggesting the desert. One scarcely pays attention to the poorly lit flats on the left and right of the stage, which will be used later.

Saïd jumps up on the first platform, one step high, and shouts toward the public: "Rose! I said rose! The sky is already pink as a rose. The sun will be up in half an hour . . . Don't you want me to help you?" Only at this moment, as in Genet's scenic direction, does the Mother appear, carrying unmatched shoes in one hand, and with the other keeping a suitcase balanced on her head. She looks for a place to sit and goes toward platform number 2, also lying on the floor. Saïd refuses to sit and stamps in place, stubbornly. He feels humiliated at being unable to afford any but an ugly woman, lacking money for a dowry. He does not understand his mother's irony: "If you laugh until you cry, your tears'll bring her face into focus." Then, softened, he becomes more compliant and kneels next to her.

Saïd's trousers are coarsely patched at the knees. His jacket is red and gaudy. The Mother wears layers of rags in faded purple; a cloth is tied around her head. The openings of her long dress leave her arms and legs free, whereas Saïd's jacket, tightly buttoned, constrains his movements of a sulky, awkward adolescent, ill at ease in his skin.

The Mother stretches, relaxed despite her fatigue, and decides to start walking again, after this short pause. They fight about who will carry the suitcase. The Mother is the stronger. She makes Saïd stumble and sits on the suitcase again, so that he can't take hold of it. Saïd squats on the floor. Both play at evoking the imaginary contents of the suitcase. Saïd uses a great many Mediterranean gestures to stress his exaggerations. Then, gently, on his knees, he smiles at his mother whom he admires, and asks her to put on her shoes. Surprised, the Mother manipulates these shoes like puppets at the tips of her fingers, puts them back on the ground. He forces them on to her feet and urges her to dance. She obeys reluctantly, and performs small, hesitant steps, her feet bruised by her high-heeled, pointed shoes. Then she grows bold and enjoys making her necklaces jingle and shake to the rhythm of her movements. She bows, chest forward, then backward. Saïd claps his hands to encourage her. The dance is not choreographed; it is a kind of improvised ritual that soon accelerates in pleasure. Mother and son excite each other; they imitate the sounds of a storm, of lightning. Saïd crawls to sweep away the dust in front of his mother. They exit laughing and fighting for the suitcase that soon opens; it is empty. All the presents of which they spoke do not exist. The two actors leave the stage. The screen, carried by an invisible stagehand, disappears at the same time, pulled along the floor toward the wing. A dimming of the light and the final line: "It's a storm. The whole wedding'll be drenched" indicate the downpour. The light is further lowered, and in the semi-darkness the undecorated white screens are set up for the following scene − the brothel.

The audience begins to participate; at every new scene new screens will arrive and new actors will appear before them, like pages of an album from which characters take shape. But the audience does not yet know that the elevation of platforms will modify the arrangements on stage. Mother and son have begun to build a unique action. The disconnected looks, the ceremony of the dance on pointed shoes, the mockery of the suitcase which is seen to be empty after its contents are enumerated − introduce a quality of fascinating strangeness.

Scene X

On the floor screens represent an orange plantation. The two colonists, wearing riding-breeches, look grotesque; Blankensee has a false belly and buttocks, red sideburns and moustache. They watch three Arab agricultural workers, bent over, weeding the ground (mime movements) and come downstage to show off. Blankensee praises the beauty of his rose garden. Blin adds a short fight between the three Arabs and Saïd, which justifies the colonist's line: "No quarreling." Sir Harold gives orders, dismisses his workers; they leave, with Saïd the last to go. The two colonists sit on chairs downstage. Oblivious, they fail to see that behind them an Arab with chalk has entered silently and is drawing a flame on a screen. Blankensee encourages Sir Harold to admire the small pad on his stomach, which, he thinks, reinforces his commanding appearance. He leans forward, then backward, revealing his orthopedic device, and showing that it permits all his movements. He sits down again. Sir Harold offers him a cigarette and takes out his lighter, while simultaneously two other Arabs set fire to orange-trees. Unnoticing, the colonists get up, commenting on the difficulties of the situation. While they walk from left to right, and from front to back, the Arabs (who blow to intensify the fire) sneak in without being noticed. (In order to simulate the fire, invisible stagehands behind the painted orange-trees shake spotlit red silk cloth at the end of a rope, making it seem like a moving flame.) The colonists notice nothing and leave, taking their chairs with them. Faint sound-effects evoke the crackling of fire. With a light change, the orange-plantation screens disappear; the platforms are raised. On the floor, at each end of the stage, two screens represent the prison for the scene with Saïd and Leïla.

Scene XI

As his speech proceeds, the Lieutenant, using the foot-bridge, goes down on the second platform, soon followed by his men. Instead of going twice into the wings to get the gloves or the binoculars, the Legionnaire Preston carries on him the whole panoply of effects necessary for the Lieutenant's accoutrement: collar, tassels, shoulder-belt, revolver, binoculars, brush, cloth, five pair of gloves of different colors. The Lieutenant himself checks every item, without which his speech would be ineffective. He talks to himself rather than to his orderly, to whom he gives orders without eye contact. For each object, Preston gives a funny little salute. The second platform is an excellent display-case for this ceremony of dressing the Lieutenant. It is high, conspicuous, and less remote than the uppermost platform. The Sergeant arrives from above; he takes his time catching up with the other Legionnaires. The Lieutenant climbs a few steps, the better to dominate his company. The lights fade on them.

The action picks up at floor level, in the prison with Saïd and Leïla. The Legionnaires are invisible. The two actions are supposed to take place about sixty miles from each other. The elevation of the platforms and the shifting play of light suggest this distance.

On the ground the Guard, Saïd, and Leïla are immersed in semi-darkness and cannot see each other. They speak without looking at each other. The walls separating them are mental walls. The three characters are soon drowned in darkness. Light falls on the first level platform, on which is seen the screen of the Blankensee house. When the couple's conversation is finished, the action returns to the prison (new lighting). Saïd and Leïla turn like whirling dervishes, competing as to who will scream the loudest. Hearing a machine-gun, they fall to the floor. A bugle-call wakes the Guard who gets up and, half asleep, leaves, taking his chair with him. Light fades on the prison; Leïla, Saïd, and the two prison screens disappear. The Legionnaires are seen getting up and leaving by the upper level. On the lighted middle level, the end of Scene XI takes place, between the Lieutenant and the Sergeant. Afterwards they proceed to the ground level by way of the inclined ramp.

Seven light changes mark the different phases of this scene, lighting in turn the first, second, or third level, and leaving in shadow the area of interrupted action. But Scene XII is in preparation, and several levels will be used at the same time: the ground and the three raised platforms. A ceremony brings together European colonists, dignitaries, and the native population.

Scene XII

The Legionnaires cross the stage, carrying two tricolored flags. The Lieutenant and the Sergeant march lockstep while a military tune sounds. Enter the Arabs. A dignitary keeps them in check in one corner of the stage. The Figures are set up on the middle level, so as to dominate the other characters. Ramparts are raised on the lowest platform, and the light is very bright. But Kadidja wants to oppose the ceremony, the fraternization with the enemy; she is silenced. A shot rings out, killing the young Communicant, the daughter of Sir Harold. Commotion. Everyone runs away. On the highest platform a European couple exhibit on a tall dummy the decorations earned by their family.

The crowd reappears below, in front of the ramparts. The flags have been removed. All is desolation, silence. The colony has suffered. Murders, fires. Time has passed. The situation has deteriorated. Sir Harold and his son occupy the lowest level, wishing to reaffirm their authority over the colony. Sir Harold harangues the natives, but they leave. Only Kadidja, yelling out her hatred, is left. Sir Harold's son kills her with one shot. The Figures disappear. Darkness on the stage.

Blue light picks out Kadidja, who gets up and encourages the Arabs to start a revolution, to shout their hatred. They come back on stage, one after the other, behind her back, without her looking at them. They invade the space and draw on the screens their guerilla acts: a revolver, a scream, a heart torn out, flames, dynamite, feet cut off, money stolen. As the dialogue continues, all levels are filled with screens; graffiti and spots of color multiply in the Arabs' unceasing movements to and fro, jumping from one level to the other in an accelerated rhythm. The stage becomes a huge mural. A new light strikes each new screen. The scurry of those who draw, appearing one after the other, the lines uttered in passing, the arm movements and the leaps from one level to the other as if to surprise an enemy, the violent spurting of paint-guns, all compose in the space a kind of poetic, feverish, revolutionary calligraphy. The Arab women are in turn invited in; first they appear frightened, ignorant of the situation; then they rush to look at the drawings.

A spot shows the arrival of the Mother. Kadidja chases her away. Fade of light to blue. Kadidja is isolated, as when the gunshot killed her, but surrounded with all the drawings of the revolt. The women will proceed with her pre-funeral cleansing. Darkness invades the stage. It is the intermission.

Scene XV

The Dead are squatting on the ground. Three single-panelled, transparent screens are punctured successively by three of the newly Dead: Kadidja, then Pierre who was accidentally strangled by the Mother (while he punctures his screen on the first level, the Mother on the middle level drags his corpse after her). Then the Mother bursts through two screens on successive levels before going down to puncture the last one on the ground. She takes longer than the others to die.

The Dead, situated at the bottom level, face the audience and look down at what is happening on earth. The spectators, however, look at the upper level which illuminates the living Legionnaires, who have climbed up there, and crawl up and down on the inclined plane. In the following scene, they die and puncture transparent screens on this upper level. While the brothel mistress, Warda, dies on the ground among the living, the prostitutes dress her corpse (a dummy) for her funeral.

On the whole, there are few light cues – only thirty-two in the first part, to punctuate transitions between the sequences, to hide the movements, and to light areas of action. Music is even more sparse – a bugle-call or a phrase of the *Marseillaise*. The richness of Genet's text and his scenic directions have inspired these appearances/disappearances of the screens, this play of colors, of many-colored rags. But the actors and their characters remain essential. Stage machinery must merely serve them.

For the first series of performances from 16 April to 7 May 1966, Blin thought that he would guide the general direction, but because the rehearsal period was too short, he did not search as deeply as he would have liked, especially in oriental theatre techniques. Apart from the second series of performances in September and October, and a German production in 1967, Blin did not again direct *The Screens*. "I never wanted to go back to it. I don't think I could have made other discoveries. I don't say that that's the best thing I ever did, but it was the production that was most important to me. There was this celebration, this anticultural jubilation."[49]

16 Rehearsal of Scene XII of Blin's production of Genet's *Screens* at the Odéon-Théâtre de France, 1966. The Arabs are on the stage floor. On the first platform at the left Sir Harold is encouraging his son. Above are the Europeans and the bemedalled dummy. At lower right Kadidja (Germaine Kerjean) tells an Arab: "Leave your fist in my mouth or I'll howl." In rehearsing the scene again from the beginning, the screen drawings, which should come later, were not erased. Ph. Acquart

Critics and audience

The whole company lived for months in anxiety. Not only did Genet make things difficult for them, but they were afraid of the scandal *The Screens* would cause. Only Blin remained calm: "Will the play shock people? I don't want to hear anything about it. I haven't done any worrying on that score for a long time. It's an insolent, moving work . . . It's a celebration, a ceremony; the purest theatre ritual. The whole should suggest what Genet wanted: lucid and accepted abjection, carried to the last degree."[50]

The Screens is a *summa* of Genet's work, and it is obvious that a 1966 audience, who scarcely knew the rest of his work, took the play like a slap in

17 Scene XVI of Blin's production of Genet's *Screens* at the Odéon-Théâtre de France, 1966. Lower left the Arab women knitting. Above the domain of the Dead, where the Mother and Kadidja welcome Warda (Madeleine Renaud) who has just burst through a white screen. Lower right at stage level two whores complete the funeral dressing of Warda (played by an actress in a costume identical to that of Madeleine Renaud). Ph. Acquart

the face, whether furious or bored at what it understood badly, or whether it rejected the whole world of Genet. During a discussion, certain spectators explained that they had not been attracted by the play's beginning; it seemed to them that there was no structure to the first scenes; they would have preferred to be moved by the story; they wished they knew Genet's other works. They admired the acting and the fact that the actors could play extraordinary characters over a period of four hours. Some were shocked by the expressions; others were not. They had come to the Odéon with the usual expectations, of a well-told story and moving characters. Some wished to see the show again after hearing Blin's explanations, but it was impossible to get tickets.[51]

The reviewers divide rather sharply into those who were furious and rejected Genet and those who were sensitive to theatre writing that left ordinary theatre behind. The Resistance-founded *Combat* reported: "It is the greatest theatre performance in years; having seen it, it is hard to remember anything else one may have seen. Everything is overthrown. In an exemplary way, Genet accomplishes a synthesis of the most implacable realism and the most brilliant lyricism."[52]

Obviously, Blin was included in this praise, since productions abroad did not arouse such enthusiasm. *Le Monde*'s reviewer was sensitive to the denunciation of social hypocrisy. *L'Humanité*'s reviewer was interested in the misery of the natives. The reviewer of *L'Express* considered the play a fragment of an immense and mocking *danse macabre*. For the well-known critic Guy Dumur the play "is addressed above all to our senses. It wants to take our breath away, to smother us with horror, to lead us to another side of ourselves. It wants us too to burst through those paper-screens burst by the Dead when they enter a paradise made in their image . . . Genet's language makes the most shocking scenes acceptable."[53]

Another intelligent critic, Gilles Sandier, wrote: "It is a great theatrical and funereal poem orchestrating the major themes of Genet as impeccably as Bach or Giotto — the liturgy of garbage, the celebration of evil, sex, hatred, death; a game of mirrors is a scandalous, violent, and lyrical confrontation; a game not only against society and its attributes, but against the failure of creation on the part of an imposter, miserable, and vicious God who does not support his saints in their quest."[54] Sandier elsewhere compliments Blin for having drawn from the bodies of the actors "magic, shrillness, incantation, fire." He praises Paule Annen and above all Maria Casarès, worthy of Peking Opera: "the laugh, the barking, the gesture of the possessed, the hands carrying worlds — everything in her was magic; everything erupted from her voice and hands — hills, wind, nettles, the night."[55]

When did the scandal erupt?

The first audiences and critics were not particularly offended. Smothered by the verbal plenitude, admiring the magnificent performance, tired of the long duration requiring close attention, they were more overcome than angered by obscenities or situations; they may have been uncertain that they understood syntactical turns or the inversion of values. There seemed to be no problem about vague references to a war in Algeria. In the press one could read: "The protest fizzled out," "The scandal is that there wasn't any." As though the bomb were defused by the poem.

A week later there were signs that one scene was particularly offensive – that of the burial of the French Lieutenant. Protests began, soon orchestrated by political parties and the press. This scene takes place after the intermission. After Genet piled up references to stench, to garbage odors in the Arab camp, he accumulated references to decomposition and putrefaction in the French camp; decadent Western society was watching itself rot. When the French soldiers saw their Lieutenant die, having nothing with which to pay him homage, each one farted in his face while exclaiming in a tone fit for Racine: "In the hostile darkness and countryside there'll be a Christian death-chamber with the smell of candles, wreaths, a last will and testament, a death-chamber set up there like a cloud in a painting." The noise of tearing cloth imitated a fart in a clown-like way. Aristophanic verve, a Carnival spirit, and lyricism meet in this mocking scene where "breaths" (to use the Carnival expression) become a gift. But in the face of a Lieutenant dead for his country! That is what enraged people.

Furthermore, Blin set on stage certain moments that Genet set off stage. In the tenth scene, for example, two colonists did not leave the stage each time an Arab set an orange-tree ablaze, but moved upstage or stood off to one side. In the eleventh scene all the Legionnaires were on stage and not in the wings; instead of leaving the stage each time the Lieutenant sent him out for something, Preston carried all the objects on his person. In the same spirit, the death of the Lieutenant and the "scene of farts" took place on stage and not behind a screen. Genet agreed with this principle, but the text was published before rehearsals and did not incorporate these changes. Certain critics read the play, and they thought that Blin had added to the shock effect. They called the scene "odious," since it "insulted the French army" and all those dead for France in Algeria. The worst of it was that this was being played in a subsidized theatre, complained Jean-Jacques Gautier in *Figaro*, whereas the *Lettres françaises* reviewer retorted: "It will be an honor for this theatre to have this play in its repertory."

Blin's mise-en-scène, in harmony with the very conception of the work as well as Genet's interdiction, was not intentionally political; it was on the contrary essentially poetic. Whatever political provocation there was existed at a much deeper level than the offending scene. Blin thought that the only political idea of the play was the lesson to the rebels; don't become organized; don't model yourselves on your former masters. Nor did hostile critics pay any attention to the lesson of the last scenes; after death all quarrels were vain; hatred disappeared. All the action was written from the point of view of the Dead.

Opponents of the play tried to stop the performance. Jean-Louis Barrault and Madeleine Renaud, aware of the danger, had shown their support by taking part in the play. Despite virulent attacks, they kept the play on the boards throughout the scheduled run.

The calendar of protests

20 April: *Figaro* mentions whistling and other reactions at the scene with the Lieutenant.

21 April: *Figaro* finds the audience "increasingly incensed. Whistling and cries soon give way to Bravos. There are eight curtain-calls, and the protesters are quiet." On the same day *Ecoutes* reports: "The scandal is that there wasn't any. Genet's supporters were installed in the upper balcony. Police cars were stationed near the Senate, but anger subsided before the courage of the company, the originality of the set, the undeniable talent of the playwright." Nevertheless, the writer Gabriel Marcel records his indignation in *Nouvelles littéraires*.

Between 21 and 30 April, anger grows, the press grows more virulent, political parties enter the fray.

30 April: (twelfth performance): *Figaro* reports that the audience is angry, and calls out to the actors. Certain spectators [the Occident Group] are as obscene as the play. The right-wing *Aurore* reports "violent incidents; Algerian veterans – parachutists and legionnaires – demand the performance to stop, with cries of 'It's a shame! It's a scandal!'" There are blows. "Enraged spectators threw seats at the stage, wounding a stagehand; an actor had to be hospitalized. A few spectators were injured. The police restored order. A quarter of an hour later the performance continued."
The Italian *Corriere della Sera* reports on the events of 30 April: "A seat thrown to the stage gave the signal. Seats, bottles, rotten eggs, tomatoes, and other vegetables were thrown to the stage. About twenty youths came down the orchestra aisle, throwing

smoke-bombs and insulting the audience. The actors were blinded by the lights and didn't see the parachutists jump from the balconies to the stage. One of them insulted Maria Casarès. Stagehands came to her rescue. The safety curtain was brought down. The tumult continued. Barrault came downstage to ask for calm: 'Let those who don't like the show leave. The performance continues.' The disturbers were expelled."

A Liaison Committee of the Veterans Association of Indo-China and Algeria (never before heard of) sent a letter to the press, protesting against this play which "threw garbage at the army," and which was "written by a deserter." A demonstration was scheduled for 4 May in front of the Odéon.

1 May: There were protests from the first moments of the performance. From the balcony about fifty youths (among them a dozen St-Cyr cadets) threw yoghurt and rotten eggs as well as smoke-bombs; one struck a spectator in the leg; a brick hit an actor in the head. The safety curtain had to be lowered twice. The French union of actors protested, demanding protection for the actors.

2 May: All newspapers reported the incidents. *L'Humanité* published the text of the Actors Union and recalled the affair of *The Nun* (a film based on Diderot's novel). The film had been forbidden just before *The Screens*, for fear of its offending Catholic audiences, and the result was a great commercial success. The same people now protested against censorship, fearing a comparable success. In a spirit of conciliation, Blin returned the Lieutenant scene to the wings, and the French flag was replaced by an anonymous emblem. He felt that the play had to be performed, but without danger to the actors. Police surrounded the theatre; volunteers manned the aisles, among whom was Patrice Chéreau, who would direct *The Screens* in 1983.

3 May: Veterans' groups specified that they had no connection with the protests, and that they would not join the demonstration of 4 May. The right-wing Occident Group said that it would join that demonstration. The jury of the University Theatre Festival at Nancy (founded by Jack Lang, who would be Mitterand's Minister of Culture) proclaimed that performances should be protected at the Theatre of France.

4 May: Six hundred youths demonstrated before the Odéon, with such cries as "Genet to the gallows! The play to Moscow!" Smiling, Genet appeared at the first-floor window. Blin was at his side. The show was in the street. Left-wing militants counter-demonstrated.

> Some sang the *Marseillaise*, others the *International*. Three policemen were wounded, and ninety-five people were arrested. The front of the building was damaged.

5 May: It was asked in the press: how many of these youths fought in the Algerian War?

7 May: Three smoke-bombs exploded at the last performance [of the series]. The Occident Group was there. Flames shot up, but the performance continued after ten minutes. Genet paraphrased Racine: "The few demonstrators from the Occident Group [for "dans l'Occident désert quel devint mon ennui"] give in to the lazy side of their nature when they see on stage a dead French officer sniffing the meticulous farts of his soldiers, whereas they ought to be seeing actors playing at being or at seeming ... Actors' acting is to military reality what smoke-bombs are to the reality of napalm."[56]

The following autumn, protests were rare at the last twenty performances. The Occident Group upset the next to last evening with firecrackers, bags of flour, dead rats; they were removed.

Veterans' organizations demanded that the play be withdrawn. Christian Bonnet, a Center-Democrat from Morbihan, requested that the subsidy of the Theatre of France be reduced, thus penalizing Barrault for having placed *The Screens* on the program. The Chamber member claimed that public funds should not support such plays. He read the fart scene aloud in the Chamber of Deputies. Genet never hoped for such glory! Bonnet abridged the poetic passages in order to excerpt the scatology from its context. Bonnet, citing earlier criticism by the well-known Catholics Gabriel Marcel and François Mauriac, invoked their names; he wanted religious conflict to add to the political one.

André Malraux, Minister of Culture, took the floor of the Chamber:

Ladies and gentlemen, liberty does not always have clean hands, but when she doesn't have clean hands, you should look twice before throwing her out the window.

It is a matter of subsidized theatre, you say. I have no comment on that.

But the reading you just heard is a fragment. This fragment was not played on the stage but in the wings. It is said that one has a feeling that the play is anti-French. If we were really faced with an anti-French play, we would be faced with a serious problem. Now, whoever has read the play knows that it is not anti-French. It is anti-human, anti-everything.

Genet is not any more anti-French than Goya was anti-Spanish. In *Caprices* you have the equivalent of the scene under discussion.

As a result, the real problem posed here is, as you phrased it, putrescence.

But there too, ladies and gentlemen, let us move slowly! For one can do anything with quotations:

"O my Beauty, tell the vermin who will eat you with kisses . . ." That's putrescence! *Carrion* was not a title that pleased the Judge of the Court, without mentioning *Madame Bovary.*

What you call putrescence is not an accident. That is what one always claimed when arrests were to be made. I am not claiming – and for that matter I don't have to claim – that M. Genet is Baudelaire. If he were Baudelaire, we wouldn't know it. The proof is that it wasn't known that Baudelaire was a genius. (*Laughter*)

What is certain is that the argument invoked – "This should be forbidden because it wounds my sensibility" – is unreasonable. The following is a reasonable argument: "This play wounds your sensibility. Don't buy a ticket. Other things are playing elsewhere. No one is forcing you. We are not on radio or television."

If we begin to allow the criterion you mentioned, we should get rid of half of French Gothic painting, for the great altar-piece of Grünewald was painted for the plague-ridden. We should also get rid of all Goya's work, which is considerable. And I return to Baudelaire whom I just mentioned . . .

27 October 1966

Bonnet's motion was not passed, but since he had read the scene of the Lieutenant's death, that text was published in the official Journal of the Chamber of Deputies.

4   In service to diverse works

Roger Blin was not only the preferred director of Beckett and Genet but also of many other playwrights of different nationalities who had sharply individual styles while being aware of contemporary reality: Adamov, Bauer, Bernhard, Billetdoux, Faye, Frisch, Fugard, Manet, Semprun Maura, and Mrozek.

SHAKESPEARE AND MODERN CLASSICS

Shakespeare

In 1972, Blin was invited to the theatre at Strasbourg to direct *Macbeth*, at a time when Pierrette Tison brought him her adaptation. He was attracted to the play's irrationality and violence. Contrary to a common tendency of our time, Blin refused to impose upon the work any allusion to the contemporary world. He thought that a classical text had to speak for itself, that one should not use it to comment on today's problems. He wanted to direct *Macbeth* "raw," as it was written, but he disapproved of the spiritual tone of Pierrette Tison's French translation, and he struggled to find a tougher, more truculent version. In preparation, Blin himself read around the play: Eisenstein on the interior/exterior parallel montage in Shakespeare's structure and Thomas De Quincey's "On the Knocking at the Gate in Macbeth."

Blin's production blended the evil magic of the night with the rivalry of gang members who were ready to do anything for power. Although actual violence is seen in fights with sword or naked fist, the theatrical magic is grounded in lighting and in the appearance and disappearance of elements of the set; vague forms arise, change shape, vanish. The background was a kind of black, spongy, burnt adobe, which suggested a decaying wall; this section of a feudal palace seemed invaded by moss or some element of plant, prairie, or forest.

For each new place a platform arrived on castors, or the lighting revealed a new area. Blin consulted prints at the library of the Musée des Arts Decoratifs, and he sketched castles, towers, flying buttresses. He was inspired by the designs of Victor Hugo. With his left hand, he rapidly sketched blackish areas and spidery lines. He would have liked to design his own set, but he finally left it to Matias, who also did the costumes.

Sets and characters were supposed to contribute to the confusion. Were the witches three or one? Of what sex? Had Macbeth seen them or dreamed? A small actress, a dwarf, and an actor wore a single garment with apertures for their heads and legs; they all danced in the same movement. The pleated curves of their garment were matched by the gestures of these gnomes. To hide their entrance and exit, a running actor unfurled an immense net over the whole stage. To this fantastic ceremony and luminous incandescence, the witches added the grotesque quality of asexual, screaming voices, and business inspired by the circus; a dwarf removed from a cauldron endless lengths of material. Statues with ironic forms gave way to people hidden behind them.

In order to introduce the fantastic swiftly, an actor dressed in the same spongy material as the set was a moving tree. The "bush" in the semi-darkness engaged in disturbing acrobatics, and the spectator could not decipher that form in motion, while strange strident noises resounded. Moreover, seen from the back, the three witches looked like bushes. Later, in Birnam Wood, the actors advanced full face, arms loaded with branches in synthetic material. Human, animal, vegetable, mineral – all have the same meaning for the artist, according to Roger Blin.

The costumes were made of the same spongy material as the set – soft, and transparent in certain lights. Vague crawling forms might be dangerous as well as disturbing. Everything was false appearance, hallucinatory vision. The soldiers' costumes, in rough material or leather, contrasted with the fluid pleats of the long robes of Lady Macbeth, Hecate, or Malcolm's cape. Most of the noise came from human mouths. When Banquo announced "The temple-haunting martlet," actors imitated the call of the martlet on Duncan's arrival. Later, an actress hidden in "holes" in the set moved her hands that were gloved with feathers.

A giant suspended crown could be lowered near Macbeth – symbol of power. The set was in constant movement. The actors themselves moved platforms on castors with their burden of banquet table and chairs, or soldiers, or Malcolm about to deliver his speech. The pieces of the banquet table were put together before the eyes of the audience; everything was merely part of a gigantic puzzle which was constructed and deconstructed, as in dreams where fuzzy images grow more distinct, and then dissolve. In Act IV, Scene I, the great door at the back of the set opened to show the eight kings, descendants of Banquo. Dressed identically, each costume invisibly attached to the next one, they advanced in profile, then turned, one by one, to show the full face, masked to resemble Banquo. During the course of the banquet Blin concretized the ghost who was visible only to Macbeth; behind a servant's head a mask of Banquo was fastened; when the servant turned, the ghost of Macbeth's vision materialized for the audience.

In Act V, Scene I, Lady Macbeth is supposed to enter with a candle. Soon the Doctor says: "Look how she rubs her hands." Nothing indicates that she has put down the candle, nor when. (Beckett, as well as Blin who spoke to him about it, remarked on the incompatibility of these two actions.) Blin, recalling Cocteau's film *Beauty and the Beast*, resorted to the fantastic. Lady Macbeth's staircase was installed on a platform. At the side of the staircase, hidden by drapes, three actors, on different stairs, seized the candle and passed it from hand to hand, thus seeming to follow the descent of Lady Macbeth, and leaving the actress with both hands free to rub away the bloodstains.

The production consisted of tricks and deliberate refusals. No elaborate means of production; no sophisticated machinery; no recorded sounds (with the single exception of the storm-sound instrument invented by Geminiani); man-made manoeuvres. Lighting created the atmosphere. The actors moved the elements of the set as often as the stagehands; an actor might melt into a tree or a chair, deceiving the audience in the creative shadow of an illusion, or, in contrast, revealing the game, borrowing from mime. Blin had faith in breath and corporeal energy to carry the action. He wooed the imagination of the audience. Against a black shadowy background with a red glow of torches, the idea of evil and bloodshed took form. It was called a red and black spectacle. Macbeth was the plaything of supernatural powers who breathed his decisions into him. Rather than draw a political lesson from *Macbeth*, Blin wanted to show the action of dark forces on the human spirit. He showed the morbid wildness of a Macbeth abused by hallucinations, inhabited by fantastic thoughts. The Macbeths, according to Blin, were "two beings who were not up to what they did."

For Macbeth, Blin made use of the qualities and suggestions of the actor J. P. Kalfon. Before the murder, Kalfon bent until he touched the ground, and Blin made him literally lie down. When he returned from Duncan's room, a knife in each hand, reporting the murder to his wife, he used his hands in speaking so that the knives gleamed, passing again and again under the eyes of Lady Macbeth who, at first attentive to his speech, finally mentioned the knives: "Why did you bring these daggers from the place?" Leaving for his last battle, Kalfon had great difficulty in putting on his armor, and Blin transformed the discomfort of the actor into a radical impediment for Macbeth, fighting for the indefensible, giving orders, still struggling but cornered and on the point of expiating his crimes.

Macbeth was deceived by nocturnal visions, by dreams in which he believed. He lived in shadow and illusion; reality escaped him. Director Blin grasped the play "in its contents of epic ingenuity, in its violent poetic imagery which, thanks to Shakespeare, is not mere imagery, but a probe into profundity of the essential human being."[1]

Ramon del Valle-Inclàn

The plot of *Divine Words* arouses pity: an idiotic dwarf is brought from fair to fair; he is the object of quarrels because people feel sorry for him and give him money, which will buy liquor for his mother, or his aunt and uncle. When dead, his body embarrasses everyone. During an orgiastic night, a demonic fever seizes all the villagers, including the Sexton. Valle-Inclàn drives this tragic farce, rooted in a miserable, obscurantist society, to the grotesque. Along with intolerance, passions are released – adultery, fornication, hunting down by forces of order – against the background of a country fair. Divine words alone restore a provisional calm: "Qui sine peccato est vestrum, primus in illa lapidem mittat."

Roger Vitrac had introduced Blin to *Divine Words* before World War II, and Barrault had suggested that he direct it at the Odéon in 1963; Blin described it:

The aristocratic aestheticism of Valle-Inclàn is such that he simultaneously shows to the bourgeoisie of Madrid the naked misery of the people, and yet he justifies this misery that nourishes a primitive religious faith that is fiercely obscurantist, in contrast to Christian rationalism. The theatre with the greatest affinity to Valle-Inclàn is perhaps the Irish theatre of Synge and Yeats.[2]

Written in 1920, the play was produced in Spain only in 1933, and it was not revived until 1961. Its virulence was feared more than the difficulty of its form. Blin continued: "Even if the mystical somersault at the end reassured believers in obscurantist *intégrisme*, the human truth that screams throughout the play continues to disturb them."

Valle-Inclàn knew painting admirably well, and one might say that he "wrote painting," evoking scenes that might create horror, or fiercely caricature society. Blin was sensitive to these visual qualities.

In order to soak up the atmosphere, Blin and his designer André Acquart went to Galicia, met Valle-Inclàn's son, visited the places where the action was supposed to happen, and photographed them. Without resorting to naturalism, Acquart designed a dark and stony set. A few critics deplored the absence of bright colors, confusing Galicia with Andalusia! The set was virtually cut in two across the width of the stage. The ground crawled with larval beings; at the end of a winding road was a small country church. Blin created a poetic intensity that gave a fantastic dimension to the wild fresco.

In looking back at the atmosphere of Blin's *Ghost Sonata*, *Divine Words*, or *Macbeth*, we can see the subterranean current to which he was sensitive. Through the literary work, what touched him was this intense, anxious life which can lead to madness or blasphemy. In *Divine Words* rage and vindictiveness are born in a stifled social class that has no other outlet than escape in alcohol or refuge in religious faith. Through the power of his style, through his poetic vision and vigorous temperament, Valle-Inclàn gave his *esperpentos* and dramas a very unusual form, comparable to the etchings of Goya. At the Odéon Blin took care not to resort to external techniques. He worked the virulence of the characters in depth; he created an atmosphere with jagged, austere, gray or steel-blue forms, over which spread a twilight, giving birth to black magic, to a force of exorcism.

To the grating music of Antonio Ruiz Pipo rolled the wagon of "the idiot with the hydrocephalic head," the dwarf, at once a pitiful victim and a disturbing monster. In the role of the Sexton, Blin brought forth the dark

18 Scene from Blin's production of *Divine Words* by Valle-Inclàn at the Odéon-Théâtre de France, 1963. Acquart's set evokes the rocky road rising toward a village church in Galicia. The uneven terrain facilitates the confrontations of the characters. Ph. Bernand

feelings of a being who is prey to the temptation of incest and to unbridled jealousy.

TOWARDS A CONTEMPORARY REPERTOIRE

Arthur Adamov

The first author chosen by Blin after the Gaîté-Montparnasse adventure was Arthur Adamov. Since the 1950s we have seen the New Novel, the New Cinema, and all of yesterday's avant-gardes that seem almost classical today, but Adamov's works were slow to be accepted. They rebelled against a form and content that were deeply rooted in habit, and in habits of mind. Adamov said of his new theatre:

Theatre as I conceive it is wholly and absolutely tied to performance. I think that performance is only the projection to the senses of situations and images. A theatre play should be the meeting-place of the visible and invisible worlds, where they collide and manifest a latent dramatic content. I want the literal, concrete, corporeal manifestation of that content to coincide with the content itself. [It is] a way of using the simplest words, those faded with use, seemingly the most precise, to restore their innate imprecision.[3]

Adamov thus rejected psychology but was adept at images and concretizations. He wanted to denounce society while coming to grips with his personal phantoms.

At the Café Dôme in Montparnasse Adamov was often in the company of Artaud, Blin, and Giacometti. Blin sometimes acted in and sometimes directed his plays. As Adamov described it: "We – Blin, Serreau, myself, others – had a similar idea of what the theatre should be. We were playwrights, actors, directors of the active avant-garde confronting the old theatre of dialogue that we condemned."[4]

In November 1950, at the small Noctambules Theatre, Jean-Marie Serreau staged Adamov's *The Large and the Small Manoeuvre* at a 6 o'clock matinée; there were usually thirty people in the theatre of 240 seats. The play is a drama of persecution: "Everyone feels himself threatened, attacked, rightly or wrongly manoeuvred."[5] In a police state a factory worker is destroyed by invisible powers; his body suffers a series of mutilations. He loses a hand, an arm, a leg; he trembles incessantly. His physical mutilations theatricalize his psychological alienation. Blin played the Mutilated One, distancing his acting into a kind of dream state. Adamov admired the performance: "Laughter ceased instantly when Blin came on stage, to be replaced by fear. He commanded respect with his understatement."[6] Critic Jacques Lemarchand praised Blin's acting in that play:

Presence. That vague word takes on meaning when applied to Blin who, far from attracting attention away from his surroundings and focusing on himself, manages to distribute attention, so that whatever he approaches – people and things – lives more intensely.[7]

After that production Adamov gradually collected enough money in 1952 for Blin to direct the previously written *Parody*. There were about fifteen spectators each evening in the Right Bank Lancry theatre. It must be recalled that this was the period when Anouilh and Salacrou dominated Paris theatre; a bourgeois public enjoyed the Boulevard comedies of Létraz and Roussin. The road was difficult for pioneers like Blin and Serreau; neither producers nor theatre managers wanted to risk a cent on their projects.

The Parody shows that all lives move toward destruction. Adamov explained its origin:

I saw all those places where people meet without seeing each other, rub shoulders without touching each other, touch each other physically without understanding each other, and that's what gave me a living image for the stage. Meeting without seeing each other, we nevertheless speak, and it is the feeling of this strange resistance of language that made me want to write dialogue. The conversations of *The Parody* mark the exact boundary not only of a language of the deaf, but most of the time of the only communication we have.[8]

Life is absurd. The city lacks a soul. Communication is absent. Nourished by Artaud, Strindberg, and the Expressionists, Adamov expresses his despair in an absurd story, devoid of psychology. Lily, the eternal feminine like Wedekind's Lulu, attracts (but never responds to) the Employee, an inveterate optimist, and N, desperate but no less inveterate. Against a backdrop by Vieira, the unlocalized city grows more and more tentacular, and on stage Lily grows more and more unobtainable. The Employee (Blin) continually moves about; he walks in every direction, even backwards. His delivery is choppy. Alone of all the characters, he ages by thirty or forty years during the performance. N (Jean Martin) is stiff; he dislikes moving. The Employee ends up in prison, and N is run over by a bus. Lily merely passes through, on her way elsewhere. At the back of the stage, a clock lacks hands. This stage world is a parody, and Adamov's play a tragi-comedy; it is a mad, bitter, disturbing drama which was bound to please Blin, both as actor and director. What he specially liked was "the absence of all psychological verbiage."[9] Everything is indeed action in the play. The lines of dialogue are brief and banal, so that the actor must have remarkable stage presence, since the discourse will not carry him. His very being is at stake, as well as his mind, his reactions, and the weight of his silences.

In his interpretation of the Employee, Blin showed what he would require of actors in plays that he directed after 1952: to be wholly committed to the climate of the work and the fate of his character and to give the characters physical exteriors and living flesh: but they should not sentimentalize. Emotion for its own sake seemed obscene to Blin. Profound conviction, mastery of the situation, modest reserve, and even a slight irony should moderate what might be excessive or lyrical.

When Barrault's Theatre of France was at the Odéon, many manuscripts were offered to him. Readers gaged their virtues and inadequacies, and a studio was founded where authors could work on their plays in the presence of a director and actors. In this situation Blin helped Jean-Pierre Faye with his *Latvia* and *Men and Stones*; the latter was then produced in the Petit-Odéon in 1965.

Through this story about three characters, a civil war is traced between Whites and Reds in 1918 in Finland. An oppressive atmosphere arises from characters trapped between two walls forming an acute angle. *Men and Stones* – one might say men and walls – spoke a new language in a dense text without links between the sentences. Blin was attracted by it: "Reading it, one is captivated, moved, trapped. Listening to it gradually reveals the lyricism of its writing; there is a slow, almost peasant-like rhythm. Characters unfold, although in reading one doesn't see what relates them to one another."[10]

Blin conceived his mise-en-scène like a ritual broken by several movements that propel the action forward. Space was also an actor in the drama; a revolution passed through the breach, the space between the two walls, which was a springboard for events that again motivated the characters.

When Barrault was dismissed from the Odéon, this studio work dissolved, but Blin nevertheless spent the rest of his life, with his slender means, as a fervent reader of young authors, offering them help either in revising their texts or embarking on a production. He acquired the reputation of being able to play the unplayable, and to give life to the most literary and hermetic of texts. From 1966 to 1968, among the many texts he read with the utmost probity, he chose several which, without being political theatre, nevertheless were concerned with two major events of our time – the Vietnam War and the Cuban Revolution.

The Carrion-Eaters

In 1966 Robert Weingarten's first play, *The Funeral of the Unknown Soldier*, had been performed by the experimental wing of the British Drama League with actors of the Royal Shakespeare Company and National Theatre. In 1967 excerpts from this 27-year-old American's second play *The Carrion-Eaters* were published in the journal of Barrault's company,[11] and in March 1968 Blin directed the play in Switzerland, with the Theatre of Carouge

Company; it played both at the Grand Théâtre of Lausanne and the Comédie of Geneva. In moving from *The Screens* to *The Carrion-Eaters*, Blin moved from the Algerian rebellion to the Vietnam rebellion. Rather than being a committed play like Gatti's 1967 *V as in Vietnam*, Peter Brook's 1966 *US*, or the Bread and Puppet Theatre's 1968 *Johnny Comes Marching Home*, Weingarten's play depicted the confusion of America. The battle was not only in the rice fields or in the napalm-burned villages, but also within the average American, torn between belief in slogans and indignation at the massacres. The play was neither realistic nor didactic; it was made up of a few concrete elements and a few theatrical signs. Vietnamese reality, shaded and filtered by propaganda, was relived in a dream of Johnny Wren, the typical U.S. Marine; or of his family awaiting his return. No Vietcong rebel appears. We see only pale images of mute Vietnamese peasants, whose presence shows the patent impossibility of communication. For Johnny in Vietnam, or for his parents in the dream scenes, these peasants have little substance; and yet they represent America's fate, which is suffering and death. The peasants perish, but Johnny, the soldier of proud America, will perish through them.

The cruel mocking image that weighs heavily on the whole performance is not so much the massacres or even the vultures hovering over their future prey (as the title might suggest) but an American parachutist over enemy territory. Throughout the play he remains awkwardly bound by his suspension-cords to a perch over a manure-heap; he is the victim of some mechanical malfunction of his costly apparatus, or of some unpredictable event, and he is condemned to die there, without being able to reach ground.

A powerful symbol, this theatrical concretization connects to the following night in which Johnny relives his adventures, both massacres and good deeds, while a Director of Dreams (a huckster of power or black marketeer) directs the waking nightmare of the Wren family – father, mother, and Johnny's fiancée; they suddenly find themselves in the presence of mute Vietnamese peasants crowding the stage; obstinate and obsessive, these peasants trouble the conscience of the Whites.

Blin was seduced by so many aspects of the play – hostility to the escalation of the Vietnam War, the prolonged suspension of the soldier over the symbolic battle, the lack of realism, and the development of dream phantoms in the average American. Stereotypes of American society who are filled with both naive good will and cruel egotism replaced the grotesque figures of the colonists in *The Screens*. Saïd the anti-hero, Si Slimane of the Arab rebellion, and the French Legionnaires whose strategy is upset by the guerillas were followed by Johnny, the indoctrinated U.S. soldier at grips with a situation that was not foreseen in his training manual, and by an invisible Vietcong enemy at once admired and hated, but never met.

In order not to betray this American vision, Blin worked closely with the young playwright, showing him the same deference as he would a famous author. The hybrid form, borrowed from Albee's *American Dream* and Brechtian "songs," permitted a transition from a nightmare sequence to musical comedy, from a sharp political awakening to chanted publicity advertisements. Werner Strub's masks on the peasant faces transformed them into Vietnamese, and the dream figures moved almost ethereally, like ghosts. Eight musicians recorded a score composed by Guy Bovet. The political/poetic impact was strong. Blin wanted to direct the play in Paris in the autumn, but he was prevented by the events of 1968, which also prevented his staging Seneca's *Thyestes*, a play that tempted Artaud.

The Nuns

Eduardo Manet came to Paris to study with the *Education par le jeu dramatique* (EPJD), where he met Roger Blin. Back in his native Cuba, he worked with a theatre company and sent his first play, *The Nuns*, to Blin. He returned to Paris for its production in 1969, and as he recalled to me: "With Roger, we talked very little about the subject of the play, but a great deal about the context. I had written two versions, one in Spanish and the other in faulty French; he helped me sharpen my vocabulary and find a more fluid style." Manet was appreciative that, unlike other directors, Blin changed none of his scenic directions; he respected the text but drew fresh nuances from it. Manet was touched by the extreme discretion with which Blin made remarks. Blin always respected the other, whether actor or designer, and there was an atmosphere of mutual confidence.

When Blin directed *The Nuns* at the Théâtre de Poche the nuns were played by men, as specified by the text. While writing the play Manet was working on Chinese and Japanese theatre, from which he took the concept of men playing women's roles as men, not only for its symbolic significance but in order to achieve distance. Manet denied any influence of Genet's *Maids*, so he was surprised when Tony Wilhem, a Bruges director, cast the nuns as sturdy women who acted powerfully and violently, although he accepted it. Despite the obvious comparison to Genet's *Maids*, according to Manet:

If my play shows any influence, it is that of Valle-Inclàn. The only critic who sensed that was Gilles Sandier. Roger Blin can always find the essential poetic transposition. He detests the theatre of daily life, which is now so fashionable. He calls it "the boulevard of the kitchen sink." He has great physical power that introduces into his mise-en-scène a kind of earthy, almost peasant realism.

This certainly described the nuns of Théâtre de Poche; they had loud voices and smoked large cigars. The Mother Superior was presented as a tragic clown, while a deaf-mute clung to the walls with a dazed expression.

The play was inspired by a Cuban incident; three women disguised themselves as nuns in order to convince a society woman to embark secretly on a boat to escape the revolution; there they planned to rob her. In the context of the Revolution, these nuns are caught in their own trap; they could be gangsters, and I therefore made them men.[12]

Outside a great revolution is being prepared – that of eighteenth-century black Haitian slaves against their masters. Tom-toms and bells sow anxiety and spread terror among the Whites, since the black Voodooists are reputed to kill and devour babies. Burlesque and tragedy invade the "nuns'" grotto, which becomes a closed chamber where the characters are smothered by their own violence.

On the small stage of the Théâtre de Poche the painter Jean Assens built a set with arcades on one side and on the other a naked wall through which one could see a second grotto in which the Señora was killed. Furniture was minimal – a table, a rocking-chair, a Christ reduced to a head and a hand. Attention was focused on the door, closed at night, lit during the day. Of his mise-en-scène Blin said:

Pierre Byland [playing the deaf-mute] can touch the ceiling. It's one of my theatre dreams that the actors can touch every part of the set which is not merely decorative. When they build that barricade before the door, they can climb it. And for them the walls should have the reality of a cave.[13]

In this limited space Blin established ritualized patterns of circular movements. He felt that on stage the shortest path between two points was a curved line. He established synchrony between the murder of the Señora in the second cave and Angela, the deaf-mute miming what she saw. In a larger theatre he would have preferred a visible orchestra with percussion and singers, but the spatial limitations of the Théâtre de Poche stimulated him. "I think that it is only honorable to serve the author with what one has available," but , "there is no reason to present him with an ugly place on the plea of lack of money. There is no reason to lack a certain beauty."[14]

The Night of the Assassins

First performed in Spanish in Paris, 1967, in the context of the Théâtre des Nations. The French première of Jose Triana's play was directed by Blin at the Récamier Theatre in 1971. Frantic acting is called for by this sharp criticism of the pre-revolutionary Cuban bourgeoisie, in which Triana tries to destroy the myth of the family and to give alienated man an active role.

The action takes place in Cuba in 1950. In *Medea in the Mirror* (1960) and *The Death of Neque* (1963) Jose Triana treated the parent/child conflict from the point of view of the parents. In *The Night of the Assassins* he treats it from the point of view of children rebelling against their education and way of life.

They take cognizance of their deeper being; they want to live and think by themselves. But incapable of throwing off paternal tyranny, they take refuge every evening in ritual – an analysis of their situation, reciprocal incitement to assassination, and symbolic murder of their parents in which they enact several roles – parents, neighbors, police, judges. The preparations for the rite are much longer than the actual ceremony, and the author is more interested in the repeated ritual of curses than in the final execution. The play speaks against the irresolution of the adolescents who, closed off in their attic, turn away from life and revolutionary action, and do nothing to change the situation.

The play is performed as a kind of improvisation. Lalo and his two sisters, Beba and Cuca, enact scenes of their daily life. Then Lalo pretends to have killed his father and mother. Cuca has not yet decided to play murder; she caricatures her mother's cleanliness and taste for order. Beba sides with her brother, and tries to convince their sister. They imagine that neighbors arrive. Lalo plays the role of his mother on her wedding-day. After the murder is finally decided upon, they imagine themselves with the police and the judge.

As in Manet's *Nuns*, there are superficial similarities to Genet's *Maids*. Although the overt theatricality has the same acting appeal, here the presentation is more direct and violent. Triana requires a rapid plunge into every situation; he forbids character development. The three adolescents shift from one role to the other without prop, costume or makeup. The actors have to rely solely on changes of rhythm, voice quality, gesture, and behavior, and in Blin's production the focus was exclusively on their performance. The stage was bare; the costumes came from the Paris Flea Market and Barrault's property room.

Blin clearly established the different levels of each role (for example, the actor plays Lalo, and then Lalo plays his mother) with its explosions, repetitions, crises. He organized the ritual with its three phases – imprecation, assassination, judgment, as well as incantation, violence, and reflections of reflections. He was able "to tear out cries, death rattles . . . to thrust to the limits of horror and grief . . . to set the speaker in motion and then stop the listener, without any break in the performance. . . . His rigor left no possibility of empty holes."[15]

The Emigrés

Paris had seen five plays by the Polish dramatist Slawomir Mrozek when the actor Laurent Terzieff brought the manuscript of *The Emigrés* to Blin, who was immediately responsive to the delicate, minimalist writing. With his customary attention to detail, the author, Slawomir Mrozek, described the environment of the action and the necessary properties. With his no less customary obedience to scenic directions, Blin asked his designer Matias to conform to them — a windowless cellar in which could be seen a sink, two beds, a table, two chairs, a screen, two valises, a naked bulb yielding a raw light, and, dominating all, a badly proportioned system of pipes which covered the walls, and in which odd noises could be heard.

An intellectual and a manual worker live together and confront one another in this enclosed space; they are two emigrés who are condemned to be together, and yet they are as solitary as Vladimir and Estragon in *Waiting for Godot*. Mrozek calls his characters AA and XX, but the acting brought out contrasting personalities. As the intellectual, Laurent Terzieff was haughty, feverish in a dressing-gown; the heavyset Gérard Darrieu played the worker, obstinate and cunning. Darrieu had worked regularly with Blin ever since his first company at the Gaîté-Montparnasse, while Blin and Terzieff had met each other through Jean-Marie Serreau. They had affinities and common tastes, such as Milosz and Rilke. Blin was aware: "There is something that tells you that you belong to the same family as certain people; a kind of filiation develops."[16] This strange filiation that develops between people makes words almost useless. And when a director like Blin works with such actors, no third person can express the alchemy by which they communicate.

There was nothing spectacular in the staging: two people spoke to one another, made economical but meaningful gestures of daily life; after-thoughts incubated; they jockeyed for power. Yet the 1974 production of *The Emigrés*, with its grating theme and clear mise-en-scène, left a marked impression on the audience. There was a world behind those walls; our world that produces emigrés who cannot return to their country; who are uprooted. "Only an emigré could be lucid enough to gash his own flesh in that way."[17]

SOCIAL DRAMA

From 1934 on, Roger Blin took part in the fight against fascism; he called for strikes and joined street demonstrations. However, he did not practice committed theatre; he knew that a revolution is not made by theatre, and he sought something else on the stage. He married provocative themes to his love/dispute with language. His productions of *Boesman and Lena* and *Minamata and Co.*, which focused on apartheid and industrial pollution, respectively, best testify to his social conscience.

Boesman and Lena

For Athol Fugard, at once author, actor, and director, the actor "in space and silence" is the essential element of theatre. When he directs, he forgets that he wrote the play; he is focused on the actor. He has said:

For me actors . . . are the instrument – as precious as a Stradivarius. An actor is total carnality – all he can use to get at you is his body, his flesh, his voice, his sense of self . . . [Acting has] taught me to write for actors. Taught me to think about them. Taught me to listen to rhythms . . . I have directed most of my plays in their first productions: not because I felt that as the author I was in possession of *the* interpretation . . . but because I have always regarded the completed text as being only a half-way stage to my ultimate objective – the living performance and the particular definition of space and silence. . . . Theatre is not words on paper, not scenery, lights, or make-up, but that magical thing that can only happen when an actor is there in the flesh, encountering a live spectator.[18]

In 1976 when Blin was offered a translation of *Boesman and Lena*, there was little discussion of apartheid in France. But, as he wrote in the program: "What mattered to me in the play was above all its profound humanity; it is social criticism in its violent portrait of the sub-proletariat. South African society humiliates and crushes the individual . . . It is a hell unknown elsewhere. All the large problems are set in mud; that's what interests me."

This play condenses into two hours the drama of a country, and its characters symbolize all the oppressed of the earth. Boesman and Lena are South African half-castes, "brown" descendants of Hottentots, European colonists, and Blacks. The browns lived in an area destroyed by bulldozers so as to be transformed into residences for Whites. The browns no longer have a stable dwelling; they move along a river in search of subsistence. They do not get along with the Blacks, who are even more miserable.

Boesman and Lena, a couple in their fifties, stand for these indigent South Africans who are constantly on the move, trying to survive. Barefoot, in rags, carrying a small bundle on head or back, they walk all day long; that very morning their home was destroyed by a bulldozer. They have nothing left; they are nothing at all. The play plunges us into the very heart of the problem of apartheid, showing us how the individual is crushed in a racist society. It is a heartbreaking cry as well as a challenge to our conscience. In their misery, husband and wife can no longer get along together, Boesman venting on Lena the blows that Whites had vented on him; nor does Boesman tolerate Lena's pity for an old Black who is even more miserable than they. He refuses to share the makeshift shelter he built, and the evening food ration – a bowl of sugarless tea and a piece of bread. Desperately, Lena tries to communicate with this exhausted Black who doesn't speak their language. She needs a witness to listen to her story – misery, wandering, stillborn babies, Boesman who snubs or beats her. The Black dies. Boesman, afraid of being questioned, decides to leave. Will Lena finally leave him? Once more she sets out behind him, estranged woman, eternal mother carrying what faint hope?

Blin first directed the play at the theatre of Cité Universitaire in 1976 and then revived it in the Gémier Theatre at Chaillot in 1978. He wanted the audience on risers so as to have good sightlines for the action, which took place at ground level.

Designer Matias made a thicker ground than in *Waiting for Godot*, so that it suggested a vague floor of odd materials, producing unevenness. Pinpoints of light suggested a road. At the back was the sky. During the action actor Robert Liensol built a shanty before the eyes of the audience; he tried to fasten a small car door over an old barrel, and close it with a plastic branch. In Liensol (Boesman) and Toto Bissainthe (Lena) Blin worked with two members of the cast of *The Blacks* who were caught up in this racial struggle. Bissainthe graduated from laughter to lament as she discovered her condition as woman and proletarian in relation to the world. Liensol raged, and another actor Tiemele remained silent. The production was at once subversive and moving. The mise-en-scène highlighted the text in both its political and poetic importance. Toward this end Blin cut the text slightly.

Only after this production did Blin meet Fugard, who invited him to watch a video tape of his South African production. Although Fugard's text contains few scenic directions, Blin found that his own blocking, based on the internal necessities of the work, bore a remarkable resemblance to that of the playwright.

Minamata and Co.

Minamata and Co., by the Japanese journalist Osamu Takahashi, deals with the battle against the Chisso Company responsible for the disease that caused 234 deaths and thousands of invalids between 1956 and 1968. The effects of eating mercury-poisoned fish – which damaged the brain, destroyed the vision, provoked palsy and speech difficulties, and harmed the foetus in pregnant women – was diagnosed a decade before the Japanese government took action. Written to publicize the charges, the play was performed by an amateur group for three years throughout Japan before the verdict was pronounced. The Chisso Company was sentenced to pay a ridiculously low compensation. The calendar of events follows:

1950   Dead fish are found in Minamata Bay.

1952   Mad crows and cats throw themselves into the sea.

1956   The first human victim of the disease appears.

1959   The Director of Chisso Hospital holds the Chisso Company responsible for the disease, but his report is kept secret.

1962   There are 121 known victims of the disease, of whom 46 die.

1965   The Minamata Disease is found at Nigata, 1000 kilometers away.

1967   The victims at Nigata bring suit against the Chisso Company.

1968   Government conclusions are published; the Chisso Company is responsible for the Minamata Disease.

1969   Twenty-nine families (a minority) of Minamata bring suit against the Chisso Company; the others are worn out by years of humiliating negotiations and decide to leave it to the government.

1970   The disease is reported in Ontario, Canada, where the victims are mainly Indians.

1973   The trial ends, and the Chisso Company is sentenced to pay 15,000,000 francs to the plaintiffs.

French ecologists realized the importance of Osamu Takahashi's play, entitled *The Accusation* in Japanese, for it publicized common dangers: yesterday a Japanese bay, perhaps the Mediterranean tomorrow; we are all threatened. Catherine Cadou translated the play into French and sent Blin a copy. He immediately wanted to direct it, telling me in 1982: "I am against all pollution – colonial pollution [*The Screens*], racist [*Boesman and Lena*],

19 Boesman (Robert Liensol) and Lena (Toto Bissainthe), driven out of their hut, take to the road with their scanty belongings in Blin's production of Fugard's *Boesman And Lena*, 1976, at the Cité Universitaire. On the ground scraps of metal from which Boesman will make a shelter for the night. Set by Matias. Ph. Yves Chériaux

ecological [*Minamata*]." But it was difficult to find a theatre that would accept the play with its painful theme. In the play no one is spared, neither the officials in power, nor the union members, one of whom is bribed. Two years were to pass before, perhaps thanks to the play's publication, a co-production was arranged between the Theatre of Aubervilliers, the Maison of Culture of St-Denis, and the Roger Blin Company.[19] (In 1975 Blin allowed a young company to use his name, but they were to find their own way.)

Osamu Takahashi kept to the facts, and his play was more documentary than dramatic. In Japan the set was realistic – on the left a fisherman's home with low roof, and on the right a smaller house with a well and a platform for town meetings. Blin wanted a theatrical event, inspired by facts and yet not didactic. He made slight changes in the text and the structure of the scenes, and asked his designer Acquart for a bare and flexible space. In Japanese houses there are paper screens that move easily. Acquart divided the stage floor into different areas without vertical walls. Platforms and bridges were brought on as needed. Footbridges were placed about 2 feet above a blue cloth representing the sea. Four of these footbridges ran the whole width of the stage; they were made of slatted boards. At one moment the many pontoons and bridges occupied the whole stage for the meeting of the fishermen. Usually, lights were focused only on the bridge or pontoon where the particular action was taking place. At larger meetings a platform permitted speeches. A puppeteer used a smaller platform for his marionettes.

In the Japanese version slides showed the audience the horrors of the Minamata Disease. Blin did not like either this mechanical procedure or the realistic aspects; he had Claude Acquart make marionettes showing stricken cats (among the first victims of the disease) as well as humans afflicted with the disease. The substitution of marionettes for living beings presented the symptoms as a kind of painful choreography. When the marionettes were not being manipulated, they sometimes lay on the stage, inert, recalling the existence of the victims even though those responsible tried to belittle the disease.

Except for one or two Japanese, neither the actors nor the set sought verism. The light makeup was vaguely Asian, and there were a few kimonos among the costumes, but these were the only signs. Blin wanted to avoid the exotic and also to imply that these events could happen in France: not only the pollution, but the denial of danger, and the efforts to conceal it.

The set was simple, functional, and beautiful; it influenced the walk, the rhythm, the behavior of the actors. Space was modified before the audience; the stagehands were visible and integrated into the action. The lighting was colorful.

Rehearsals were difficult because the subject became an obsession, causing

20 Book-cover of the French translation of *Minamata and Co.* by Osamu Takahashi, on which Blin based his production. Cover by Chantal Petit

nightmares to the actors. The militant ecologists were tense. A Japanese film on the subject was unbearable. And, above all, they kept asking themselves how to present these afflictions to the audience without having recourse to the horrors of reality. Only one actor played a badly afflicted victim.

Blin made a brief montage at beginning and end of the performance; the puppetteer manipulated his convulsive cats; there was a sonic mix of sea waves, cat cries, crows croaking, a baby's hysterical crying, and the noise of knife-sharpening. A voice called out: "I accuse," recalling the play's original title of *The Accusation*. Then the first words were spoken. During the course of the action that same sound mix was occasionally and effectively introduced.

The character Sato spoke a long monologue in the original, but Blin fragmented it, integrating her remarks into various sequences:

Old Shige, unable to bear the sight of her husband diminished physically and mentally, tries to strangle him. Neighbors rush in at the cries of fright by the invalid. Actress Andrée Tainsy expressed the distress and pitiful rebellion of this woman overcome by an inhuman fate.

Before the Municipal Council, Dr Okawa of the Chisso factory describes symptoms he has seen. Under the cloak of a scientific discourse, actor Jean-Pierre Jorris shows the embarrassment of a medical man employed by an establishment that he dares not openly accuse; besides, he has not yet completed the necessary scientific proof. In counterpoint, Sato continues her story. The fishermen worry because nobody wants to buy their fish.

At the hospital, no one knows how to treat those whose nervous system is tainted with mercury. Giichi prefers to go home; his grandfather succumbs.

At the Chisso Company, there is concern at a report from the University of Kumamoto, blaming the waste products of the factory. Dr Okawa decides to make cats drink the polluted water.

To a sound effect of the waves, Sato evokes the past; she used to like to go boat-fishing with her husband. Since she became ill, she dreams of returning to the sea.

From scene to scene, different pontoons slide in to diversify the space. Two groups co-exist, without true dialogue between them – the diseased and those responsible for it.

Protesters demand rapid action, compensation, solutions. To the sound of the shamisen, at an inn, the Director of the Chisso Company tries to make an ally of the President of the Fishermen's Union. Through a series of manoeuvres, the trial drags on. In Dr Okawa's laboratory, the cats howl, twist, go mad. That is the proof that the waste-mercury of the factory polluted Minamata Bay, leading to hundreds of deaths and incurable paralysis. Only later, after Dr Okawa's retirement, will the official report be published, blaming the factory.

The Crime of Minamata

Blin later wrote a preface to Catherine Cadou's translation:

Our body is our only possession. By the body, we feel a solidarity with those whom we love, close or distant. With the pretext of progress, industrial society claims to be working for our well-being. Actually, through the aberration of profit, it leads to the destruction of our bodies more slyly than through wars. The body is assaulted through all its orifices, all its pores. In the cities, who can breathe deeply? Who now can trustingly take into his mouth bread, vegetables, fish, meat? In what sea, and soon in what river, will we dare immerse our bodies?

All this happens subtly, until suddenly the crime takes place, the crime explodes. The Minamata affair is one of those crimes, and we would say it was one of the most "spectacular" if that word didn't have an odor of estheticism. This crime was committed in Japan a few years ago, and its consequences are still with us. The play of Osamu Takahashi is a rending cry, the cry of victims; not a lyrical and vague complaint against fate, but a cry of ferocious and detailed accusation, which concerns us all, for though the suffering ones whom we see are Japanese, we know that murderers are among us too.

Takahashi calls his play "didactic." So were the Greek tragedies, in one sense. But if the old gods with their caprice and fantasies represented the unfathomable in Nature, modern gods in spectacles and well-cut jackets are cold monsters, lacking in fantasy and interested only in the arabesques of the stock market.

When Catherine Cadou introduced me to Takahashi's work in her beautiful translation, I thought that it would be exciting and useful to present it to a French public, for a strong and exemplary dramatic architecture was present in the intrigues of the Chisso Company to conceal the affair, the complicity of the government, the many legal tricks, the corruption of experts and union officials, the intimidations; in that architecture the center would be the body of exploited man, the naked body of the poor creature whose only riches were poisoned – the right to live.[20]

Blin respected the scenic indications of the playwright – noise of the fishermen's protests, breaking glass of the rebels, shamisen music, a childish song about 30,000 yen. A laugh described as "homeric," and "open-throated" was amplified by Blin; he recorded it, sent it through an echo chamber. At the end of the performance there was a repetition of the sound mix of the beginning.

With the consent of the playwright, Blin and translator Cadou added an ecological meeting with signs and rhythmic slogans – As / sas / sins! As / sas sins! Chisso / to the gallows! A protestor concluded vigorously: "The sea can't be both a food source and a garbage-dump."

21 Acquart's model for the set of Blin's production of *Minamata and Co*. Striped background for the sky. Above the polluted water of the sea, bamboo pontoons that slide or contract during the action. A platform for speeches. Photo Acquart

The performance lasted about two hours. Without any sentimentality, it grasped one by the throat, but the critics were hostile to this nightmare. One of them dismissed it as an "ecological complaint." The production disturbed those who came merely to see a show, although Blin included beauty and emotion in his rendition of a problem that embraces more than Minamata – for example, the Mediterranean. The production disturbed certain Japanese. Would this give a bad impression of Japan? The production displeased militants on the left; was it really necessary to show a corrupt union official? (Even though the playwright followed the facts.)

The theatre was half empty, and the cast abandoned a planned tour to the ports of Marseille, Brest, and Corsica, where audiences might have reacted more directly to the problem. Nevertheless, there were passionate discussions at Aubervilliers. The best performances were those of student matinées. Blin commented: "We performed that play three years too soon for it to have an impact on France."

THE EYE LISTENS

This Claudelian title captures an aspect of the phenomenon of theatre and the mobility of its signs. Sometimes theatre signifies through the visual and sometimes through the verbal, but the radio listener has only sound to orient him; the author or director woos his imagination by dialogue, commentary, sound effects, music. The set that is described or suggested is not a visible object on the stage but a sum of possibilities, a dreamlike universe because it is dreamed by an imaginative listener.

Radio writing therefore demands specific qualities, and production involves a knowledge of auditory reception. Clarity, richness of suggestion, care with technique, but also an invitation to what is strange and fantastic. Far from being a handicapped form of expression, radio permits subjects and forms that would be impossible on a theatre stage. It frees one from rational constraints; it permits instant change from one place to another, as well as the most unpredictable metamorphoses. Effects of simultaneity, echo, distance, or closeness can lead to new kinds of dramaturgy; the character becomes a voice; act/scene structure explodes; Aristotelian laws disappear. Soliloquies are permissible; large casts are less problematic.

Conscious of this, National French Radio for years urged playwrights to write for radio, thus compensating to some extent for an absence of a politics of culture in the area of theatre. Very much aware of new works in this area, Roger Blin sometimes drew upon them, and he was particularly adept at transferring to the stage what had been conceived for the airwaves. He advised experienced playwrights like François Billetdoux or Carlos Semprun Maura, and the less experienced Jean-Louis Bauer.

Name's Isabelle Langrenier

In 1977 a friend showed Roger Blin a manuscript consisting of a 29-page monologue of a woman who relives a past, but there was neither anecdote, conflict, suspense, nor development. Although words turned in her head, she found it difficult to bring them across her lips; they stumbled over faulty articulation, coming apart or catapulting. In the prey of a delirious logorrhea, Isabelle speaks, stutters, gets tangled up in words. There is a hiatus between her thought and its expression.

Twenty-six-year-old Jean-Louis Bauer thought he had written a Beckettian play, intended for the mouth of an actress, without intervention of her body. Blin thought it was a radiophonic text, but it was a challenge to stage it. Syntactically disturbing, without logic or dramatic structure, diaphanous, it unrolled its discontinuous, repetitive phrases. Assonant syllables are

22 Protests of the victims of *Minamata and Co.*, Théâtre de la
Commune d'Aubervilliers, 1978. Ph. Roger-Viollet.

inventively telescoped *à la* Queneau. Beneath them lies a drama, in the
memory-nightmares of Isabelle, in danger between Eros and Thanatos. This
effort at direct writing, transcribing thought without rationalizing it, foreign
to theatre language, showed a lack of experience. No director would have
wanted it. At the same time, it gave evidence of a clear poetic gift. This
rejection of the prosaic asked for a special tone. Repeated syllables, words
invented by association, incomplete phrases recalled the autistic universe of a
Bob Wilson, where movement and images substituted for words. In Jean-
Louis Bauer's universe, words sought their own salvation; they were neither
at the service of a character nor of a story: "Where words no longer exist
where the Word becomes matter." There are holes, obstructions: "how many
times have I dreamed of this past   together." In a deformed,

deforming vision, chronology slips away: "it was another day"; geography dissolves: "it was another place"; grammar goes wild, with genders and persons invading one another: "my knife your knife youall knife." To the harmony of the leitmotif "Once I was Persian and I wrote Persian letters," succeeds a strange mathematical eruption: "the eight came up three times in succession / the eight / but the three answered him because the four said / and the eight came up. . ." The protagonist asserts herself: "My name is Isabelle Langrenier," but then she retreats into the third person: "She claims to be Isabelle Langrenier"; at the end words escape her increasingly: "I am
years old and I   three black men in front of   ." Only silence can close a story that is impossible to relate.

Roger Blin was touched by the aphasia of the protagonist, and by a style distant from realism, through which could be discerned a poetic talent and restraint of expression. The influence of Marguerite Duras showed in the seeking of the essence, in the quest for silence, for time dissolved. Blin did not know what to do with the text in the state he received it. But could he abandon this embryonic author who might never write anything else for lack of guidance and advice? Blin made the acquaintance of Bauer, spurred him to rework the manuscript, but without giving him precise directions. When, two years later, he directed *Name's Isabelle Langrenier*, it was not to add another production to his own credentials, but to help an inexperienced author learn his craft by seeing his first work performed.

Blin did not claim the right to cut, arrange, or recompose this material; that was not his role. Jean-Louis Bauer tried to discover what his text narrated, the better to formulate the story without betraying the structure. He dissociated characters and ruptures of style; he cut imperceptibly. He concretized two characters mentioned by Isabelle (the Painter, the Grandmother), and in the production at the Petit-T.E.P. (Théâtre de l'Est parisien) he himself played the Painter who had turned into the Black Man. An actor (Claude Aufaure) played the Grandmother. The introduction of a third character, the Singer, induced Roger Blin to accept a musical accompaniment for the first time; he explained:

Up to now I was satisfied with the human voice, which moves me more than any instrument. I have often created sound effects with the voice, for example in *The Blacks* and *Minamata*. But for *Name's Isabelle Langrenier* I can say that, with the musician Joel Wissotsky (who is doing his first score for the theatre) and the singer Laurence Schumann, we work on the text second by second.

In the composition – live piano and percussion, tape of flute and cello – the mathematical lines ("the eight came up three times in succession," etc.) became a counting rhyme recorded by a child's chorus or a tune hummed by Isabelle.

Blin asked for part of the text to be rewritten in the present tense, to make it more active; he expected the author to cut slightly during rehearsals, and he had Isabelle lose her voice as the play progressed. The characters around her did not belong to the real world, and could not carry on a dialogue with her. Sometimes, the lines of the Black Man and the Grandmother crosscut one another, without connecting. Aside from a few lines, the Singer sang; she thus expressed herself in another register. One speech was sung on a single note while Isabelle silently mouthed the same words. The Black Man spoke the scenic directions aloud. The Singer and the Grandmother relieved an Isabelle who was faltering, aphasic. Solitary although surrounded, contradicted rather than comforted, prisoner Isabelle ended by making-up as an old woman, marking her face with black lines like her grandmother, before being killed by her alter egos.

The designer Chantal Petit saw an association between Bauer's text and Velasquez' *Maids of Honor* in which we see a half-child, half-adult Infanta (Isabelle), a painter (the Black Man), and a somewhat monstrous woman (the Singer). Exploding the text into several characters allowed the expression of Isabelle's thoughts as doubles, as projections of the protagonist; this indeed is reminiscent of Velasquez and the doubling of the painter looking at himself in the painting in progress. Blin did not make this association; instead, he quoted a literary reference of the poet Milosz – "little girl suddenly grown old" – but the idea amused him, and he blocked the actors as in the Velasquez painting.

In her sketches and paintings, Chantal Petit revealed a terrible and mocking inner world, an effervescence that blended rage, harmony, and humor. Roger Blin remembered a curious armchair with human back and arms, which he had seen in a London antique shop, and one was constructed to become the main, totemic element of the set. It was perched on a pedestal of steps, vaguely like a pyramid. The sanded, polished, reddish wooden arms were prolonged by long, thin hands. Above the chair's back, the actor playing the Grandmother (hidden behind the chair and mounted on a pedestal) could show his head and lean it on the chair as on a chinrest. At certain moments he moved the chair-arms as though they were his. The Grandmother, joined to this chair and yet endowed with moving arms, became a surrealistic creature, a huge deadly spider that ended by enclosing Isabelle seated on his knees (the chair-seat). A piece of dark cloth encircled his neck. The chair-back revealed a grotesque, tall, narrow torso, endowed with two breasts made of strips of cloth; a machine made them swell and "breathe." At the top was a relatively small head surrounded by a large head-dress of bunched-up net through which light played. At the bottom were two very exaggeratedly long paws; the legs of the armchair were carved in the form of gigantic human legs, adding to the strangeness. Made up in white with features emphasized in

23 Scene from Blin's production of *Name's Isabelle Langrenier* by
Jean-Louis Bauer at the Petit-T.E.P., 1979. Isabelle (Hermine
Karagheuz) is seated between the "legs" of the Grandmother
(Claude Aufaure), in a fantastic ensemble. Ph. Yves Chériaux

black under his head-dress, with parts of the black costume falling over the armchair, the Grandmother spoke in a strange, almost sexless voice. A text which was originally radiophonic acquired extraordinary visual power.

Isabelle (Hermine Karagheuz) wore a reddish-brown satin dress with removable elements. Her chest was enclosed in a blouse with smock-stitches and pleats that also evoked a spider. The swan-robe specified in the text could not be obtained for the Singer, who appeared beside a swan-form on a platform, and moved away from it at certain lines. Her melodic flights were accompanied by this image of a mythological animal, which was absurd in this situation. On her dress were small wings with brilliant ribs, suggesting an insect. The Black Man wore a pointed hat, with the point weighing down; he wore large shoes and a jacket whose coat-tails ended in a point. He also suggested a black insect. Around the armchair, netting supported by stiff threads suggested a spider-web spun by the Grandmother, in which Isabelle might be caught. This world of sharp, stinging insects contributed to Isabelle's disturbance; lost internally by aphasia, she was opposed externally by an inhospitable world.

On the Petit-T.E.P. stage the characters glided among black nettings to appear and disappear. At the brightly lit center Isabelle could permit herself only rare displacements; she was soon the prisoner of the armchair and her own nightmare. She evolved less in scenic space than in the winding of her thought. Delicately, Blin allowed the mental universe to loom up. The only property was a knife whose brilliant blade was made of a double-sided mirror, and whose hilt was made of carved glass. At times this knife gleamed in the dark; Blin's spare lighting recalled the phantom aspect of his *Ghost Sonata*. At the beginning of the performance, light gradually revealed the sculptural armchair, then the details of the face and chest of the Grandmother; then it revealed Isabelle bent over, tirelessly rereading the letter she had just written. Then one could distinguish the Singer and his fabulous swan, and finally the Black Man.

The critic Gilles Sandier liked the unique, spellbinding ceremony, the sonic repetition, and the fixity of the totemized Grandmother. In general the reviews were favorable, and the Petit-T.E.P. was always full. Each rehearsal strengthened Bauer's desire to write, and several of his plays have since been produced. In accepting the challenge of directing an almost formless play of a beginner, Blin encouraged the birth of a new playwright, and the lead actress, Hermine Karagheuz, was also inspired to write a play.

THE OTHER SIDE OF THE MIRROR

Triptych

Following the presentation of the Zurich Schauspielhaus productions of *Biedermann and the Firebugs* and *The Great Rage of Philippe Hotz* at the Théâtre des Nations in 1958, all the major dramatic works of the Swiss-German Max Frisch had been performed on the French stage. Frisch was therefore hardly unknown when Blin directed *Triptych* at the Odéon in 1983, using actors of the Comédie-Française, but he was an author with a limited audience. Is this because translations always betray an original work, or are Frisch's density and humor less evident in a rational language like French? Or are the French repelled by the severity of his themes? In any case Blin did not choose an easy path in directing this author who was not popular in France in spite of his international reputation, and this work in particular demands reflection about death at a time when audiences prefer to see life through rose-colored glasses.

Triptych is not macabre, and this was not the first time that a playwright has put an after-life on stage, whether it be the hell of Sartre's *No Exit*, the beyond of his *The Chips are Down*, the transitory passage of *Outward Bound* by Sutton Vane, or the no man's land of *The Screens* by Genet. But Frisch's work is doubly disturbing; on the one hand because it reminds us of the ineluctable human destiny that we daily try to forget, and on the other hand because it emphasizes that nothing can be changed in an existence that has been lived, actions that have been performed, words that have been spoken. As we were, we will remain in the memory of those who knew us. If we are believers, that is how we will appear on Judgment Day, without any possible revision. Frisch's theme is therefore less the suggestion of what awaits us in death than an inspiration to reflect on what we do in life. We can never return to the past; our actions are definitive.

Frisch's warning is indirect. He expresses himself not so much in situations and words, as in what is not said, and in analogies and differences. In the play of cunning mirrors implied in any theatre performance, each stage image sends the spectator back to his own lived experience, and he bristles at this call to order against his negligence or frivolousness.

Before publication of the play, Laurent Terzieff procured a copy of Henry Bergerot's French translation and gave it to Blin to read. Immediately interested, Blin proposed it to several theatre managers, but Jean Mercure, Patrice Chéreau, Jean-Louis Barrault either couldn't or wouldn't accept it. Finally Jacques Toja, head of the Comédie-Française, put it on the program of the Odéon. It took nearly three years, as in the case of *Waiting for Godot*. Toja said: "Blin is one of the greatest men in our theatre, and it was important for me that he be able to direct this play."[21] Journalists tried to reassure their readers about *Triptych*, and if they are to be believed, Blin spoke only in negatives defending himself against possible detractors: "The play is certainly not macabre." "The play is not political . . . I don't believe it teaches anything." and "I am not attracted by metaphysical theatre." They do report that he found the play "beautiful, attractive" and that "it moved me very much." Suffering from heart trouble, this play may have added to his pain. Who knows whether, as in the case of Molière, right in the middle of a rehearsal . . . "That would be formidable!" joked the director whose comic sense was in perfect harmony with that of Frisch, leaving no room for morbidity.

The play pleased Blin because it was disturbing. "Certain plays pleased me because I saw that they could lead to performances against the establishment – Beckett, Genet . . . I'm not looking for scandal, but if there is a simultaneous kind of provocative jubilation and beauty, that pleases me wholly."[22] *Triptych* seemed to Blin a work *à clé*; the springboard might have been a middle-aged man's sight of a beloved young woman in a rocking-chair. "If there is a moral, it is simply 'Carpe diem.'"

At the Comédie no actor was available for the protagonist Proll, so Blin cast Maurice Garrel who would not theatricalize unduly. He is there, he exists, and that is amazing enough because he plays the part of someone dead. But that's the point; the actor brings to it his humanity and good faith; the character is perhaps a militant but certainly an Everyman. Blin was fond of a certain kind of "not acting." He wanted the actor to enter the global situation of the play, bring his own personality and experience to it. The spectator perceives this experience but beneath the interpretation, especially for the dead Proll, and the Aged Lady.

In the first part of *Triptych*, which takes place on earth, the dead man Proll is in his armchair. There is some social criticism but also comedy; manners of the petite bourgeoisie are slapped down humorously. During the expressions of sympathy that follow the funeral, we see pettiness and egotism. Max Frisch and Roger Blin both proceed with small details, so they are difficult to dissociate. Blin scrupulously followed the scenic directions of the author, rendering them effectively – the bell that rings before the curtain rises, the empty stage with one part in the light, where we see a white rocking-chair; that empty stage without furniture is the symbol of the home left by Proll, and it seems empty to his widow. Bordering the forestage are pebbles and earth, suggesting a recent burial. Designer Acquart described it to me:

What is this place? A house? Part of a cemetery? I left this ambiguity about exterior and interior; I didn't want to enclose the space; I didn't want to trap the people of the first part, but the playing area should nevertheless be small. The central part is about five yards by four and a half. It is limited in height by a low glass roof which lets the light shine through and creates an atmosphere. Actors can walk around it, and on the side there are stylized holly-bushes about as high as a low wall; black lines create a rhythm in the space, and a black backdrop limits the stage depth.

The characters appear on the central part of this set, facing us in their petty behavior; then they disappear through large apertures, going to take refreshments served in an offstage garden, or directly out onto the street. One can interpret the glass roof marked with irregular black ovals as a broken window with large cracks.

The scenic directions are followed exactly in the sobs of the Widow, and her long black veil, the pipe of the First Guest (invited for the burial or the refreshments? Frisch leaves it ambiguous), the group entrance of the others, and at the edge two people, Roger and Francine, who will reappear in the play's third part. But Blin wanted to modify the serious tone of the opening, and he took advantage of the presence of a child. With the heedlessness of his age, the boy sits down in the dead man's rocking-chair and begins to rock; his mother slaps him when she sees it.

The embarrassed guests have nothing to say to the Widow. The arrival of refreshments creates some diversion, but Blin sends the guests into the offstage garden a little more quickly than indicated by Frisch, and he begins a sonic counterpoint to the main dialogue – various laughs, a breaking glass, exclamations, commotion. As soon as they leave, we see dead Proll surreptitiously stealing into his rocking-chair, as indicated in the scenic direction. Motionless, profile to the audience, he sees no one, and no one pays attention to him. Theatre convention indicates the separation of the living and the dead, physically close but unable to communicate.

Frisch specified certain costumes – Francine in light slacks while the others are in dark clothes, and Roger in turtle-neck sweater; he specified certain objects and their use – Francine smokes, Ilse distributes napkins. Blin is faithful to these specifications, but in the short Roger/Francine conversation she looks at the Pastor, mute at their side. Blin's "invisible mise-en-scène" informs us of a dissonance between two people who will live together without understanding one another. Furthermore, Francine's finesse enables us to understand how Roger's words have disturbed the clergyman in his faith. "The first scene mixes genres – bitter comedy, social criticism, and then starts investigating the beyond."[23]

The danger for the actors playing the guests is to do too much, to move in the direction of Boulevard comedy, whereas Frisch satirizes lightly, without caricaturing. One can imagine that the instruction here would be to exercise moderation. "My job is to prevent it from being natural, Boulevard, everything that I hate," declared Blin.[24]

The first part of *Triptych* centers to a large extent on Proll's Widow, who was played by Denise Gence. She had recently played a widow and victim in Henri Becque's *Vultures*, directed at the Comédie-Française by Jean-Pierre Vincent. And she is a widow here, a petite bourgeoise whom her husband has not always treated too well, and who speaks up now that he is no longer there. She dares address him with lucidity, good sense, humor, and tenderness. Denise Gence has a sense of the comic, without ever resorting to obvious tricks; she works in half-tones. One feels that the actress is not the dupe of her character. Having removed her widow's veil she makes awkward and clumsy movements with her handkerchief, crying and also laughing. She lacks the sophisticated elegance of the model that attracted her husband late in life. She has difficulty realizing her new situation, and she converses with the dead man as though he were alive and able to answer her. Her broken gestures, her movements to the side and back, reveal the absurdity of her situation. She has a way of taking a few uncertain steps backward, which undercuts the perfect assurance of her words – "We will see each other again." Blin encouraged her to play with certain phrases, but to play the situation very seriously.

The First Guest blows smoke in her face, the boy refuses to shake her hand when he leaves, the Invalid shakes both her hands vigorously for some time. These little signs are more meaningful than the flat words with which the guests take leave. The guests have already returned to their personal preoccupations; they scarcely see the Widow, who no longer interests them. They are of course blind to the dead man who has escaped from his coffin to witness their behavior. Only the Widow senses this unusual presence and finds it quite natural. It is this mixture of truth and absurdity that renders the scene simultaneously comic and disturbing. A kind of surrealism undermines what might be a conventional scene. The lights dim; the dead man rises and leaves the room in a very ordinary way. When she sees the empty chair, the Widow is stupefied. For the spectator death is light, and the plot rather humorous. Francine and Roger have just met; perhaps they will fall in love.

Frisch did not write *Triptych* for the stage, so he differentiated its three parts without worrying about unity of form or style. The second part takes place underground in the region of the Dead. After the comedy of manners in the first part, the floor of the veranda (which had chains at the side) is slowly raised to become the ceiling; the three holly-bushes also rise. From this ceiling and these bushes now hang giant roots that can suggest dandelions as well as a humus that the lighting renders white and dreamlike.

All the living guests of the first part are walking on their future tombs. Even if it was only a technical requirement to have the set of the second part already present in the first, symbolically the arrangement reminds us that death is contained in life.

Blin added a private joke to this idea. The dead Proll of Part I in his rocking-chair was only an extra, masked to resemble Maurice Garrel, who played Proll. Blin amused himself by concealing the entrance of this false Proll; a young Guest wore on his back the mask of Maurice Garrel; during a group movement that hid him, he sat down in the chair and donned the mask. No sooner did this stage double leave at the end of Part I than the real Proll, Maurice Garrel, entered from the other side with his fishing-rod. (In the same way, Blin in *Divine Words* had arranged the disappearance of a false dwarf in a carriage, and the reappearance of the actual dwarf.) Comparably, too, as the rocking-chair was raised to the flies when the floor went up, from the wings stagehands manoeuvred an identical rocking-chair toward the stage, ironically rocking.

How to portray the beyond, the void, the luminous whiteness specified by Frisch? "A white choreography had to be invented for this place that is neither hell, purgatory, nor heaven. One might think of it as limbo."[25] In the program at the Odéon Blin specified that it was an opalescent limbo. In this void Frisch does not say how the people make their appearance, nor how they are grouped, nor how they move on stage. It seems that they just well up out of the void at the moment that they speak; then they go away, or fade away, to become visible again at another moment.

Blin had the main characters enter normally. Downstage, Proll fished at the edge of an imaginary stream, observed by the Garage Mechanic who will prove to be his father. Since he died young, the Garage Mechanic is younger than his elderly son. Can these dead people be taken seriously? In the center of the stage Proll's mistress is seated in the rocking-chair, slowly rocking. This was Frisch's seed-image for the play in 1978 – a young woman in a rocking-chair. She was alive, and then she was no longer alive.[26]

The ground was slightly raked and raised about a step. Proll was seated by the river bordered by pebbles. Blin had the other characters arrive unnoticeably and slowly; he freed them from the weight and clumsiness of two-legged creatures by having the ground move under them. Toward that end he had individual turn-tables installed in the floor. These slow symmetrical turns made the characters move strangely, destroying their corporeality; like zombies, they advanced without walking; they could not move of their own will; they were moved by a mechanism that is unknown to them and to us. There is no more free will.

Except for the white chair, the set was empty, but lit from below and behind. Behind the turn-table zone were two steps. The black backdrop has disappeared, revealing thick rolls of white gauze, about a yard and a half in width and ten yards in length; they overlap to make a glistening white background. Behind them one can see blue (coming from blue lights). At the same time as this suggestion of sky, we hear the chirping of birds (recorded).

The inhabitants of Limbo also hear them and raise their heads, realizing that another spring has arrived on earth. Blin explained to me (1983): "The birds indicate the passage of time; earthly time passes more quickly than the time of the dead."

A scene in which a child plays ball with his Pilot father was to be played before the white gauze, but Blin moved it behind, which distanced them even further. There were thus two pale images of the domain of the dead, which added to the dreamlike quality, like the background in a painting. Only the slow rhythm signalled the other-worldliness. Using the same principle as in *The Screens*, and giving a final blow to realism, Blin had the Tramp comment on the ball-game behind him while he looked straight forward at the actual audience in the theatre.

The last detail that distinguished the realm of the dead was the characters' pinkish complexions – a completely anti-realistic idea, like the symbols of traditional Chinese theatre, where facial paint designates the social position or temperament. Already in *The Screens* Blin had marked the face of the Dead with a white gash. This time he painted the faces pink, the color he most hated, being that of digitalis pills (for his heart ailment).

This second part inspired Blin with a creative vertigo; he was challenged by the technical difficulties. He told me: "Frisch wants white light everywhere, but he didn't visualize the trajectory of the characters who have to loom up miraculously at a given point, to be ready for their speech. In cinema it would be easier; on stage we don't have a zoom effect or comparable tricks." Blin wanted the characters to appear and stroll in an unreal way, like phantoms on the River Styx, but he disapproved of real water, sand, and smoke on stage. He talked to Acquart about slides, springboards, roller-skates, appearance from below, or descent from the flies. And then they arrived at the idea of individual turn-tables. There were five, mounted on an axis, turning at different speeds, either in the same direction or its opposite. Blin explained to me:

When we tried the turn-tables in the Sarcelles workshop, I was seized by a kind of obsession. The characters strolled independent of their own will; then they were unloaded by the turn-tables. Sometimes I had to figure out their departure a quarter of an hour before their arrival, or I had to change the speed of rotation so that the arrival would happen on the right line of dialogue. The stable fixed elements are the fisherman Proll with his fishing-rod (which was fastened to the ground when Proll moved away), the rocking-chair in the center, and the Tramp on the ground.

In harmony with these slow rotations, the actors' bodies were relaxed, and their words were delivered slowly. The spectator, fascinated by the moving set, is caught up in slow rhythms or words and gyrations. The dead are often ridiculous on stage, but these dead profit from a hypnosis induced by the

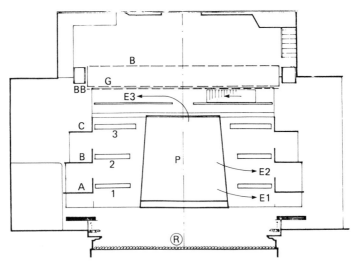

1, 2, 3	stylized holly bushes		B	hidden white backdrop
A, B, C	L-shaped flats		G	hidden rolls of white gauze
P	podium; area under the glass roof		BB	black backdrops
E1, E2	exits to the street		R	row of pebbles
E3	exit to the garden			

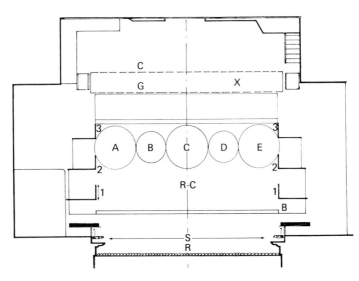

A, B, C, D, E	turn-tables		G	rolls of white gauze 10 m long, piled up
R-C	rocking-chair			to 1.5 m in height constituting a
R	row of pebbles			glistening background
1, 2, 3	L-shaped flats reflecting		S	space for the Styx
	white light		C	white cloth
B	border one step high		X	place for the ball-game

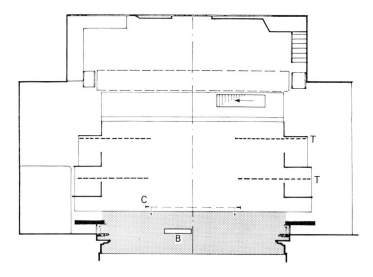

B   bench
C   black curtain brought slightly forward
T   track for curtain
▭   playing space reduced to shaded area

24 Acquart drawings for Blin's production of *Triptych* at the
Théâtre National de l'Odéon, 1983
Part I is played mainly on the limited central area.
In Part II five turn-tables, three large and two small, take up the
entire width of the stage.
Part III is played on the forestage.

tempo. We look at them differently. It may be that a text has never before
relied so deeply on kinetics to control the dynamic of the action.

Characters who rotate without wishing it confer status on the speakers
among the dead, gaining credence for their disconnected utterances,
continually reminding us that they are no longer living, that their memories
are part of the past. And all this even though the actors act like living people.
The Aged Lady, for example, is serene and glad to be there. Andrée Tainsy,
who played that part, told me: "Blin instructed me not to think that I was
seventy-seven years old, but to be rather healthy and even truculent. I was
not to enact a corpse. Her husband is forty-one years old, her son seventy. It's
amusing. I don't know whether the audience was aware of that." This
rallentando from which the dead cannot escape theatricalizes the ineluctabil-
ity of their fate. They continually remember, recapitulate scenes that they
have lived, words they have spoken and heard. But they can change nothing,

since the words are fixed once and for all in their past. They cannot go back on their actions to improve their image. All is over.

While Catherine rocks in her chair, repeating an old action in slow motion with an absurdly real chair, her monotonous oscillations increase the gyratory effect of the characters displaced on turn-tables according to a steady rhythm. At the same time Proll downstage manipulates his real fishing-rod with precise gestures, and each time he catches nothing, but he doesn't care. "At the water's edge, I feel free," Frisch has said.

The first person to be brought in on a turn-table is the young Pastor with the dark silhouette, whom we have seen in the first Part. He enters on the left turn-table, and soon Xavier and the Flautist enter on the right. Imperceptibly, they change turn-tables at the end of a rotation, to find themselves at the other end of the stage, but it takes a long time, as if the transition were interminable. Time and space seem to expand. The time of the dead does not obey our clocks; the dead move in an infinitely large coordinate, if not within infinity.

The neighbor who played the flute always plays a false note at the same place; he cannot progress, and his exercises irritate the dead as much as they did the living. A tramp enters, bag over his shoulder, wearing an old cap over his bald head, and big boots that recall those of Estragon in *Waiting for Godot*. The role was played by François Chaumette (who played an elegant and big-bellied Pozzo in Blin's production at the Comédie-Française). Frisch's tramp is educated; he quotes Diderot, but who listens to him? Sprawled on the ground, he tries to take part in the conversation, but no one pays any attention to him. Is it because he is a tramp? He talks to himself. Blin had a weakness for this character, playing him any time that Chaumette was absent from rehearsal.

Another failure of communication separates (old) Proll from his (young) father. Seated side by side, Proll evokes the past, with his mother not very happy and himself misunderstood. The father doesn't listen, interested only in the fishing-rod, eternally teaching his son who will never know how to fish properly. In passing, fragments of events filter through; the problems of their past are absent — the Spanish Civil War, unemployment, ecological preoccupations. Around Catherine gravitate her failures in love with Xavier and Klas, before she met Proll; then her suicide at age thirty. "How did you die?" is the refrain of the Pastor every time he sees someone. He is ever-watchful even though he cannot do anything for anybody; he is dead, like the others. Blin called him "the police scout," because of his probing into the causes of death. He wasn't allowed to preach in the first part, where he was shaken in his faith by the guest Roger, and in the second part he is condemned to repetition.

Sometimes a scene of past reality enters Limbo. The dead recall it, replay

25 Scene from Part II of Blin's production of *Triptych* by Max
Frisch at the Théâtre National de l'Odéon, 1983. The (dead) Pilot
is reunited with his (dead) son and plays with him behind the
gauze. Ph. Yves Chériaux

part of it, echo the words they pronounced on earth, unable to change the
dénouement – as a music-box cannot change its refrain. Thus Klas appears on
all fours in his pyjamas to pick up newspapers that Catherine habitually threw
on the floor. Blin took advantage of these relived situations to sketch a fight
between the Tramp and the Flautist who was once a policeman, beating-up
tramps. But the guilty one escapes into the brilliant side of the stage with its
distorting reflection, so that the Tramp cannot seize the character he wants to
attack. The gestures of the dead are ineffective; everything slips through their
fingers; everything crumbles or dissolves. Thus, the designer Acquart
explained: "On the sides I placed L-shaped reflecting material oriented
toward stage-center and at the same time reflecting images and breaking

sightlines. Velvet covers the side that faces the audience, but they nevertheless extend the stage laterally, while breaking sightlines; set and characters are reflected in these mirrors."

The entrance of the Aged Lady seems particularly slow because she turns several times on the same turn-table, on the right side, unable to reach the other areas of the stage. She is Proll's mother, the wife of the Garage Mechanic; she is confined to a wheelchair pushed by Ilse, her grand-daughter. Ilse is dressed in black in the first part, and she carries a tray of refreshments; in

26 Part II of Blin's production of *Triptych* by Max Frisch at the Théâtre National de l'Odéon, 1983. Set by Acquart. The ground of Act I is above the "dead" in Act II, and its roots are visible. At the back swathes of white gauze let the light through. At ground level on the left the Garage Mechanic (Nicholas Silberg) at the edge of "the stream." Behind him (and reflected on the brilliant wall) is the Pastor (Yves Furic). In the centre Catherine (Geneviève Casile) and Proll (Maurice Garrel). At the back the Flautist (Jacques Destoop). On the right the Tramp (François Chaumette). Ph. Yves Chériaux.

Limbo she is dressed as a nurse. None of these theatre dead suggests a corpse; there is neither sickness nor suffering. The Aged Lady smiles; her physical ailments have disappeared. Ilse is fresh as a spring. Not being able to move, the Aged Lady is twice handicapped; like the others, she is at the mercy of her turn-table, but also she needs somebody to push her wheelchair. When the Garage Mechanic wants to approach his wife, whom he never knew so old, and of whose troubles he has just heard, he is carried by another turn-table through a long series of curves before he can stop near enough to the wheelchair of the Aged Lady to talk to her. In other words, Blin anticipated this movement of the Mechanic and had him on the turn-table long before his conversation with the Aged Lady.

In another use of a turn-table an airplane pilot is in his cockpit before his plane crashes. His legs are stretched out; he is dressed in blue shirt and black trousers, with earphones on, and a map in his hand. He turns continually, prisoner of an invisible cockpit. Xavier, the soldier, was the victim of an avalanche during a military exercise, and he tells the amnesiac pilot about the accident that claimed his life. These gyrations of the turn-tables reflect the Pilot's thoughts; he seems to have forgotten everything.

Carlos, a young Spanish militiaman, is dressed in tight trousers and khaki shirt. He is supposed to clean his rifle, but Blin will elaborate this direction to have him mime his death in slow motion; his arms are spread out as he turns around while the machine-gun crackles. This is a reminder that Frisch was much affected by the Spanish Civil War, but it also suggests the pointlessness of all war. The Child, the Pilot, the Soldier, and the Militiaman all die young. The Militiaman cannot get over being dead at nineteen. As the actor told me: "He will stutter his death throughout eternity."

The second part of *Triptych* contains two scenes separated by the sounds of church bells and a recorded *Te Deum*. Blin intended to put the intermission at this point; the actors return to the stage on turn-tables; it was an extraordinary image, but unfortunately their rhythm was broken by the intermission. During a run-through, the two scenes were linked together, and the acting improved considerably. Blin therefore suggested dropping the intermission, and Frisch agreed. In this way, only four or five actors return on turn-tables, while the others are already on stage.

The second scene of the second Part is more painful. We learn of how difficult it was to live – reproaches, wounds, and even crimes, since the young bank employee whom Ilse thought of marrying was killed in a hold-up by a criminal who afterwards regretted it. He will regret it forever. The criminal seems a pale descendant of Frisch's Count Oderland (who was inspired by a news item, but Frisch makes him a force for slaughter, a man who confuses himself with his murderous ax.) But this criminal is remorseful, and he cries on

stage that he would so soon have been freed. Catherine does not appreciate
the reappearance of men she has loved. Here is the one who always brought
roses, and center-stage fills with a vase of thirty-five red roses that look real.

While the Tramp with amnesia tries to remember the lines of Hamlet,
whom he played when an actor, the Aged Lady reminds Proll of his
childhood. Son and Mother are almost the same age now, and this disturbs
the audience. We are trapped too in these false données. But Mother and Son
get along well, and this is enhanced by the casting. Maurice Garrel and
Andrée Tainsy look at each other, and give to their characters as dead people
a very human authenticity. Somehow they convey to us their own lived
experience on earth in an archetypal mother/son relationship. No sooner do
they leave, son pushing his mother's wheelchair, than the child appears,
playing ball. When his Pilot father arrives, they play together. Death here
seems light and diluted.

The set is so well integrated into the action that it seems to inspire it. The
Invalid is the victim of the turn-table which doesn't carry him where he
desires. He raises his two canes to try to attract Proll's attention, since it takes
so long to reach him, but it turns out that Proll didn't want to see this old
reactionary. Politics had separated them, and the Invalid cannot make up for
his slander. The turn-table carries him away, with his indelible past. The
others keep repeating their words. Proll and Catherine are most lucid, since
neither of them expects anything or has anything more to discuss.

One might recall Frisch's earlier play: *Biography: A Play*. There the author
quoted Chekhov: "What if this life were only a rough draft?" (*Three Sisters*).
What is final and unchangeable in our existence? Theatre permits us to
explore all the biographical possibilities of an individual; one can stop some
events, return to the past, envisage a variant or another dénouement. That is
what happens in *Biography*. The protagonist Kürmann is invited to live his life
differently. A master of ceremonies helps him find the key moments of his life
"as in a chess-game when one lays out the pieces to see what we could have
done differently." A woman awaits him, his wife; they will replay their first
meeting among a group of guests. We think of the meeting of Francine and
Roger, among the guests at the burial in *Triptych*. But *Biography* flaunts its
theatricality. Lighting changes indicate whether it is a rehearsal or a
performance, and another change when it is a variant. Because it is theatre,
Kürmann can return to his past, make other decisions, orient his life
differently. As one of the characters says: "Theatre permits what reality does
not; we can modify, begin again, experiment with another biography."

Elements of *Biography* are found in *Triptych*; some phrases are echoed –
"It's two in the morning," "a taxi," "I can hardly stand up," "laughter of the
guests offstage." Comments repeat and criss-cross: Kürmann's father drank

27 Scene from Part II of Blin's production of Frisch's *Triptych* at
the Théâtre National de l'Odéon, 1983. The 77-year-old Woman
in a wheel-chair is driven by her Mechanic husband, dead at age
41. On the ground the Tramp. Ph. Yves Chériaux

and had debts. A bicycle was given to Kürmann and to Proll as a child. Catherine commits suicide like Kürmann. As *The Screens* summarized Genet's earlier plays, *Triptych* is built with some of the material of *Biography*. One might say that the character of Kürmann has split into Roger (in his union with Francine), the imprisoned criminal (Kürmann too is imprisoned and pardoned), the Aged Lady (Kürmann in a wheelchair is pushed by a nurse). In *Biography* we already have the roses, revolver, false notes on a musical instrument. In *Triptych*, however, we can no longer resort to theatre to change decisions. Life is left behind, without any possible recourse. Words spoken last forever. We are like the music-box dolls that fascinated Kürmann: "These characters make the same gestures when the same melody is heard." Life can be lived only once.

The set for the third part of *Triptych* consisted of a narrow area in front of the step of the second part; it was closed off with black curtains, and at the left was a bench. On the black netting were large round balls. Acquart wanted a photographic enlargement of a building that looked disturbing; at the foot of the building would have been a road with moving lights on it. Thus the city would be present. A frame would have occupied the stage, behind which one would have seen streets and luminous points as traffic. Projectors would have made it real and unreal at the same time. But Acquart told me: "Roger Blin didn't want any photographs of buildings, and we didn't have enough time to make the street and the moving lights."

A little before the beginning of the third part, Blin brought in Francine on a turn-table. In tailored suit and carrying a handbag, she discovers this world that is new to her and these people whom she doesn't know. She seems absent but still tense. The mirroring material of the second Part now turns its opaque side. The black net curtains half close, and after a blackout only a small area is lit, with a bench on the left. On it is seated Francine, dead, and the still-living Roger (who met her at the funeral of Proll). They are at the place where they separated after their life together. Blin used the turn-table to anticipate the entrance of Francine so as to link the second and third Parts of the play, and to indicate to us the status of Francine, for there is little difference between the two people on the bench. They are in the same acting area; they are lit the same way; they are both dressed like the living, and Francine does not even have a pinkish complexion (since the actress refused this distinguishing makeup of the dead). Their dialogue seems to be logical; they replay fragments of scenes they have lived. Francine is living only in Roger's memory.

In this long scene for two people, slight dissonances alert us to the invisible boundary between them. Their dialogue begins to fragment; she doesn't hear or doesn't listen to what he says; he lights her cigarette too late; she repeats her phrases a few times in the same monotonous tone because her intonations have been erased from his memory; she gets tangled up in words; she cannot go beyond the words that she has already spoken, and, like the Mummy in *Ghost Sonata*, she is caught up in words. The actress can no longer play the present; she has to put herself in the past; she cannot play in the same time as her partner, and the audience grows uneasy. We don't share Roger's problems; we are not concerned that this couple didn't get along, and that after another failure in love, Roger will commit suicide. There are too many suicides in this play for us to be moved; too many dead people for us to think about death itself. It is this strained and impossible dialogue that is disturbing; this mystery of a beyond that takes form and is concretized in a unique relation between the bodies of two actors. The drama in this scene is in the deafness of Francine, who has remained young, to the words of Roger, who has aged. He cannot engage in a new dialogue with her, which would modify the past or justify his perhaps bad conduct. We never see ourselves clearly; or it's too late.

Behind the black netting there is a hint of a highway with cars on it; by the sound and by a play of lights from left to right or right to left at ground level, Blin suggests a passing automobile with bright lights on. The dead woman is aware of it, reacting to its sounds. Actually, though, she is underground and Roger above. It is only by their looks and by the recollection of the underground set of the second Part that Blin activates the imagination of the audience, even while simplifying Frisch's sonic directions. (Between the green and red traffic lights the author provided for numerous automobiles every fifty seconds, and sometimes a bus on the main street, with other automobiles on the side street.) Toward the end we hear an ambulance siren that interests Francine but not Roger.

All the scenic directions about cigarettes are meticulously obeyed: "she takes a cigarette," "she smokes," "he stubs out a cigarette underfoot," "he gives her a light." Francine smokes as she smoked in the first Part. She is cold and closes her collar; she speaks to a policeman who disturbs them; he is scarcely visible in the shadow, and he leaves immediately. She buys a newspaper from a newsboy; she is more alive, more corporeal than the others. Roger tries desperately to engage her in dialogue because his own father, whom he nevertheless criticizes, consulted his dead wife in all his decisions. By exactly recalling Francine's phrases, perhaps he can catch a sign. Roger plunges madly into this hope and illusion until he drowns. He even confuses reality with the scene in which he saw Francine in a dream. Christine Fersen, the actress playing Francine, maintains her calm, almost motionless except for the moment when she withdraws slightly into the shadow to return above Roger on his bench. Roger (Toja) is prey to the anxiety that haunts many of the living, and particularly this living creature who grows old while imagining that the woman he lost remains the same age. At times the dead woman makes a familiar gesture; she puts on lipstick while looking in a hand-mirror; she puts on glasses to read an actual newspaper. Gradually, the traffic noises decrease, signaling the passage of time.

Blin would not allow great passion to Francine, even when she repeated a scene of the past. She is only a faded bloodless image. Her tone is flat. Her phrases crumble, and the dialogue no longer dovetails. Roger can only disappear. The lighting grows red in the distance, and a rumbling spreads over the empty stage, louder and louder.

The play had too strong a resonance not to trouble the actors. During rehearsals Blin often had to joke in order to break through the gloom. More than ever before, he refused to be directive. The actors had to be extraordinarily attentive to capture, between wisecracks, an indication or the hint of a direction. The profound theme of the play must have been close to Blin, who was in bad health. He admitted: "This play touches me closely. If I weren't old and sick, I probably wouldn't have directed it."[27]

In two weeks the detailed blocking was done. The actors rehearsed for three months without the turn-tables, which appeared three weeks before the opening. Three months to immerse themselves in that life/death, and accomplish the osmosis between the actors of the Comédie-Française and those from outside it. Three months during which slight physical afflictions appeared in the actors, sporadic but revealing.

The reviews were lukewarm, but Blin didn't care. He told me: "I want to satisfy the author, not the reviewers." There was no virulent attack, but no delirious enthusiasm either. The mise-en-scène was called "clear and simple" (Le Monde), "wise" (Figaro), the setting was "ingenious" (Le Monde), "Curiously 1925 . . . spare and luminous" (Figaro). The actors were praised: Denise Gence had "a true and striking sense of comedy, like a Daumier" (Figaro); Maurice Garrel was "astonishing, with an inner life despite the fixity of his facial expression," and Jacques Toja was "swallowed up as a victim of drowning" (Figaro).

For the France-Soir reviewer François Chalais, Blin's mise-en-scène "leaves nothing to chance, as if at the end of each scene everything was locked up to prevent gestures and words from straying into unforeseen paths." There it was – the invisible mise-en-scène to which no actor could testify; they have the impression that Blin told them nothing and that he never formulated a clear direction; that he let things go their own way. But that was his conscious method, and the small touches that he added each day constituted the essential steps of a ripening process. What he hated was prior analysis: "I am against those dramaturgs who explain why and how to me. I make discoveries while I work. By trial and error. I say more [his view only] to the actors so that they will do less. I don't write anything in advance. But one can be obsessed by images, and that is what directing comes from; everything passes through the hands."[28]

François Chalais judged the work of this visionary as "fascinating as a master painting," and he concluded: "This is the way a proud and solitary creature works – one of the last magicians of our contemporary theatre."[29]

After *Triptych* Blin thought of directing Sylvain Itkine's *Hussy*, as well as plays by Brendan Behan and Arnold Wesker. He recorded a monologue for radio. He was preparing a Beckett program, a collection of texts chosen in consultation with Beckett, and he was supposed to play at Avignon in the French première of Thomas Bernhard's *Minetti*. Illness prevented completion of any of these projects. In December 1983, he was hospitalized. He died on 20 January 1984. His friends filled the cremation room at Père Lachaise Cemetery. His desire was to leave no trace.

5   An ethic of theatre

Roger Blin always had at least two careers – actor and director – and he therefore never relinquished the actor's viewpoint. *Actor* meant much more to him than a mere interpreter; he was above all a person and a citizen of the world. Although he probably would have liked to act in and direct more films, he continued to act and direct in the theatre within the possibilities of that art. He never forgot Charles Dullin and the Atelier or the challenging spirit of the October Group. He had a nose for what was new, a Beckett or a Genet, and he produced plays at moments that were not necessarily favorable for them. Let us cite a few milestones in his career – Artaud, the art of radio, work with actors, and imaginative use of stage space.

BLIN AND ARTAUD

They met frequently in the 1930s at Montparnasse, in the company of Desnos and Hemingway. At that time Artaud amused and fascinated Blin: "He taught me a great deal, but I didn't agree with him about the omnipotence of the director."[1] Less impressed by *The Theatre and its Double* than by Artaud's poems, Blin didn't want to be either the disciple or the explicator of his friend, whom he defended against "voyeurs and sightseers." Rather than influence, it was a sharing of tastes and distastes. They shared a taste for the mystics, metaphysics, Jarry, Ribemont-Dessaignes, Büchner, German cinema, oriental theatre, painting, color; they both despised realism, bourgeois conventions, colonialism, Claudel, Giraudoux.

Both men sought a way to master spoken language, to make a kind of sonic material out of the voice. Artaud wrote: "and words will be construed in an incantatory, truly magical sense, side by side with this logical sense – not only for their meaning, but for their forms, their sensual radiation."[2] And what is too often forgotten in the popular image of an anti-verbal Artaud: "We do not intend to do away with dialogue, but to give words something of the significance they have in dreams."[3] It is in accord with these views that Blin played the Student in his 1949 *Ghost Sonata*, although at that time he didn't know Artaud's production notes. The remorse of the Old Man is concretized in the silent apparition of the Milkmaid; she represents the person he killed, and is only an obsessive image in the conscience of the Old Man, beyond reach. She has to be played in a different register from the other

150

actors. As played by Blin, the Student seems to have a sixth sense for perceiving evil; intense, he can read into secret truths and lies of characters, beyond their words. If there is cruelty in Blin, it is in his unsentimental view of the world, in his critical lucidity to the least detail; it does not translate into aggression against the audience. His staging relies on nuance, subtlety, suggestion; it is dreamlike. His conception of death was not at all macabre; it was seen through a veil; the dead have slow gestures that resemble dance; they rotate by themselves or on turn-tables; they slide; they are not realistic.

Blin and Artaud were similar in other respects. In Blin's staging he often denounced through laughter. The laughter of Hamm was nervous and measured as he clung to his power in his home. The victim of criminal pollution in *Minamata* had a resonant laugh, deformed by an echo.

Roger Blin remained a Dadaist in spirit, and perhaps that explains his astonishing youthfulness. Among friends he played poetic games of breaking down everyday language; he was a friend of the two Dadaists who never became Surrealists — Tristan Tzara, the poet of the deconstruction of language, and Georges Ribemont-Dessaignes, that violent and abstract poet without pathos. These three friends sought to translate a Beyond of consciousness by a Beyond of words. Blin did not direct their works, any more than he directed those of Jarry whom he loved. He wanted to direct new works and not revivals.

He had a gift for phrases: possibly he could have been a writer. Sometimes he told his friends about an idea for a play, but as far as we know, he never wrote one. Perhaps he thought that was not a role for a director. Perhaps it was because he wanted to leave as little trace as possible.

Hungry for poetry and metaphysics, Blin was attracted by the spoken word, but he also fought against language: not only because of his Dadaist commitment but also because his stuttering kept him at continual grips with his rebellious pronunciation. On the stage or in the studio (even when a television program was "live"), he mastered his stuttering. He entered a kind of superior state in which the poetic stream welled up in him; his unconscious was somehow freed, and he no longer stumbled over syllables, probably at some cost to himself. To reach this level, Blin passed through a network of non-verbal communication, and that accounts for his dislike of explaining things with words, either to his actors or even to his friends, with whom he might remain silent for long periods. That didn't mean that silence separated them. The waves were circulating.

Playing in about thirty stage plays and over a hundred films, Blin also took part in many radio programs that were especially difficult. In all media his voice possessed a kind of vibrato, a personal music acquired through constant struggle against his own affliction. He might play an elegant dandy in a light voice or a dignified tramp in a deep voice. His intonation was never banal; it could ridicule or elevate. An atheist and a revolutionary, a destroyer of the power of family and religion, a denouncer of the establishment, Blin was also an officiant at a ritual, at a stage ceremony. He carried oral expression to a pinnacle. Through the rhythmic melody of words, he was an earthy actor with a living voice. Through his attention to gesture, he showed "anthropological nobility" of an authentic human being. Blin integrated into his acting his difficulty of being, his uneasy relation with the world and he did this in spite of his rebellious pronunciation.

More secretly, Blin also expressed himself in drawing. His pen drew ritualized forms that transcribed his anxiety. He corresponded to the description of anthropologist Marcel Jousse: "Every man who knows how to maintain his naive freshness is able to throw [something] on a canvas, to mould clay, to create rhythm with sound, or to express orally in words aspects of a still unknown and unsuspected reality."[4]

WORK IN RADIO

The Studio d'Essai was founded secretly by Pierre Schaeffer in 1942 during the Occupation. It was succeeded by the Club d'Essai of which the poet Jean Tardieu became head in 1946. In this Experimental Studio (which would give birth to the Experimental Section of French National Radio) directors, musicians, actors, and writers discussed the relationship between words and music, words and sound effects, sonic environments, the importance of monologues. The specific qualities of radio art were sketched out and, since it dealt with speech, there was some overlap with theatre. Blin recorded for Marcel Herrand or François Billetdoux; Billetdoux recorded in the same Babylone Theatre where Blin rehearsed. Sometimes they used the same actors – Maria Casarès, Jean Martin, Pierre Latour, Lucien Raimbourg – the last three in *Godot*.

At the Club d'Essai enthusiastic actors lent themselves to experimental broadcasts involving research on the voice, breath, sounds that were then broken down in makeshift apparatus with microphones, echo chambers, and resonance boards. Their equipment was nothing like that of today's sophisticated studios; they worked with primitive materials. Roger Blin recorded his role of Railway Watchman (adapted from a Dickens story) in the cellar of their studio, since his voice had to come from a tunnel. Blin was of course attracted by their research on voices, sounds, Martenot waves, concrete music. And the experimenters were attracted by his rare voice with its strange timbre and unconventional cracks. The hallucinated Railway

Watchman, imagining an accident and running in front of the train to stop it, found in Blin a disturbed and disturbing actor. He was often cast in radio (as in theatre and television) because of his temperament, his refusal of traditional styles, his physique and grating voice, his sensitivity to and understanding of texts that were supposed to be difficult; thus he played unique characters who were set off from others in non-realistic, poetic, and polysemic texts.

Unlike actors who pull apart a poem and translate it into an action to play, he respected the written word, the atmosphere of a work, the matrix from which the words soared. He knew how to control his voice in long periods, without getting lost in syntactical detours. He recited Lautréamont's *Songs of Maldoror* and Rimbaud's *Drunken Boat* as no one else could. He rendered long passages in *The Maritime Ode* of Pessoa. He broadened the sonic horizon; he navigated on the high seas. When he recited, the poem flowed; he could sing/speak without lingering over each syllable, without accenting one word rather than another. He paid little attention to intermediate punctuation. Sometimes an offhand inflexion showed his spirit of fun. After a humorous parenthesis, he again took up his personal lyricism.

François Billetdoux told me:

He knows one thing that too many actors forget, which is that you have to find that source that makes music of words. Not a singsong but music. When the music begins, he doesn't stutter any more. He never stutters before a microphone or in a scene. When he finds that lit... spark, that little springboard for the music, then it's all lyricism. There isn't a gratuitous sound. It becomes a form of respiration and phrasing. The most important aspect of a word is its sound. It's the sound that gives the full sense; it's not a question of meaning but of intonation. This is evident in great languages like Finnish, Sanskrit, or Hebrew. Sixty percent of the language is intonation. And that's Roger Blin.

In recording studios he was appreciated for his professional conscience, his imperturbable calm, and his patience with the inevitable retakes. He was given texts by poets René Char and Pierre Reverdy. He took part in a series by Jean Lescure, "The Birth of Language"; he was a ventriloquist in a Swedish play. He read several parts in a single work, for example, Knut Hamsun's *Hunger*.

Nor is it digressive to insist on how Blin read on radio, along with his familiarity with written texts, and his experience and taste for the spoken word, for he brought that experience and taste to the theatre. He was essentially a man of words, even though he could have become a painter or designer, and though he visualized a play immediately, and then made it live in space. That is why a man like Beckett would come to him, or he to Beckett; that is also why he several times staged works originally written for radio. From *Isabelle Langrenier* to *Did I Mention That I'm A Hunchback?*, from Beckett to Frisch, he put himself into the text; he worked at the image *and* the sound.

BLIN WITH ACTORS AND DESIGNERS

Jean-Marie Conty's Education by Theatre project (EPJD), in which Blin participated, was an ideal to which he remained faithful. As a school it influenced the training of many actors, authors, teachers. Although far from the usual theatre training school, it did have forerunners in France − in particular Jacques Copeau's Vieux-Colombier School and then Dullin's School. Both favored improvisation, which today is a familiar training technique. Traditional training gave way to exercises that would develop the personality and inventiveness of the actor, stressing corporeal expression as well as diction.

Before, during and after World War II various disciples spread the ideas of Copeau and Dullin. Decroux and Barrault developed abstract mime; Jacques Lecoq emphasized corporeal expression; Jean-Marie Conty developed training courses for those who did not intend to make a career of theatre. After the Liberation, the TEC (Travail et Culture) was an umbrella organization for a number of courses − drama, music, fine arts. They fell foul of political interference, and Jean-Marie Conty then founded EPJD in studios in Paris and Montrouge, where he was joined by Barrault, Blin, Marie-Hélène Dasté, André Clavé, Claude Martin, Jean Vilar, as well as other actors who later became well known in France.

The program not only opposed traditional actor training. It also attacked the bourgeois prejudices and religious precepts of all conventional education, and in particular the Western rationalism that separates mind from body. The courses were concerned with spontaneous expression, with the unconscious, with biology; they aimed at a total integration of being, and, in order to establish new ethics, they demanded radical social change. At EPJD the focus was more on a sense of life than on stage techniques. The principles were published collectively under the title *To Make Living Beings*.[5]

The exercises liberated vital energy by spontaneous expression, then controlled it, and used it creatively. They made for decontraction, independence of gesture, rallentando. Today we are familiar with these group techniques, which may be therapeutic, or may serve an experimental group such as the Open Theatre. But in 1947 EPJD was a precursor. Mute improvisation, closer to Decroux or Barrault than Copeau or Dullin, helped the actor mobilize his physical, sensory, and emotional skills. According to Conty, it was appropriate "to balance the play of life between two poles: lucidity devoid of feeling and trancelike possession by the character."

This contradicted the classical training of the actor in France, based on the dominance of the text and on a cerebral rather than respiratory process. Throughout Blin's career, one can trace his irritation with the traditional actor who forgets to be a living being; and his preference for the actor "by nature," who risks his deepest being, even while knowing how to control it.

Actress Hermine Karagheuz told me: "With [Blin] the work at the table is soon over. He makes us move right away. Instead of explaining, he plays the part, and that's a huge indication. He gives the rhythm and the humor. Then the actor has to get away from it. Sometimes he tells a story that doesn't seem to have anything to do with the play. Or he lets the actor search."

Other directors who spend longer "at the table" also direct by example – like Giorgio Strehler or Roger Planchon. A choreographer shows a group of dancers the step or exercise to do. Too rational an approach may freeze the actor and block his imagination. Instead of imposing a single style of acting, a single series of gestures, a given pace, rhythm, or interpretation, Blin cut away and eliminated whatever clashed with the spirit of the work or with his personal hatred of realism. His demonstrations were suggestions and not examples to follow: "Leïla limps; I'll show you how she can limp," but actress Paule Annen invented her own limp. That actress told me:

Blin takes off from the body to move into the whole space. When he directs a Beckett play, if the character is supposed to shake, he shakes. In *Boesman and Lena*, Lena is supposed to become more and more repulsive; she is increasingly deformed. Toto Bissainthe started with her own body to show that downfall. Blin doesn't give detailed instructions. He takes a page of the text, begins to read it and play it; the actor changes and integrates it.

Blin listens, open to whatever the actor can offer him.

Blin never insisted on a direction to a faltering actor. He never theorized. He gave everyone a chance to express himself within the context of the play. He was not prodigal of blame or compliments. He had a small smile that said he was not a dupe. Sometimes after a play opened, the timing might grow lax, the makeup might not be applied so rigorously, a line of dialogue might be skipped, an actor might overact; unannounced, Blin would slip into the theatre, along with the audience. He would notice these faults, and after the performance he would go into the dressing-rooms but say nothing. There was no need. Everyone knew he had seen everything, and the next night everything would play as it should.

Even though he liked consistency of performance, Blin was disappointed that in subsidized companies, both in France and abroad, skillful actors were disciplined into passivity; they were merely waiting for his strict orders. He needed cooperation, and even argument. He never wanted to destroy a personality or to force it into a pattern. He was tolerant and open to suggestion. He hated textual analysis and pedagogical explication. He was interested in the meeting-point of the actor and the character. He lacked the cruelty of Artaud, who wrote him in 1946: "I need actors who are first beings on stage, who are not afraid of the true feeling of a knife-wound, or of labor pains in childbirth."[6]

At the beginning of the century the great actor Lucien Guitry stated that directing took care of itself, if the casting was properly done. Blin was also adept at casting, even though it might occasion surprise; he knew his own criteria and did not adhere to role-models. For example, Beckett did not know what the characters of *Godot* looked like; Blin took Lucien Raimbourg from another milieu to cast him as Vladimir, less because of his skill (as a cabaret entertainer, he had never been in a play) than because of his human quality. When Blin had to replace tall, thin Jean Martin for the tour of *Endgame*, he chose small, stocky André Julien who had alternate reactions of submission and protest, which gave life and credibility to Clov. For *Happy Days*, Blin was mainly preoccupied with the difficulty of memorizing and speaking the text, and he therefore chose Madeleine Renaud.

Blin told me in 1966: "The actor should be free in his body without being conditioned by any school and without trying to be charming." Similarly for speech. Indifferent and even hostile to too precise a diction and the physical aspect of the actor's role, Blin was sensitive to the deepest self of the actor, even to disturbed areas that might be hidden. Blin liked rare and strange people like O'Brady, Jean Martin, Paule Annen, Christine Tsingos, Hermine Karagheuz. He was always on the lookout for people who had roots and were close to the earth without flaunting it. He polished the pronunciation of the Griot Company so that they would be audible; he attenuated their accents. He loved discreet people under whose surface he perceived hidden uneasiness. He could tell a film director about an actor or actress whose "madness" would enrich a character. He was faithful to his tastes and friendships. He needed to work with ethical people with a sense of civic responsibility, and yet he liked a certain marginality. He needed people with a sense of poetry.

Without telling them, he helped launch careers, for example those of Laurent Terzieff and Gérard Lorin. Even those who suffered under his silence and lack of verbal communication came to appreciate how meaningful these silences were, after they had worked (unhappily) with more verbal directors. Blin always chose the most direct and simple way; he found luxury and sophistication useless. He made himself understood by jokes: "The origin of theatre is a drunk on a street corner; he begins to tell his life. People gather round."[7] As Jean-Louis Barrault told me in 1984:

Roger Blin was a fraternal being, full of tact, modest, very sensitive, able to break into sobs when a play moved him deeply. He was a marvelous actor, doing rare things. When he directed us, I obeyed him with confidence. He had a profound knowledge of theatre and a very sure judgment, which he expressed by dropping a brief phrase.

For Blin theatre could happen anywhere. One can live anywhere – in a wagon, a room, the street. One can play anywhere – a square, a barn, a proscenium stage, theatre in the round, thrust stage, in the Théâtre de Poche or the huge Chaillot. He was indifferent to dimensions and forms of exterior architecture. He adapted and had a gift for adaptation. His mise-en-scène could also adapt; between its première at the Petit-Orsay and its revival at another small theatre, *The Emigrés* went on tour, and it played at the 2,000-seat Opera of Luxembourg. With or without budget, he managed. He was not prey to costly gadgets, which he thought harmful. Except for *The Screens* and *Triptych*, all his productions could tour inexpensively, without trucks. His principles of ethics and esthetics placated the conscience of those who never gave him subsidies; for that matter, he almost never asked for any.

He directed in the little theatres of the Left Bank which spawned the creativity of the 1950s – Noctambules, Babylone, Lutèce, which today are cinemas or developers' land. He directed at the Petit-Odéon, the experimental theatre that Barrault carved out of the large Odéon, and that today is named for Roger Blin. He directed at the Récamier, which was rented by Vilar and then by Barrault. But he also directed at the large theatres of the Odéon and the Comédie-Française.

From Beckett's no man's land with its slender tree in a desert, he went on to the complex set at several levels of *The Screens*. After having worked with painters Thanos Tsingos, Vieira da Silva, Atlan, Jean Assens, he worked mainly with two designers – André Acquart and Matias. At the age of seven, Blin was already drawing. Afterwards he showed a few friends some of his two thousand odd drawings, (a collection of which will soon be published under the supervision of Michèle Meunier). He gave a self-portrait to Laurent Terzieff. He himself did sketches for several of his sets and costumes. He was attracted by makeup, and each evening the actors in *The Screens* made up their faces in accordance with his sketch. When he played a leper in *Pacific*, he pasted colored crepe-paper on his face for bloody sores, and pieces of sponge constituted a torn ear. His care for colors and lights is that of a painter, and it is worth studying the relationship between his drawing and theatrical work.

He boasted: "I always work closely with the designer. I like to work with people. I tell him what I have in mind, and we develop our ideas together. I prefer an architect or sculptor to help me with my sets."[8] From *The Blacks* on, Blin called on André Acquart when his set necessitated a transformable architectural construction at several levels – *Divine Words, The Screens, Minamata and Co., Triptych*. From *Happy Days* on, he called on Matias to work on a ground-cover or a fixed set – *Boesman and Lena, Macbeth, Dream Play, Waiting for Godot* at the Comédie-Française, *The Blue of Eau-de-vie*.

He was confident of the skill of his designer friends, but at the same time uneasy about their final products. A rendering on reduced scale does not always predict the full-scale set, and the director is suddenly aware of the distance between the original common project and its concretization in space.

Concretization is a barbarous word for the visionary poet/painter who dreamed of an almost abstract support for his play, and who suddenly sees a materialized ground, a heavy construction to carry the bodies of actors and objects which have to be calculated in kilograms. The artist–designer in his studio had prepared an esthetic and functional object; the director had turned over ideas and worked with the minds and bodies of actors. Suddenly his stage is invaded; the surface and volume are burdened with uprights, squares; exits are narrowed and obstructed. Terrified, the director given to "poor" theatre has to rethink his blocking (as in *The Screens*) or accept superabundance (the simple square of light above an empty chair in the first act of *Triptych* became a white pedestal adorned with glass roof and bushes, and this was more luxurious than necessary for the living-room of a book salesman). Designer Acquart told me: "When Roger chooses a decorator, he leaves him entirely free. When he doesn't agree, he doesn't say so openly, but you can see it in his reticence. He would have preferred something more modest than the white ground of *Triptych*. But he was interested in the glass roof because of its effect on the light. I changed the white ground into off-white tiles to decrease its importance."

Blin bragged about not using smoke on stage, as so many directors do today. He said in 1983: "In my productions the actor who speaks is well lighted and visible. Even in Strindberg's *Dream Play*, when the castle has to go up in flames, I produced that effect by hands waving red and yellow cloths." He seeks "total reality in the set, in that it should live, move, breathe, be human." A street should "be shown as it looks at night, drunk." Profound reality interests him, but he hates *verism*. Or, as he told me: "You have to push it to the limit, so that a bottle taken out of the frigidaire should have visible frost on it." In *The Blacks* he loved Acquart's multi-levelled architecture which took different forms, tones, and colors under different lights.

When the playwright indicates a stage movement, Blin prepares the actor to perform that movement as though it flowed from a source. Otherwise he waits for the text to be decanted so that the action itself prompts a gesture or arranges itself in space. The actor, delivering a text that he had to take in without the director's personal commentary, may, in uttering the words, feel the need to move. Then Blin may approve of a precise movement or channel excessive impetuousness. He insists upon the power of breathing and the rhythm immanent in the text to propel the actor's body, without mediation. He does not try to arrange estheticizing images nor draw significant, symbolic, concerted diagrams. He does not project a spatial construct parallel to the play. The paths on his stage do not obey any outside intention. He is concerned only with putting his actors in the mood in a given space and with letting the text grow flexibly.

In *Men and Stones* by Jean-Pierre Faye, two walls form an acute angle at the end of which is a passage, a deliberate fissure. Events reverberate on these walls before they suffuse the actions of the characters, who show their feelings by their position with respect to one wall or the other, by their proximity or distance from one another. Two sides oppose each other in an extremely limited space. In *The Emigrés* Mrozek leaves his two characters seated for about twenty minutes. Blin waits for one of the actors (Terzieff) to show a desire to get up and move. In *The Blue of Eau-de-vie* by Carlos Semprun Maura, the two friend/enemies use evasions and stealth in their dialogue. Similarly, their movements betray their instability, their hide-and-seek at a distance. They turn their backs to one another or draw together face to face, Alain seated on a step, Pierre wallowing on the bed or venting his anger on a stool, one or the other looking at the audience as though there were a window at stage-level.

Blin arranges a specifically theatrical space in *Men and Stones* or *The Screens*, with laws and conventions appropriate to the particular work. In *The Emigrés* or *The Blue of Eau-de-vie* the space is "natural"; it does not reconstitute a slice of life, but the blocking blends with social and anthropological qualities. Studying these movements of the characters, one arrives at the same conclusions as Edward T. Hall in *Hidden Dimension* or Erving Goffman in *Presentation of Self in Everyday Life*. What seems like simple empiricism corresponds to a deeper science that refuses to advertise itself as such, and that betrays itself only in a global osmosis.

LIKE A LIGHTHOUSE

The "invisible" mise-en-scène of Roger Blin, unlike the forceful affirmations of certain directors who advertise their technical skill, develops like a firm network of many threads. Immersed in the work and proceeding by increasingly fine touches, he seems to mould a carefully measured amalgam, which remains suspended in the air for a long time. He brings the work to the stage at the same time that he brings the actors to the work, seeking a common rhythm.

Roger Blin never wanted to create a mise-en-scène about which one could say confidently: "That's a Blin." Each of his productions conformed to the rhythm of the playwright, without addition or subtraction. He left no disciple, school, or style. His career is exemplary in the sense that it is a unique example of its kind. But one can make several points about it:

Direct only new authors.

Seek works that are challenging in form or content.

Do not graft personal ideas onto a work, but reveal the thought of the author and give weight to his words.

Use only simple theatre techniques, relying on the actor rather than machinery.

Respect a balance between daring and sobriety.

Blin's influence spread far beyond his own productions of work by new or relatively unknown playwrights. Many young and less young people are Blin's debtors for a pertinent remark, a helping hand in the profession, a presence at moments of doubt. Few directors were as devoted as he to reading manuscripts, to helping rework them (whether or not he finally directed them), to being present at first readings or at rehearsals. Often he saw a fault and suggested a better solution. He made a practice of seeing his colleagues' productions, and was always curious about theatre in process, even when the choices were different from his. He went out to the suburbs, interested in unknown companies, careers at their start. He might recommend someone enthusiastically, helping him or her along.

Even more than his esthetic, Blin has left us an ethic. He is a beacon to our conscience, like those that guide sailors lost at sea. Before certain excesses on the contemporary stage, he recalls us to balance. He has shown us the path of rigor in the struggle for a new theatre and a new human being – even at personal cost to himself. Like Dullin, Artaud, or Van Gogh, Blin was less a professional than an artist of the absolute.

Blin chronology

Unless stated otherwise, all Blin's direction is in French.
Asterisks denote premières.

1907   Born in Neuilly near Paris, the first of five children in a bourgeois family.

1914   Blin's father, a doctor who refused to leave wounded soldiers, is captured by the Germans during World War I. During the two years of his imprisonment, the family suffers poverty.

1926   Enrolls in the University of Paris to study literature. Meets Surrealists.

1927–29 Studies art at the Grande Chaumière; draws charcoal nudes. Will continue to draw throughout his life.

1928   Meets Artaud, Sylvain Itkine, Jacques Prévert.

1932   Meets Barrault.

1933–34 Plays minor roles in films, and will continue to play in films throughout his life. Works with Pierre Chenal on scenario and direction of *The Nameless Street*.

1935   Joins the October Group and remains with the group until its dissolution in 1938.
Assists Artaud in his production of *The Cenci* and plays a mute assassin.

1936   Supports the Popular Front.
Plays a speaking part in *The Wonder Show* by Cervantes, first produced in Barrault's Augustins attic, and then with the October Group.

1937   In addition to continued film work (including Pierre Chenal's *Alibi* with Eric von Stroheim), plays in Barrault's production of *The Magnificent Cuckold* by Crommelynck and plays several parts in Barrault's production of *Numantia* by Cervantes at the Théâtre Antoine.
Plays in Itkine's production of *Ubu Enchained* by Jarry at the Comédie des Champs-Elysées.
Plays in Douking's production of *The Broken Jug* by Kleist at the Théâtre des Ambassadeurs.

1939   Plays with Barrault in latter's adaptation of Hamsun's *Hunger* and Granval's production of Laforgue's *Hamlet*, a double bill at the Théâtre de l'Atelier.

1940   Plays in Maurice Tourneur's film of *Volpone*.
        Plays Buckingham in a revival of Dullin's *Richard III* at the
        Théâtre de l'Atelier.

1941   Plays in Raymond Reynal's productions of Synge's *In the
        Shadow of the Glen* and *Playboy of the Western World* at the
        Théâtre Monceau.
        During the war he teaches mime and acting at EPJD
        (*Education Par le Jeu Dramatique*).

1943–44 Plays sporadically in film and on stage during the Occupation,
        notably in *Tragedy of Love* directed by Fernand Ledoux at the
        Vieux-Colombier.

1945   Plays the Narrator in a ballet produced by Roland Petit,
        Rendez-vous.

1946   Plays his first lead in a film of Gréville adapted from a Zola
        story – *For a Night of Love*.

1947   Plays the Devil in *Epiphanies* by Pichette at the Théâtre des
        Noctambules.
        Plays in a double bill at the Vieux-Colombier – a revival of
        Synge's *In the Shadow of the Glen* and the creation of Shaw's
        Blanco Posnet.

1949–51 Heads a company at the Théâtre Gaîté-Montparnasse, where
        he begins to direct.

1949   Plays in Cocteau's film *Orphée*.
        Directs *The Moon on the Yellow River* by Denis Johnston at the
        Gaîté-Montparnasse. Design Thanos Tsingos.
        Directs *The Ghost Sonata* by Strindberg and also plays the
        Student at the Gaîté-Montparnasse. Design Thanos Tsingos.

1950   Directs *The Executioner is Impatient* by Jean Silvant at the
        Gaîté-Montparnasse. Design Thanos Tsingos.
        Plays The Mutilated One in Adamov's *Great and Small
        Manoeuvre*, directed by Jean-Marie Serreau at the Théâtre des
        Noctambules.

1952   Directs Adamov's *Parody* at the Théâtre Lancry. Design Vieira
        da Silva.

1953   Directs Beckett's *Waiting for Godot* at the Théâtre de
        Babylone and plays Pozzo. Design Sergio Gerstein.
        (Directs *Godot* in German at the Schauspielhaus, Zurich, in
        1954, in Dutch in Arnheim, Holland 1955, in Toulouse 1964,
        in Paris revivals in 1956 at the Hébertot, 1961 at the Odéon,
        1970 at the Récamier. In 1978 he directs a new mise-en-scène
        at the Comédie-Française, which is revived in 1980 at the
        Odéon.)

1956   Directs *Low Tide* by Jean Duvignaud at the Théâtre des
        Noctambules. Design Atlan.

1957   Directs and plays Hamm in Beckett's *Endgame*, first at the
        Royal Court Theatre, London, and then at the Studio des
        Champs-Elysées, Paris. Design Jacques Noël.

1958   Directs *Endgame* (in German) at the Fleismarkt Theatre of
        Vienna.
        Directs the Griot Company in Synge's *In the Shadow of the
        Glen* at the Théâtre du Faubourg St-Jacques, as well as helping
        them with other productions.

1959   Plays Bishop Tikhone in Camus' production of his adaptation
        of Dostoyevsky's *Possessed* at the Théâtre Antoine.
        Directs Genet's *Blacks* at the Théâtre de Lutèce. Design André
        Acquart. (Revival at Théâtre de la Renaissance in 1960; also
        directs London production in English at the Royal Court in
        1961).

1960   Directs French première of Beckett's *Krapp's Last Tape* at the
        Théâtre Récamier.
        Directs *The Lion* by Amos Kenan at the Théâtre de Lutèce.
        Design Acquart.
        Plays Davies in Jean Martin's production of Pinter's *Caretaker*
        at the Théâtre de Lutèce.
        Signs the *Manifesto des 121* supporting the right to
        insubordination during the Algerian War, and is therefore
        barred from all government-subsidized media.
        Plays the Envoy in Peter Brook's Paris production of Genet's
        Balcony at the Théâtre du Gymnase.

1963   Directs and plays the Sexton in Valle-Inclàn's *Divine Words* at
        the Odéon-Théâtre de France. Design Acquart. (Directs it in
        Slovenian in Yugoslavia, 1972.)
        Directs French première of Beckett's *Happy Days* with
        Madeleine Renaud. Design Matias. Opens at the Venice
        Drama Festival and plays almost continuously thereafter in
        Paris and on tour. (Directs an Italian production at Teatro
        Stabile of Turin, 1965. Design Matias.)

1964   Plays Cardinal Cibo in Raymond Rouleau's production of
        Musset's *Lorenzaccio* at the Théâtre Sarah Bernhardt.
        Directs the Griots in a reading of Césaire's *Tragedy of King
        Christophe* at the Festival of Experimental Art at Knokke le
        Zoute, and then at the Théâtre de Lutèce.
        Plays in a television piece directed by Pierre Prévert, and
        continues to play in television until 1980.

1965   Directs *Men and Stones by Jean-Pierre Faye at the Petit-
Odéon.

1966   Directs *The Screens by Genet at the Odéon-Théâtre de France.
Design Acquart. (Directs a German production at Bühnen der
Stadt, Essen, in 1967. Design Acquart.)
Directs Genet's Balcony (in Dutch) at Nieuw Rotterdams
Toneel, Holland.
Plays on television in O'Neill's Ile and Bound East for Cardiff.

1967   Plays Rapaccini in the Octavio Paz adaptation of Hawthorne's
Rapaccini's Daughter.

1968   During the events of May participates in plans for a radically
different university of theatre.
Directs *The Carrion-Eaters by Robert Weingarten in
Switzerland at Théâtre de Carouge, Grand Théâtre of
Lausanne, and Comédie de Génève. Design Jean-Marc Stehle,
with masks by Werner Strub.
Plays the Watchman in The Beet-Garden by Roland Dubillard,
directed by the author at the Théâtre de Lutèce.

1969   Directs *The Nuns by Eduardo Manet at the Théâtre de Poche-
Montparnasse. Design Jean Assens.

1971   Undergoes open heart surgery.
Directs *The Night of the Assassins by Jose Triana at the
Théâtre Récamier.

1972   Directs Macbeth at the Théâtre de Strasbourg. Design Matias.
Directs *Where the Cows Drink by Roland Dubillard at the
Théâtre Récamier. Design Matias.

1973   Plays the lead in Claude Accursi's film Dada au cœur (still
unreleased).

1974   Directs *The Emigrés by Slawomir Mrozek at the Petit-Orsay.
Design Matias.
Plays The Solitary One in The Black Pig by Roger Planchon,
directed by Planchon at the Théâtre National Populaire in
Villeurbanne.

1975   Directs Peter Weiss's German translation of Strindberg's Dream
Play at the Schauspielhaus, Zurich. Design Matias.
Exhibition of his drawings at the Gallery Ortemp.

1976   Formation of the Roger Blin Company by young actors.
Directs Boesman and Lena by Athol Fugard at the Théâtre de la
Resserre, Cité Universitaire. Design Matias. (Revival in 1979
by the Roger Blin Company at the Théâtre National de
Chaillot.)

Receives Grand Prix National des Arts et Lettres for his
theatre work.

1977   Directs *Lady Strass by Manet at the Théâtre de Poche-
Montparnasse. Design Matias.

1978   Directs the Roger Blin Company in *Minamata and Co. at the
Théâtre de la Commune d'Aubervilliers. Design Acquart.
Plays in Adolescence, film directed by Jeanne Moreau.

1979   Directs *Name's Isabelle Langrenier by Jean-Louis Bauer at the
Petit-T.E.P. Design Chantal Petit.

1980   Directs *Did I Mention I'm a Hunchback? by François Billetdoux
at the Petit-Montparnasse. Design Chantal Petit and Christian
Gallet.
Directs Thomas Bernhard's President at the Théâtre de la
Michodière. Design Matias.
Directs *The Blue of Eau-de-vie by Carlos Semprun Maura at
the Petit-Odéon. Design Matias. (Revived 1982)

1982   Plays leading roles on French television.

1983   Directs *Triptych by Max Frisch at the Théâtre de l'Odéon.
Design Acquart.
Illness interrupts his direction of *Black Street by Any Diguet
at the Cartoucherie of Vincennes.

1984   Dies in the hospital on January 20. Cremated at Père Lachaise
Cemetery.

Notes

Introduction

1 Unless otherwise indicated, quotations from Blin come from his various remarks to me, over the course of the years.
2 Alfred Bouchard, *La Langue théâtrale* (Paris, Arnaud et Labat, 1878).
3 Arthur Pougin, *Dictionnaire* (Paris, Firmin-Didot, 1885).
4 Jacques Copeau, "Le Théâtre du Vieux Colombier," in *Critiques d'un autre temps* (Paris, NRF, 1923), p. 246.
5 *Revue théâtrale* no. 23, 1 April 1903.
6 Alexandre Blok, "Du Théâtre," 1908, tr. Nina Gourfinkel in Odette Aslan, *L'Art du théâtre* (Paris, Seghers, 1963), p. 246.
7 Erwin Piscator, "Conférence du Centre français de l'ITI at the Theatre of Nations," 1 June 1956.
8 Claude Régy, *Littérature. Arts. Spectacles*, no 1, May 1983.
9 Emmannuelle Riva, *ibid*.
10 Patrice Pavis, *Voix et images de la scène, essais de sémiologie théâtrale* (Lille, Presses universitaires de Lille, 1982), *passim*.
11 Bettina Knapp, "An Interview with Roger Blin," in *Tulane Drama Review*, 19 (1963), 121.
12 John Willett, tr. *Brecht on Theatre* (London, Methuen, 1973).

1 In search of Roger Blin

1 Roger Blin in Michel Fauré, *Le Groupe Octobre* (Bourgois, Paris, 1977), p. 264.
2 *ibid.*, p. 244.
3 *ibid.*, p. 268.
4 *ibid.*, p. 265.
5 Blin in Paul-Louis Mignon, *Le Théâtre d'aujourd'hui de A à Z* (l'Avant-scène/Michel Brient, Paris, 1966), p. 56.
6 Fauré, p. 288. Between 1928 and 1930 Blin contributed to *La Revue du Cinéma*, from which quotations in the text are drawn.
7 Mignon, *Le Théâtre d'aujourd'hui*, p. 56.
8 *ibid.*
9 "Their shadows [Blin and Chauvet] rise, turn like tops, cross in a flash of lightning," Guillaume Hanoteau, *Ces nuits qui ont fait Paris* (Fayard, Paris, 1971), p. 588.
10 Blin, "Qui était Sylvain Itkine," in *Revue d'histoire du théâtre*, September 1964.
11 Henri Béhar, "Une mise en scène surrealiste: *Ubu enchaîné* de Sylvain Itkine," *Revue d'histoire du théâtre* 1, 1972.
12 *Arts*, 24 February 1950.
13 Gérard Philipe in *Paris-Presse*, 31 October 1947.
14 Jacques Lemarchand in *Combat*, 5 December 1947.
15 Henri Pichette in *Combat*, 22 November 1947.
16 Hazards at the dress rehearsal caused *Woyzeck* to be dropped, and *Ghost Sonata* was played alone.
17 Jacques Lemarchand in *Combat*, 8 November 1949.

2 Beckett's plays

1 Roger Blin, *Le Nouvel Observateur*, 26 September 1981.
2 Blin interviewed by Pierre Hahn, *Paris-Théâtre* no. 201.
3 Jacques Lemarchand, *Figaro littéraire*, 15 January 1953.
4 Pierre Aimé Touchard, *Revue de Paris*, February 1961.
5 Pierre Mélèse, *Beckett* (Paris, Seghers, 1966), pp. 145–50.
6 "Portraits pour Jean Genet," *Masques*, no. 12, Winter 1981/82.
7 Cf. Ruby Cohn, "*Godot* par Beckett à Berlin," *Travail théâtral*, no. 20, Summer 1975.
8 Aldo Tagliaferri, *Beckett ou la surdétermination littéraire* (Paris, Payot, 1977), p. 119.
9 Geneviève Serreau, *Le Nouveau Théâtre* (Paris, Gallimard, 1966), p. 88.
10 Mélèse, *Beckett*, p. 48.
11 Beckett letter of 29 December 1957 to Alan Schneider, in Samuel Beckett, *Disjecta* (London, Calder, 1983), p. 109.
12 Israel Shenker, "Moody Man of Letters," *New York Times*, 6 May 1956.
13 Andrée Waintrop, "Les Mises-en-Scène de Beckett par Roger Blin," mémoire de maîtrise, Paris III, 1969.
14 Mélèse, *Beckett*, p. 147.
15 Waintrop, "Les Mises-en-Scène de Beckett."
16 *L'Express*, 8 February 1957.
17 Alain Robbe-Grillet, *For a New Novel* (New York, Grove Press, 1965).
18 Mélèse, *Beckett*, p. 154.
19 John Fletcher, "Roger Blin at Work," *Modern Drama*, February 1966.
20 Robbe-Grillet, *For a New Novel*.
21 Mélèse, *Beckett*.
22 Fletcher, "Roger Blin at Work."
23 Waintrop, "Les Mises-en-Scène de Beckett."
24 Myriam Louzoun "Fin de partie" in *Les Voies de la création théâtrale*, vol. 5, Paris, CNRS, 1977, pp. 443–5.
25 Waintrop, "Les Mises-en-Scène de Beckett."
26 Louzoun, "Fin de partie."
27 Pierre Marcabru, *Arts*, 8 May 1957.
28 Jean Duvignaud, *Gazette de Lausanne*, 4 May 1957.
29 *France-Observateur*, 17 October 1963.
30 Peter Brook, "*Happy Days* and *Marienbad*," *Encore*, Jan.–Feb. 1963.
31 Gilles Sandier, *Théâtre et Combat*, Paris, Stock, 1970, p. 48.
32 *Figaro littéraire*, 14 October 1963.
33 Waintrop, "Les Mises-en-Scène de Beckett."
34 *Figaro littéraire*, 14 October 1963.
35 Brook, "*Happy Days*."
36 Waintrop, "Les Mises-en-Scène de Beckett."
37 *ibid.*
38 Mélèse, *Beckett*, p. 150.
39 *Figaro littéraire*, 14 October 1963.
40 Waintrop, "Les Mises-en-Scène de Beckett."
41 Gian Renzo Morteo, "Incontro con Roger Blin," *Quaderni del Teatro Stabile di Torino*, no. 3, 1965.
42 *ibid.*

3 Genet's plays

1 "Entretiens avec Jean Genet" in Jacques Poulet, *Aveux spontanés* (Paris, Plon, 1963), p. 110.
2 Bernard Dort, "Genet ou le combat avec le théâtre," *Le Théâtre moderne depuis la deuxième guerre mondiale* (Paris, CNRS, 1967), pp. 57–69.
3 The quotations in English from Genet's plays are by Bernard Frechtman.
4 *Théâtre populaire*, no. 36, 1959; *Arts*, 11 November 1959; *Encore*, March–April 1960; *Lettres nouvelles*, 11 November 1959.
5 Richard N. Coe, "Pouvoir noir et poésie blanche," *Cahiers Renaud-Barrault*, no. 74, 1970.
6 Genet's preface to the French translation of *Prison Letters of George Jackson*.
7 Poulet, *Aveux spontanés*, p. 112.
8 *Playboy*, April 1964.
9 Bernard Poirot-Delpech, *Le Monde*, 4 November 1959.
10 Leonard B. Pronko, *Avant-garde* (Berkeley, University of California Press, 1962), p. 153.
11 Coe, "Pouvoir noir et poésie blanche."
12 Geneviève Serreau, *Histoire du nouveau théâtre* (Paris, Gallimard, 1966), p. 129.
13 *Nouvel Observateur*, 30 March 1966.
14 Duvignaud in *Lettres nouvelles*.
15 Document of the Griot Company.
16 Jean Duvignaud, "Roger Blin aux prises avec *Les Nègres*," *Lettres nouvelles*, 28 October 1959.
17 Duvignaud, *Lettres nouvelles*.
18 *France Observateur*, 20 February 1958.
19 *Tulane Drama Review*, Spring 1963.
20 Poulet, *Aveux spontanés*, p. 113.
21 *Playboy*.
22 Jacques Lemarchand, *Figaro littéraire*, 7 November 1959.
23 Oddly enough, Genet authorized Peter Stein's 1982 German production of *The Blacks* with white actors in black makeup.
24 Rolf Hochhuth's *Deputy* dealt with the behavior of Pope Pius XII during World War II, and especially his silence about Auschwitz. When it played in Paris in 1963, five out of thirty performances were interrupted, and the actors were threatened.
25 See Aslan's comparison of six productions of *The Screens* in vol. 3 of *Les Voies de la création théâtrale* (Paris, CNRS, 1972), pp. 11–107.
26 *Playboy*, no. 4, April 1964.
27 *Libération*, 10 June 1983.
28 Frantz Fanon, *The Wretched of the Earth* (Harmondsworth, Penguin, 1967).
29 Hubert Fichte, "La Fin dernière d'une révolte," *Magazine Littéraire*, no. 174, June 1981.
30 Jean Genet, "Letter to Roger Blin" in *Reflections on the Theatre*, tr. Richard Seaver (London, Faber & Faber, 1972), pp. 11–12.
31 Jean Genet, *Playboy*, no. 4, April 1964.
32 Jean Genet, "How to Play *The Maids*" in vol. 4 of *Oeuvres complètes* (Paris, Gallimard, 1969).
33 Jean Genet, *Reflections*; the phrase in parenthesis is omitted from the Seaver translation.
34 "Dossier Jean Genet, Roger Blin," *Masques*, no. 12, Winter, 1981.
35 Jean Genet, *Reflections*, pp. 23–4.
36 *ibid.*, p. 25.

37 *Combat*, 3 June 1966.
38 Jean Genet, *Reflections*, pp. 27, 28, 29.
39 Jean Genet, "How to Play *The Balcony*," in *Ôeuvres*, vol. 4, p. 275.
40 Maria Casarès in *Masques*.
41 *Masques*.
42 *Masques*.
43 *Tulane Drama Review*, Spring 1963.
44 Paule Annen, television interview, April 1966.
45 Maria Casarès, television interview, April 1966.
46 *Le Monde*, 14 April 1966.
47 *Libération*, 10 June 1983.
48 Jean Genet, *Reflections*, pp. 38–9.
49 *Libération*.
50 *Nouvel Observateur*, 30 March 1966.
51 Discussion at the Maison du Spectateur, 23 April 1966.
52 Jean Paget, *Combat*, 23 April 1966.
53 Guy Dumur, *Nouvel Observateur*, 3 May 1966.
54 Gilles Sandier, *Arts*, 3 May 1966.
55 Gilles Sandier, *Théâtre et Combat* (Paris, Stock, 1970), p. 28.
56 Jean Genet, *Reflections*, pp. 49–50.

4 In service to diverse works

1 Blin, "Les vers du nez" in *Macbeth*, edited by Pierrette Tison (Paris, Stock, 1972),
    p. 165.
 2 Blin in *Lettres françaises*, 21 March 1963.
 3 Adamov in *Combat*, 18 March 1950.
 4 Adamov, *L'Homme et l'enfant* (Paris, Gallimard, 1968), p. 97.
 5 Adamov in *Combat*, 10 November 1950.
 6 Adamov, *L'Homme et l'enfant*, p. 99.
 7 Lemarchand, *Figaro littéraire*, 18 November 1950.
 8 Adamov, *Arts*, 29 May 1952.
 9 Blin in *Combat*, 4 June 1952.
10 Blin, *Nouvel Observateur*, 24 January 1965.
11 *Cahiers Renaud-Barrault*, 63, October 1967.
12 Manet in *Action théâtrale*, no. 2, 1969.
13 Blin in *Action théâtrale*, no. 2, 1969.
14 *ibid.*
15 Bastide in *Nouvelles littéraires*, 8 April 1971.
16 *Acteurs*, 3 March 1982.
17 Jean Vigneron, *La Croix*, 3 November 1972.
18 Mary Benson, "Fugard on Acting", *Theatre Quarterly*, 28, 1977.
19 Other controversial works were produced at the Théâtre de la Commune
    d'Aubervilliers. *The Investigation* by Peter Weiss also posed the problem of theatre-
    documents: how could the horrors of Auschwitz be staged?
20 Blin, preface to *Minamata and Co.*, Osamu Takahashi, translated by Catherine Cadou,
    1977.
21 Jacques Toja to Armelle Héliot, *Le Quotidien de Paris*, 17 June 1983.
22 Emmanuel Klausner, "Roger Blin et la comédie amère," *La Croix*, 10 February 1983.
23 *ibid.*

24 Jean-Pierre Thibaudat, "Je ne peux jouer que les princes ou les clochards," *Libération*, 21 February 1983.
25 Josanne Rousseau, "Un entretien avec Roger Blin," *Comédie-Française*, 116, February–March 1983.
26 Max Frisch interview, *Nouvelles littéraires*, 3–9 March 1983.
27 *La Croix*, 1983.
28 *Libération*, 1983.
29 *France-Soir*, 21 February 1983.

5 An ethic of theatre

1 Blin in *Libération*, 21 February 1983.
2 Antonin Artaud, *The Theatre and its Double*, tr. Victor Corti, London, John Calder, 1970, p. 83.
3 *ibid*, p. 72.
4 Marcel Jousse, *L'Anthropologie du geste*, Paris, Resma, 1969, pp. 74, 161.
5 Michel Garnier, Maurice Martenot, Jean-Marie Conty, *Faire des vivants*, Paris, Editions de la Nouvelle France, 1947.
6 Letter of 25 March 1946, published in *Libération*, 21 February 1983.
7 *ibid*.
8 Blin speaking to Bettina Knapp, *Tulane Drama Review*, 19, 1963.

Bibliography

Adamov, Arthur, *L'Homme et l'enfant*, Paris, Gallimard, 1968
Artaud, Antonin, *The Theatre and its Double*, tr. Victor Corti, London, Calder, 1970
Aslan, Odette, *Jean Genet*, Paris, Seghers, 1973
    (ed.), *L'Art du théâtre*, Paris, Seghers, 1963
    "Les Paravents" in *Les Voies de la création théâtrale*, Paris, CNRS, vol. 3, 1972,
      pp. 13–107
Beckett, Samuel, *Disjecta*, London, Calder, 1983
Benson, Mary, "Fugard on acting," *Theatre Quarterly* 28, 1977
Bonnefoy, Claude, *Jean Genet*, Paris, Editions universitaires, 1965
Bouchard, Alfred, *La Langue théâtrale*, Paris, Arnaud et Labat, 1878
Brecht, Bertolt, *Brecht on Theatre*, London, Methuen, 1973
Brook, Peter, "*Happy Days* and *Marienbad*," *Encore*, Jan.–Feb. 1963
Coe, Richard N., "Pouvoir noir et poésie blanche, *Cahiers Renaud-Barrault*, 74, 1970
Cohn, Ruby, *Just Play: Beckett's Theater*, Princeton, Princeton University Press, 1980
Copeau, Jacques, *Critiques d'un autre temps*, Paris, NRF, 1923
Fanon, Frantz, *The Wretched of the Earth*, Harmondsworth, Penguin, 1967
Fauré, Michel, *Le Groupe Octobre*, Paris, Christian Bourgois, 1977
Fletcher, John, "Roger Blin at work," *Modern Drama*, Feb. 1966
Garnier, Michel, Martenot, Maurice, Conty, J.-M., *et al*, *Faire des vivants*, Paris, Editions
    de la Nouvelle France, 1947
Genet, Jean, *Lettres à Roger Blin*, Paris, Gallimard, 1968
Hanoteau, Guillaume, *Ces nuits qui ont fait Paris*, Paris, Fayard, 1971
Hassan, Hanan Kassab, *L'Espace et l'objet, étude structurale des Paravents*, Thèse de 3ème
    cycle, Paris III, 1983
Jousse, Marcel, *L'Anthropologie du Geste*, Paris, Resma, 1969
Louzoun, Myriam, "Fin de partie" in *Les Voies de la création théâtrale*, vol. 5, Paris, CNRS,
    pp. 377–445
Mélèse, Pierre, *Beckett*, Paris, Seghers, 1966
                Adamov, Paris, Seghers, 1973
Mignon, Paul-Louis, *Le Théâtre d'aujourd'hui de A à Z*, Paris, L'Avant-scène/Michel Brient,
    1966
Pougin, Arthur, *Dictionnaire*, Paris, Firmin-Didot, 1885
Poulet, Jacques, *Aveux spontanés: Entretiens avec Jean Genet*, Paris, Plon, 1963
Pronko, Leonard, *Avant-Garde*, Berkeley, University of California Press, 1962
Robbe-Grillet, Alain, *For a New Novel*, New York, Grove, 1965
Sandier, Gilles, *Théâtre et Combat*, Paris, Stock, 1970
Serreau, Geneviève, *Histoire du nouveau théâtre*, Paris, Gallimard, 1966
Waintrop, Andrée, "Les Mises en scène de Beckett par Roger Blin," maîtrise, Paris III,
    1969

Index